# HOLLYWOOD
## ABROAD

Audiences and Cultural Exchange

Edited by
Richard Maltby and Melvyn Stokes

 Publishing

First published in 2004 by the
British Film Institute
21 Stephen Street, London W1P 2LN

The British Film Institute promotes greater understanding of,
and access to, film and moving image culture in the UK.

Cover design: Barefoot Graphics
Cover image: (detail) The Subaruza movie programme, 18 November 1947, for *All This and Heaven Too* (Anatole Litvak, 1940)

Set by Servis Filmsetting Ltd, Manchester, UK

Printed in Malta by Interprint

British Library Cataloguing-in-Publication Data
A catalogue record for this book is available from the British Library

ISBN 1–84457–018–5 (hbk)
ISBN 1–84457–051–7 (pbk)

# Contents

# Notes on Contributors

**Charles Ambler** is Dean of the Graduate School and a member of the history department at the University of Texas at El Paso. He received his Ph.D. in African history from Yale University. His current scholarship focuses on ideas about difference in debates about alcohol in the British empire and on the social and cultural history of modern Africa, including most recently a special issue of the *International Journal of African Historical Studies* on the history of leisure.

**Anne Bittner** is employed by an academic publisher in promoting online journal content. She completed her Ph.D. thesis 'A Balanced Show: A Cultural History of the Relationship Between Stage Attractions and Film in Australia from 1920 to 1935' at La Trobe University, Melbourne, in 2000.

**Kate Bowles** is Senior Lecturer in the School of Social Science, Media and Communication at the University of Wollongong. She has a Ph.D. in film history and is currently working on the research and design of a digital archive of local oral history interviews, the 'Memories of Cinema' database.

**Raphaëlle Costa de Beauregard** studied miniatures of the Elizabethan period for her Doctorat d'État in France and currently teaches Film Studies at the University of Toulouse Le Mirail, where she is a Professor. She has published two books: *Nicolas Hilliard et l'imaginaire élisabéthain* (Paris, 1991) and *Silent Elizabethans* (Montpellier, 2002). She founded SERCIA (Société d'Études et de Recherches sur le Cinéma Anglophone) in 1994 and has edited two volumes of conference proceedings: *Le Cinéma Se Regarde* (1994) and *Le Cinéma et Ses Objets* (1997). She is currently writing a book on the colours of melodrama from Shakespeare to early cinema.

**Nezih Erdogan** teaches at Bahcesehir University, Istanbul. He is the author of a book on *Cinema and Spectatorship*. He has also published articles on Turkish popular cinema and censorship. He is currently working on the history of entertainment and spectatorship in Turkey.

**Michael Hammond** lectures in film at the University of Southampton. His book *The Big Show: British Cinema and the Great War* will be published by Exeter University Press in early 2005.

**Nancy Huggett** has recently completed her Ph.D. at Wollongong University, Australia, on the Cultural History of Cinema-going in the Illawarra region of New South Wales. She currently works as a Senior Policy Officer at Wollongong University, where she assists in the development of the 'Memories of Cinema Online Archive' and gives lectures on audience studies.

**Priya Jaikumar** teaches in the Department of Cinema and Television at the University of Southern California. She has published articles on British cinema, Indian cinema, and film policy, and is currently completing a book entitled *Cinema at the End of Empire*.

**Hiroshi Kitamura** is a visiting assistant professor at SUNY Oswego, where he teaches U.S. and world history. He is currently working on a book about Hollywood's export campaign in Japan during the Allied occupation.

**Richard Maltby** is Professor of Screen Studies and Head of the School of Humanities at Flinders University, South Australia. His publications include *Hollywood Cinema: Second Edition* (Blackwell's, 2003), *Dreams for Sale: Popular Culture in the Twentieth Century* (Harrap, 1989), as well as numerous articles and essays. With Ruth Vasey, he is currently writing *Reforming the Movies: Politics, Censorship and the Institutions of the American Cinema, 1908–1939*.

**Philippe Meers** is assistant professor in Communication Studies at the University of Antwerp. His publications on media culture, film audiences and international fiction flows have appeared in journals such as *Media, Culture and Society* and *The Journal of Popular Film and Television*. He is co-editing a reader with Daniël Bilereyst and is also co-editing a book series on 'Film and TV Studies' for the Academia Press.

**Melvyn Stokes** teaches film and American history at University College London. He is the editor of *The State of U.S. History* (Berg, 2002). His co-edited books include *Race and Class in the American South since 1890* (Berg, 1994) and *The Market Revolution in America* (University of Virginia, 1996). He is co-editor, with Richard Maltby, of *American Movie Audiences* (BFI, 1999), *Identifying Hollywood's Audiences* (BFI, 1999), and *Hollywood Spectatorship* (BFI, 2001). He is currently writing about *The Birth of a Nation*.

# Preface

This is the fourth of a series of books we have edited for the British Film Institute on the reception of Hollywood films. The first, *American Movie Audiences: From the Turn of the Century to the Early Sound Era* (1999) explored how American audiences responded to films and the film-going experience in the first four decades of the twentieth century. It also dealt with the differing ways in which audiences were perceived, especially by movie exhibitors or those who saw themselves as champions of the prevailing morality and culture.

The second volume, *Identifying Hollywood's Audiences: Audiences and Cultural Identity* (1999), analysed two major themes: what Hollywood knew – or thought it knew – about its own audiences from the 1920s to the 1990s, and the effects of this knowledge in terms of production strategies; and, secondly, what audiences have made of the films they watched and the meanings they have constructed from them.

The third volume, *Hollywood Spectatorship: Changing Perceptions of Cinema Audiences* (2001) attempted to test the validity of theoretical, text-based constructions of spectatorship in the light of historical evidence on how films were actually received by both audiences and critics and as a consequence of shifting viewing patterns resulting from recent technological changes in distribution and exhibition.

The present volume explores the reception of Hollywood films by audiences outside the United States, from the 1910s to the contemporary consumers of the megaplex. Its contributors demonstrate the complexity of the processes by which foreign audiences have interpreted and reinterpreted American movies through the perspectives conferred by their own national culture. We argue that such audiences create meanings through their negotiation of a set of cultural relations that extended well beyond the boundaries of any individual film.

We would like to offer our thanks to Andrew Lockett and Tom Cabot of the British Film Institute for their work on the book; to Robert C. Allen and Janet Staiger for their help and support for the project from its beginnings; and to Leigh Priest for preparing the index.

*Richard Maltby and Melvyn Stokes*

# Introduction
## 'The Americanisation of the World'

Richard Maltby

> Every film that goes from America abroad, wherever it shall be sent, shall correctly portray to the world the purposes, the ideals, the accomplishments, the opportunities, and the life of America . . . We are going to sell America to the world with American motion pictures.
>
> *Will H. Hays, 1923*[1]

> All the world thinks of the United States today as an empire, except the people of the United States. We shrink from the word 'empire', and insist that it should not be used to describe the dominion we exercise from Alaska to the Philippines, from Cuba to Panama, and beyond. We feel that there ought to be some other name for the civilizing work which we do reluctantly in these backward countries . . . The only effect of this refusal to admit that we are assuming imperial responsibilities is to turn over the management of our empire to business men with a personal share in it and to our second-rate and least experienced diplomats.
>
> *Walter Lippmann, 1927*[2]

> The meanings of even the most universal of imagery for a particular population derive as much from the historical experiences and social status of that group as from the intentions of purveyors . . . images and cultural traditions do not derive from, or descend upon, mute and passive populations on whose *tabula rasa* they now inscribe themselves. Instead, they invariably express the identities which historical circumstances have formed.
>
> *Anthony D. Smith, 1990*[3]

> I only liked the bioscope. Horses, cowboys, big hats, America.
>
> *Mrs W., Lusaka, 1988*[4]

In 1926, a US State Department official observed that without the legislation restricting immigration passed in 1921 and 1924, American movies would be bringing 'a flood of immigrants' to the United States. Instead, he suggested, 'the longing to emigrate is changed into a desire to imitate'.[5] Two years later, a film industry representative declared that motion pictures 'are demonstrably the greatest single factors in the American-isation of the world and as such fairly may be called the most important and significant of America's exported products'.[6] In discussing the reception of Hollywood movies outside the United States, the essays in this volume are inevitably concerned with issues of transnational cultural transmission, 'Americanisation' and the globalisation of culture. While these concerns dominate both popular and academic discussions of Hollywood's reception abroad, they seldom surface in accounts of American domestic audiences, as if Hollywood's dissemination of an 'American' culture within the United States was an unproblematic and inconsequential part of its cultural function, rather than a key component in the formation of a domestic discourse of 'Americanism' in the 1920s and 1930s.[7]

Contributors to the previous volumes that Melvyn Stokes and I have edited on the multiple histories of Hollywood's audiences have made it clear that the place of motion pictures in American domestic culture has in fact been a constant site of contestation and debate, and that American audiences have been far from univocal in their interpretation – or their acceptance – of the movies.[8] There remains, nevertheless, a common assumption of what we might call national ownership over the cultural images and mythology circulated abroad by Hollywood. In *Gunfighter Nation*, the final volume of his monumental analysis of the historical development of the Western as 'a *national myth/ideology*', Richard Slotkin justifies his concentration on the production of Westerns rather than the 'complex and various' modes of their reception by arguing that this narrowed focus permits a closer study of 'the dynamics of myth-production in the particular cultural site that has acquired the power to address us *as if* it spoke for an "American" national culture'.[9] Slotkin's formulation is one of several critical attempts to describe Hollywood 'as if' it were a national cinema. In his history of the American musical, Rick Altman claims that however much non-American critics may understand 'the context and meaning' of a movie such as *Singin' in the Rain* (1952), they will inevitably lack the familiarity with American culture that equips them to translate the movie's 'raw thematic material into . . . the culture's master themes', which 'are not actually *in* the text, yet the text is produced in such a way as to evoke them for a particular interpretive community'.[10]

Altman seems to be suggesting that however much a foreigner attempts to acquire an intellectual understanding of a text's encoded, resonant symbols, he or she can never approach the depth of intuitive understanding of the native. Like Slotkin's, Altman's formulation implies that an 'American' sensibility can define, for the rest of us, what the mythology of 'America' represents. Such accounts, however, do not necessarily describe the recontextualised sign 'America' and the signifying process 'Americanisation' when conducted or represented or viewed elsewhere. What 'Americanisation' has represented abroad is not necessarily what any individual or official ideology has privileged, supposed or assumed, since what circulates beyond the boundaries of the United States is not a full-blown mythology but rather its icons, its random fragments, which – as non-Americans interpret them – may take on meanings only tangentially related to those recognised at its point of origin.

One of the paradoxes of transnational cultural history lies in the way in which a cultural artefact of demonstrable semantic complexity at its point of production and initial domestic consumption is liable, when exported, first to be simplified and then rendered semantically complex in different ways by the conventions through which the artefacts of its originating culture are perceived in the second, host culture. Hollywood movies are no less liable to this process than West African masks or Kwakiutl totem poles.[11] In order to be integrated into the complexity of a host culture, a foreign artefact must lose at least some of its own domestic cultural complexity, so that it can be interpreted in a more simplified way. This new form, however, renders it open to reinterpretation within the cultural matrix of the host culture, which may provide a radically different context from that of its point of production. This context may, indeed, be sufficiently different to destabilise any critical capacity to ascribe ideological meaning or cultural function through the procedures of textual analysis alone.

As Altman implies, the foreigner's viewing position is necessarily different from that of the native American. While the American recognises diversity within his or her native culture, the foreigner receives 'American' cultural artefacts not '*as if* [they] spoke for an "American" national culture', but *as* 'American' national culture. The foreigner is not equipped to understand the artefact, or indeed the whole 'American' culture it represents, as complexly resonant since, in his or her experience, it is not. Unlike the evident diversity of his or her own cultural artefacts, the imported object appears comparatively simple, sometimes even childish or vulgar. Historically, this is the predominant opinion that Europeans have expressed towards 'American' culture, perceiving resonant symbols as stereotypes, and national myths as children's stories. This is particularly true of Hollywood, and within Hollywood, it is particularly true of the Western.

My childhood, in a dour Scottish city reluctantly emerging from post-war austerity, was pervaded by Western imagery. My toy guns were not, for the most part, replicas of those with which my father's generation had actually fought a decade before, but cap pistol versions of Colt 45s and Winchester rifles. Like the children of the Rhodesian Copperbelt discussed by Charles Ambler, I dressed up as a cowboy, and for several years my most prized possessions were cowboy and Indian figures and the Western town and fort they inhabited in my re-enactments of Western history. By the age of eight, I was fully familiar with the terminology of the West, my almost encyclopaedic knowledge of Western lore acquired almost entirely from Hollywood sources.[12]

In describing the Americanisation of my imagination, I am also describing the terms in which, as a child, I came to understand and then emulate the distinction between right and wrong, the proper activity of gendered roles, the ideal of heroism. These les-

Richard Maltby and Melvyn Stokes, both in the youthful grip of American exceptionalism

sons were learned as an American discourse or, perhaps more exactly, in American accents.[13] My imagination was Americanised because the iconography and plots of my childhood play were those of the lore of American exceptionalism. They were not, however, exclusively so. My cowboy toys cohabited unproblematically in my toy box with British soldiers, and sometimes joined them on the same battlefield if the game were sufficiently elaborate or my imagination sufficiently elastic. The cultural identity of these toys was not predetermined by what they were supposed to represent, but subject to my eight-year-old narrational whim. While their accents affected my identity, my culturally complex sense of self determined theirs.

Andrew Higson has argued that the concept of national cinema is most often used 'prescriptively rather than descriptively, citing what *ought* [Higson's emphasis] to be the national cinema, rather than describing the actual experience of popular audiences'. Higson describes the process of identifying a national cinema as involving 'both the production and assignation of a particular set of meanings, and the attempt to contain, or prevent the potential proliferation of other meanings'.[14] Definitions of national cinema commonly involve 'the construction of an imaginary homogeneity of identity and culture, an already achieved national identity', apparently held in common by what Benedict Anderson has called 'the imagined community of the nation'.[15] In the process Higson describes, Hollywood figures most often as the cultural Other against which 'national' cinema production has been defensively defined in other countries. Critical conceptions of national cinema almost invariably focus on issues of production rather than reception. The production of a national cinema is understood as 'a means of asserting national autonomy', an activity of resistance to a dominant international cinema understood to be 'American'.[16] By constructing a binary opposition between nationalities as a defining condition of cinematic identity, this process has largely excluded consideration of the manner and extent to which Hollywood has been 'an integral and naturalised part of the national culture, or the popular imagination, of most countries in which cinema is an established entertainment form'.[17] It has also privileged national identity over other forms of identification; not merely those of class, race or gender, but also the local identities that audiences may recognise as constituting communities to which they belong.

Hollywood has itself seldom been constrained by any obligation to behave as if it were a national cinema of the kind Higson discusses. The 'Americanisation of the world' has actually involved the circulation across national boundaries of a multinational popular culture which recognises no frontiers. The 'American culture' resisted by nationalists elsewhere has been a national culture only outside the geographic boundaries of the United States, when national identity has been thrust upon Hollywood as the name of its cultural Otherness. The 'America' of the movies has presented itself to its audiences less as a geographical territory than an imaginative one, which deliberately made itself available for assimilation in a variety of cultural contexts, becoming what Richard Kuisel terms 'everyone's second culture'.[18] What Dick Hebdidge has called 'the ubiquitous spectre of Americanisation' has, however, functioned as a trope of displacement, migrating from its economic base into the virtual geography of cultural nationalisms revolving around fears of homogenisation and anxieties over the desire to imitate.[19]

Since the mid-1920s, when cultural nationalists began to draw their governments' attention to the potential effects of Hollywood's commercial dominance, Hollywood has figured as a bad object: seducer of the innocent; representative of the Great Satan; over-paid, over-sexed, and over here, 'poisoning the souls of our children' and turning them 'into the docile slaves of the American multimillionaires'; dangerous to cultural elites because of its radically democratic challenges to hierarchies of discrimination, taste and class.[20] To a significant extent, 'Americanisation' was defined by European cultural nationalists through their encounter with Hollywood. Conversely, Hollywood was accorded a national identity – akin to those of European nations – so as to charge it with contributing to 'Americanisation'.[21] Hollywood's commercial success in foreign markets led to its identification as 'American' by self-interested parties, such as rival film producers, as they constructed an argument that served competitive commercial purposes by invoking higher cultural objectives. The process of 'Americanisation' was one of alienation of cultural patrimony, and the charge was principally levelled by those who either believed themselves possessed of cultural patrimony or those who wished to lay claim to it. Paradoxically, the defenders of 'traditional' national cultures exaggerated the influence and transformative power of 'American culture' in order to demonstrate how threatening it was.[22]

The opponents of Americanisation have frequently failed to recognise the extent to which both American purveyors and American critics of 'American' commercial culture do not perceive these products as part of a specifically national culture. Optimists of the will from Will Hays to Joseph Nye have argued that 'America has always had a syncretic culture, borrowing freely from a variety of traditions and continuously open to the rest of the world', advertising 'the values of democracy, personal freedom, upward mobility, and openness'.[23] A well-established tradition of American intellectual pessimism has, however, bemoaned the absence of a clearly identifiable American national culture and held Hollywood and other forms of commercial popular culture responsible for the lack.[24] It is, indeed, arguable that American commercial culture has only received official *imprimatur* as an expression of American national aspirations since its products began receiving serious critical attention as cultural artefacts in the late 1960s, at the same time that the American political process adopted the entertainment industry's marketing strategies and its culture of celebrity. During the preceding two decades, when the CIA was in effect acting as America's 'Ministry of Culture', it promoted the idea of a *pax Americana* among the intelligentsia of western Europe by celebrating the achievements of American 'high culture' and undermining negative stereotypes of America's perceived cultural barrenness.[25] Pursuing a campaign of conscious, ideologically motivated Americanisation from 1950 to 1967, through agencies such as the Congress for Cultural Freedom, the CIA very consciously chose its instruments of cultural propaganda in order to contest European perceptions that America was, in Malcolm Cowley's phrase, 'a mass-cult hell'.[26]

As a term, 'Americanisation' harbours a number of definitions competing for semantic hegemony. It also has a lexicological history. The State Department official and movie industry representative cited at the beginning of this chapter were among the first to refer to 'Americanisation' as an export activity. Before the mid-1920s, it was primarily a domestic term, identifying a consciously ideological project seeking to 'assimilate and amalgamate' recently arrived immigrants 'as a part of our American race, and to implant in their children, so far as can be done, the Anglo-Saxon conception of righteousness, law and order, and popular government'.[27] According to Will Hays, President of the Motion Picture Producers and Distributors of America, Inc. (MPPDA), the motion picture was an ideal instrument for the Americanisation of immigrants:

> They are coming to a strange land to live among strange people. Their language in most cases is different from ours. Their customs are different. What is America like?, they ask themselves. The motion picture is able to answer that question, to teach them ... The picture says to [them]: 'Here is America. See what America, your new home, is like. Look at me and love America.'[28]

Histories of the domestic Americanisation campaigns of the 1920s unanimously agree that they had little effect on the individual assimilation of recent immigrants, not least because, as Constantine Panunzio suggested, immigrants already possessed a firm 'idea of America' that they brought with them to Ellis Island.[29] This observation applies equally to the CIA's post-war campaign to alter foreign perceptions of American culture. The overtly ideological intentions of both campaigns were at odds with their audiences' pre-existing perceptions and desires, derived in large part from their consumption of popular culture's images of 'America' as a democracy of consumption. Panunzio's comment also illuminates the contemporary recognition that the consumption of American popular culture has not brought with it an assimilation of American values in large parts of the world. During the 1990s, after *Dallas*, CNN and satellite television had apparently won the Cold War for democratic capitalism, the US government scaled back the extent of the public and cultural diplomacy it had previously conducted through such entities as the US Information Agency, while US news networks cut back their foreign news content by two-thirds. At the same time, the global market for American-sourced popular culture expanded more rapidly than at any time since the late 1910s, to the point where, in 2001, Motion Picture Association President Jack Valenti proudly declared that the motion picture industry was the only sector of the US economy 'in trading surplus with every country in the world'.[30] In April 2001, State Department spokesman Richard Boucher justified the level of state disengagement from cultural diplomacy, declaring to the *Advertising Age* that his department had now 'taken the view that to know us is to love us'.[31]

The shock following September 11 was not merely President Bush's amazement 'that there is such misunderstanding of what our country is about, that people would hate us'.[32] It was also the shocked and apparently sudden recognition that the abandonment of cultural diplomacy to corporate commerce had not resulted in 'the triumph of American ideas'.[33] Instead, suggested House International Relations Committee Chairman Henry Hyde, 'the country that invented Hollywood and Madison Avenue has allowed ... a destructive and parodied image of itself to become the intellectual coin of the realm overseas'.[34] Viewed from abroad, where the concept of Americanisation has long carried fewer positive connotations and has more frequently been a term hovering somewhere between critique and abuse, the catastrophic failure of the ideological project encapsulated by Hays and Boucher seems much less surprising, since Hyde's comments echo those repeatedly expressed by American diplomats since Charles Evans Hughes declared that their 'false distortion of American life' produced 'a pernicious distortion among other people with respect to the way in which our people live'.[35] The dissonance between the commercial and political effects of American cultural hegemony might, however, lead us to reconsider the terms in which Hollywood's role in 'the Americanisation of the world' has commonly been understood.

The essays collected here contribute to a history of 'Americanisation', but the history they describe is one very different from the conventional, unidirectional process articulated in theories of cultural and media imperialism, in which commercial hegemony leads to ideological dominance.[36] Most theses relating to cultural imperialism have been constructed with little direct address to – or questioning of – those assumed to have been rendered subservient by such imperialism.[37] In much the same way that our previous volumes on Hollywood's audiences have suggested that the behaviour of empirical viewers does not resemble that of film theories' spectators, several of the essays in this volume make it clear that in the specific cultural contexts of their everyday existence, the Jaffa-rollers of the Illawarra and the cowboys of the Copperbelt did not behave as the theorists of media imperialism have argued that they should. Indeed, Charles Ambler argues in his chapter on cinemagoing in Northern Rhodesia in the 1940s and 1950s that theories of cultural imperialism owe an uncomfortable intellectual legacy to the theorists and practitioners of Empire who sought to regulate the content of their supposedly 'unsophisticated' subjects' media consumption. Priya Jaikumar, similarly, notes the overlapping concerns of British imperial censors and Indian nationalists: both treated Hollywood movies primarily as political objects, capable of having a direct impact on colonial relationships and providing a pretext for a confrontation over colonial inequities. Despite the best efforts of the censors to preempt the possibility, Indian nationalists used their critiques of Hollywood strategically, to emphasise the ways in which the imperial government neither represented nor protected Indian interests.

The essays in this collection broadly follow Andrew Higson's suggestion that we shift emphasis away from an 'analysis of film texts as vehicles for the articulation of nationalist sentiment . . . to an analysis of how actual audiences construct their cultural identity' through their engagement with cinema.[38] Rather than providing confirmatory descriptions of hapless audiences deceived by irresistible texts into abandoning their cultural patrimony to become 'temporary American citizens', these essays describe the activities of local agents accommodating and adapting Hollywood movies to the cultural topography of their immediate environment.[39] From a variety of critical and methodological perspectives, they analyse the place of Hollywood within national, local or regional cultures of exhibition, reception and consumption, and interrogate the identification of international strategies of distribution with 'Americanisation'.

Because of the paucity of direct documentary evidence about audience reception and response, the contributors make use of a range of sources to ask a series of overlapping questions about Hollywood's relationship with its foreign consumers. Some of the essays in this volume are primarily concerned with examining the aims of groups exercising control over the distribution and exhibition of movies, and with these groups' commercial and ideological construction of the audience for Hollywood's product. Other essays focus attention more directly on audiences themselves, exploring the cultures and contexts of viewing and the activities that accompanied and contextualised it.

Priya Jaikumar, Nezih Erdoğan and Hiroshi Kitamura are primarily concerned with the institutional context of reception, but the scale of their concerns ranges from

Jaikumar's overview of the politics of distribution in India to Kitamura's focus on the history of a single cinema in post-war Japan. Kitamura, Anne Bittner and Michael Hammond provide histories of individual cinemas which are also histories of the geography and demographics of the communities they served.[40] Raphaëlle Costa de Beauregard and Melvyn Stokes, Nancy Huggett and Kate Bowles, Charles Ambler and Philippe Meers provide broader accounts of the social and cultural context of the audiences they examine.

Only one of the essays in this collection concerns itself principally with the reception of an individual picture: Michael Hammond's account of a local screening of Thomas Ince's *Civilization* (1916) in Britain. Writing of an exhibition occasion for which we have no witnesses, Hammond conjectures a fictional pair of spectators to witness the première of *Civilization* at the Palladium theatre, Southampton, on 31 August 1917. Unlike theoretical spectators but like actual audience members, these fictional characters bring a collection of expectations and prior experiences with them to the occasion, and view it through the multiple prisms of those expectations and experiences. Fictionalisation is a useful strategy by which to articulate these prisms of interpretative possibility; methodologically, its defence lies in its plausibility, its 'adequacy to the real', a characteristic it shares with the selective documentary evidence used in institutional accounts and the claim to authenticity provided by the personal declaration of oral history.

These essays also contribute to the social history of cinema as a cultural institution. Such a history asks significantly different questions from those concerned with the textuality of films, acts of interpretation of textual meaning and theoretical approaches to these acts of interpretation which have preoccupied film studies to date. As several of the essays in this volume suggest, for most of the history of cinema, the primary relationship that most audiences have had with the cinema has not been with individual movies but with cinemagoing as a social experience. The cinema has provided a site and an occasion for particular forms of social behaviour and within that general truism, individual movies have further specified the nature of the site, the occasion and the behaviour. The enquiry into Hollywood's relation to everyday life is an enquiry into the production of meaning, but that meaning is social, not textual. However little we may actually know about them, the spectators in whom we are interested are not theoretical constructs.

Historically, Hollywood's dominance of the world's screens preceded the appearance of anxieties over 'Americanisation' by approximately a decade. In Raphaëlle Costa de Beauregard and Melvyn Stokes' discussion of French audiences' 'infatuation' with American cinema before and during World War I, the movies' national origin does not generally feature as either an attraction or a concern in itself, any more than it seems to be for the Flemish teenagers interviewed by Philippe Meers in 2001. According to the contemporary accounts they cite, French *populaire* audiences were principally attracted by the commercial and aesthetic superiority of Hollywood's product: the linear plots stimulating a range of emotions and ending 'in a bright, happy, denouement'; the naturalistic performances of Hollywood's early stars; the energy, zest, and 'almost ferocious smile' of *Perle Vite* (Pearl White); the *photogénie* of Hollywood's 'expressive details'; the association between the technical quality of Hollywood's lighting, costume and set design and its budgetary extravagance. These characteristics summarise the essential features of Classical Hollywood Cinema's commercial aesthetic as it was being formulated in the period up to 1917, rather than any explicit or covert ideology it may have expressed.[41]

Michael Hammond's account of a young woman's experience of the Southampton première of *Civilization* in 1917 certainly acknowledges her awareness of the picture's origins, but also recognises that the issue surrounding the picture was less its nationality than its attitude to the war which dominated the city's everyday life. The adaptation of *Civilization* involved the amelioration of its American pacifist discourse and its modification into 'Civilisation: What Every True Briton is Fighting For'. Hammond illustrates not only how this American movie was adapted for a local market by the institutions of distribution and censorship, but also how the exhibitors' advertising strategies worked to bring the picture's publicity into line with the public image that the Palladium theatre itself had within the community. Hammond uses this evidence to speculate about the range of probable interpretations of the picture available to the theatre's audiences.

The adaptation of *Civilization* was explicitly ideological and largely institutional. Much more often, however, accommodations and adaptations were made at a more local and individual level, involving only the exhibitor and the audience, and had more to do with enfolding imported content in a more appropriate local cultural context. Anne Bittner discusses these smaller-scale strategies of acculturation by focusing, like Hammond, on a single performance, examining the organisation of a typical evening's entertainment in 1922 at the York picture theatre in Adelaide, South Australia. Placing this performance within its cultural context involves shifting interpretative focus from the cultural objects exhibited to the relationships between the participants in this cultural event: the performers, the theatre management and the spectators. Like the Palladium, Southampton, the York theatre had a specific niche in the cultural topography of its city, and its management's programming strategies were designed to appeal to an identified target audience. Given the limited control that the exhibitor had over the pictures he received, the movies themselves were, ironically, the programme component over which the theatre management had least influence, even before distribution strategies of block booking further restricted the local manager's control over what he showed. As a result, programming strategies had to find ways of re-packaging the 'prurient rubbish' he sometimes received from Hollywood into something that would pass muster as respectable Australian entertainment.

Bittner's essay examines the content of the entertainment programme that surrounded the two features, demonstrating how it situated Hollywood's product in a local context. The York theatre itself was proudly and assertively Australian in its architecture – 'the work of Australian genius and material', as the local newspaper had described it on its opening. The tyranny of Australian distances also ensured that, with the exception of a few first-run theatres in Sydney and Melbourne, the live performances accompanying Australian cinema exhibition were occasions for the display of local talent. Child singer Baby St Clair was one of the many girls and young women who performed in their neighbourhood or city theatres. Their audiences, familiar with the local entertainment industry as parents or neighbours, were themselves as much participants in the programme as they were spectators of it. These familiar performances provided a means of localising the cinemagoing experience and diversifying its appeal by balancing the titillation of the imported feature with home-grown sentimental respectability.

Detailed accounts such as Bittner's and Hammond's demonstrate that, however explicitly 'American' the feature pictures were on any given occasion, they were also encased within a programme that balanced the exotic with familiar local performances and offered the theatre's regular patrons a diversity of attractions. Nancy Huggett and Kate Bowles take this argument one stage further by examining the local context of exhibition in the Illawarra district south of Sydney, Australia, in the 1930s. The oral histories they conducted with audience members and theatre managers are much more concerned with the routines and rituals of cinemagoing as a public event – 'who sat where each week, and with whom, and what they wore' – than with the memories of particular movies: 'to the extent that interviewees recall specific movies at all, they do so largely in order to tell stories about the community'.

Audiences projected existing social, economic and religious distinctions onto the informal social segregation of cinema seating arrangements. While the move from 'peanut alley' to the upper stalls was one of several rites of passage through childhood, adolescence and courtship were charted by attendance at particular theatres and times. The cinema also provided a relatively safe public space in which 'individuals challenged authority in minor ways, made reputations and starred in their own serial dramas'. These descriptions of 'larrikinism' and local ingenuity challenge both conventionally nationalist accounts of Australian and other audiences as hapless collaborators in Hollywood's hegemony, and more general descriptions of spectatorship which imagine the viewer as an icon of modernity, an isolated, anonymous and implicitly metropolitan figure fixated on the screen.

Huggett and Bowles argue that if audiences are envisaged only in terms of their response to exhibited screen content, they will appear homogeneous, with the same movie constructing the same audience wherever it plays. Investigations of localities, on the other hand, reveal how members of one community used their respective cinemas as one means of comparing themselves with their neighbours. Huggett and Bowles stress the role that this audience parochialism played in incorporating and accommodating the American content that occupied their screens into the dominating everyday context of local concerns and community experiences. They also raise questions about whether small regional communities in different countries may have, albeit unknowingly, shared common discourses about the role of cinema in community life. Above all, they emphasise the resilience of the local culture they examine, and its 'tactical and self-confident accommodation' of Hollywood to 'the everyday routines of childhood, courting and ageing'.

Huggett and Bowles' oral histories suggest that the content of the movies was, at least in the long term, the least memorable part of the social experience of cinemagoing. This evidence leads them to argue that Hollywood's interests were adequately served wherever audiences formed the habit of going to the pictures for reasons to do with their local circumstances, no matter what played on the screen. In the most radical critique of theories of cultural imperialism offered in this book, they argue that 'it was also pre-eminently in Hollywood's interests that the movies were designed for widespread smooth adaptability and, by implication, only minimal cultural impact'. Their conclusion may perhaps underestimate the transient influence of this movie or that star performance on manners, behaviour, gesture or even morals, transmitted and negotiated through long-forgotten conversations in the milk bar or coffee-house, or any of the other locations of the post-movie experience, but it affords a salutary reminder that only histories of the audience can reliably tell us about the practical extent of Hollywood's influence.[42]

As Bittner's examination of occasions of exhibition in Adelaide indicates, the earliest and strongest concerns over the dominance of American screen product had primarily to do with its moral suitability rather than with its national origin. The concerns of the ladies of Adelaide were in fact little different from those of the Daughters of the American Revolution, the colonial censors of the British Empire, or State Department officials worried about 'the unwholesome moral effect of such pictures, especially on certain illiterate or ignorant races of the Far East'.[43] By the mid-1920s, however, both proponents and opponents were talking of Americanisation. While this delay in recognition may in part be attributable to the delay between a process of cultural change and its observation, it also suggests that, by the mid-1920s, factors other than cultural influence were in play. In the decade after World War I, Hollywood became the most visible signifier of an unparalleled American economic expansionism, as the United States 'flooded the world with products, branch plants, and investment capital', while American radio and cable companies, wire services and airlines built the foundations of the American communications empire in what Owen D. Young, head of the Radio Corporation of America, described as the 'economic integration of the world'.[44]

Fuelled by the United States' position as a creditor nation and managed by an informal alliance of businessmen, central bankers and government officials, US international economic policy in the 1920s sought to rebuild the economies of Europe as markets for American goods and politically stable fields for American investment. 'Film America', as the German trade press called Hollywood, was a powerful agent of this policy, as both a sales apparatus for American goods and as a demonstration of what Victoria de Grazia has characterised as 'the enduring capacity of the American "empire without frontiers" to discover, process, and redistribute techniques, styles, and tastes of global provenance'.[45] To proponents such as Young and Hays, America's expansion was inherently benign, since it was based 'not on military force or government design but on the wonders of its private industry, the skill of its experts, the goodness of its philanthropists', and the ubiquity of its communications technologies. 'The power of communications is a greater power than that of the combined armies and navies of the world', Young believed: 'no international understanding . . . can ever function adequately to preserve the peace of the world unless we can get communication so cheap, so free, that all the people of all the nations will understand all the questions and problems of the world.' And that, he asserted, 'is the business of the Radio Corporation of America'.[46]

As historian Emily Rosenberg argues, however, the apologists for an American economic imperium were entrapped in 'misapplied notions of nineteenth-century liberalism and myths of America's exceptional mission', and 'only obscured understanding of the process by which Americans expanded their influence'.[47] The ideology of liberal developmentalism underlying the United States' global economic expansion after both world wars presumed that other nations could and should replicate the American pattern of development, without acknowledging that this also required them to relinquish a conception of nationhood that presumed sovereignty over culture.

Less explicitly, the syncretic, assimilationist construction of American culture was offered as a means of advancing a cultural integration of the world, a dissolution of homogeneous national traditions and secure cultural boundaries in imitation of American cultural exceptionalism. In many respects this version of Americanisation conformed to the vision of Hollywood as an advertising agent for American goods articulated by the State Department's dictum of the 1920s that 'trade follows the film' instead of the flag. The Americanisation achieved by emulation rather than emigration represented that version of American 'dreaming' that economist Christine Frederick identified in 1929 as 'Consumptionism . . . the greatest idea that America has to give to the world; the idea that workmen and masses be looked upon not simply as workers and producers, but as consumers . . . Pay them more, sell them more, prosper more is the equation'.[48] More recently, historian Gary Cross has argued that 'consumerism, the belief that goods give meaning to individuals and their roles in society', was the 'ism' that won the political and ideological engagements of the twentieth century 'even though it had no formal philosophy, no parties, and no obvious leaders'.[49] Cross's account of consumerism emphasises that the 'essential ambiguity of consumer goods was and is fundamental to their meaning and continued appeal'. The semantic malleability and complexity of consumer products have, in his analysis, been the source of their power to divert great social disharmonies into small, individualised disharmonies, to help 'individuals contend with social conflict and ambiguity, evade clear-cut choices, and even hold contradictory desires'.[50]

We have by now an accumulation of evidence for the semantic malleability of Hollywood's products, and their susceptibility to what Phil Rosen has called 'local meanings, practices and even rituals'.[51] Ruth Vasey and I have argued that there is textual and documentary evidence to demonstrate that as texts, Classical Hollywood's movies accommodated themselves to the varied conditions of their reception through the deliberate adoption of strategies of semantic indeterminacy and ambiguity, and did so out of their very nature as themselves consumer products in search of the largest, least differentiated audience and thus the largest profit. Textual indeterminacy is a structural property of Hollywood movies, resulting from the economic conditions of their circulation: their distribution to a multiplicity of venues for a multiplicity of audiences, and the requirement that the single object serve multiple audience pleasures.[52] Cross's arguments suggest that in this indeterminacy they both represented and embodied the semantic fluidity of consumerism itself. In inculcating the central premises of consumerism – the democracy of goods and the democracy of desire – they were teaching their audiences the possibilities of pleasure in the democraticisation of meaning and of the power to interpret.

Beyond the established national boundaries of 'old Europe', Hollywood's relation to questions of nationality and existing alignments of power was even more complex than the cultural nationalists' derogatory definition of mass culture as 'American' allowed. Priya Jaikumar provides a detailed description of film distribution in India in the 1930s, together with an account of the arguments over class, caste and racial divides among audiences in their preferences for American or Indian pictures. Declaring some movies unfit for Indian viewers, British authorities sought to construct a hierarchy of audiences, while Indian nationalists simultaneously attacked Hollywood's racist representations and drew attention to the state's discrimination between audiences along race and class lines.

While, as in other markets, the physical location of a theatre and its pricing policy maintained a de facto separation of its audience by class, race and nationality, the segregation of audiences was entrenched by the exhibition practices of importers catering primarily to Europeans and elite Indians. Like other non-metropolitan audiences, rural Indian audiences saw movies on their tenth or eleventh run, and these distribution and exhibition practices 'reinforced a hierarchy of audiences by class and education'. Indian film-makers, by contrast, self-consciously sought to break down the segregation of domestic Indian viewing and establish a national audience through their deliberate development of a 'national' visual and linguistic idiom for cinema. The success of these strategies should also be noted by anyone concerned to interrogate the cultural imperialism thesis: 'By the early 1940s, Hollywood no longer dominated the subcontinent. It existed as a parallel cinema', part of 'a generic "foreign" cinema while Indian films were identifiable in all their national and local variations'.

Since its development in the 1930s, popular Indian cinema has been probably the most enduring national-popular cinema functioning as an alternative to Hollywood. Its success may, as Jaikumar suggests, have significantly to do with its capacity to adapt and re-codify elements of Hollywood practice in an Indian cultural context, and thus to gain dominance in its domestic market through its cultural specificity rather than through an imposed state policy. These re-codified elements are stylistic rather than overtly ideological. Jaikumar argues that Hollywood paradoxically served as 'a template by which Indian films became progressively differentiated from their Western counterparts in the sound era', offering 'an aesthetic that was a point of both reference and alterity for Indian cinema'.

Hiroshi Kitamura's study of the Marunouchi Subaruza theatre in Tokyo between 1947 and 1950 provides an example of Hollywood's product being used explicitly for ideological purposes, in offering American cinema as a sophisticated and culturally elevated product for Toyko's educated mainstream audiences of office workers, *sarari men*, public officials and students. Following John Dower's account of the post-war period in Japan, Kitamura argues that Subaruza's enthusiastic engagement with Hollywood identified it as 'an interactive space in which the Japanese "embraced" the victor's values and meanings in reconstructing their new identities under America's neocolonial presence'. Subaruza deliberately courted an elite audience, including senior politicians, academics, artists and members of the Imperial family, and encouraged them to treat the Hollywood movies they saw in this 'chosen' theatre as a 'serious' cultural phenomenon, from which the Japanese could, as the American Movie Culture Association put it, 'learn the finest things that America is spreading across the world', using movies to aid 'Japan's reconstruction into a democratic and cultural nation'.

Apart from the viewing conditions themselves, Subaruza highlighted the quality of the pictures they showed through printed programmes featuring articles that outlined American customs, beliefs and lifestyles, celebrated Hollywood's representation of 'high culture' and provided endorsements of the pictures' artistic status. The programme for *The Best Years of Our Lives* contained an essay on 'American Society and Life', in which cultural critic Nakano Goro considered the movie as a representation of what he saw as the essence of America: a 'democracy in action', concluding that this 'great picture based on a great idea' could ultimately stimulate, facilitate and encourage Japan's own 'democratisation'.

While Kitamura's analysis draws attention to the conscious use of Hollywood movies for ideological effect, he nevertheless challenges the notion that the American film programme in occupied Japan was a 'forced Americanisation'. Rather, he argues, local agents actively consumed, appropriated and reinvented Hollywood entertainment in ways that facilitated its penetration across the war-damaged nation. While the movies were not themselves textually altered in this process of appropriation, they were contextualised. Kitamura's account of Subaruza's post-war history reveals that, even in a context in which the ideological work that Hollywood movies might perform was acknowledged and reinforced, the movies themselves were seen as insufficient agents of social transformation.

Hollywood established its commercial hegemony in Turkey in the 1940s. Nezih Erdogan uses Turkish film magazines of that decade to demonstrate how Turkish audiences adapted Hollywood's product to their specific cultural concerns. The magazines, Erdogan argues, constructed an image of the 'American way of life' through the image of Hollywood that they promoted. Taking their material from Hollywood's publicity output, amplified by contributions from Turkish journalists living in the United States, the magazines' discourse concentrated on matters of romance, consumption and the material success attendant on stardom. Erdogan argues that there was a culturally specific inflection to their implementation of these typically 'Americanised' concerns – in the ways in which prevailing Turkish ideas on beauty and desirability constructed the local characteristics of American stardom, for example. For American audiences, he suggests, Lana Turner was a star, but for Turkish audiences she was an *American* star, an image which coalesced with a wider American dream that Turkish audiences appropriated from Hollywood's images in order to construct what Erdogan evocatively calls 'our America' out of their own cultural imagination. As one magazine talent competition expressed it, 'We are looking for a Betty! A Betty [Grable], but a Betty of beautiful Istanbul.' Hollywood's erotic intensity was evident in the envious attention paid to the experience of Turkish men lucky enough to hover near the flames of Hollywood glamour. Accounts of actor Turhan Bey's relationship with Lana Turner constructed him as an 'agent of fantasy' for Turkish audiences at the same time that it provided the opportunity for the articulation of a much more conservative view of gender relations. 'Our America' would have been unrecognisable in Los Angeles. It could be imagined only in Turkey, but it was not itself in Turkey, since it represented a range of behaviours that could only be imagined as occurring in some Other, utopian, inaccessible place. As the editor of *Hollywood Dunyasi* advised one of his readers seeking advice about emigrating, 'It is impossible to go to America right now. And even if it was possible I wouldn't advise you to do so . . . Do not let yourself be deceived by dreams.'[53]

Like Erdogan, Charles Ambler uses the evidence provided by his account of the 'Copperbelt cowboys' of Northern Rhodesia in the 1940s to suggest that 'the often disjointed and exotic images of the "Wild West" . . . comprised a crucial repertoire of images' through which the young urban population could 'engage notions of modernity'. Ambler argues that the moviegoing experiences of audiences in the Copperbelt challenge the confident assumptions of mass media products' powers to persuade by exemplifying the ways in which audiences appropriate media products for purposes barely connected to, and never communicated to, the point of production. The movies those audiences watched, at almost the farthest extreme of the global distribution chain, had been subjected to a panoply of physical deconstructions, to a point where their plots would have been barely discernible to an audience equipped with the linguistic and cultural competences to 'follow' them – which Ambler's protagonists were not. To make these artefacts make sense, these audiences had to reconfigure them into patterns of symbol and behaviour which might mean something in the context of their viewing. They thus found ways to use the characters and action of their B-Western diet as 'a kind of guide to urban modernity and sophistication' in central Africa, 'weaving witchcraft and kinship politics into discussions of the meanings of particular sequences'. Like the Indian nationalists in Jaikumar's chapter, these audiences also used the movies they watched as an opportunity to critique the colonial order under which they lived. The vernacular modernism thus created, however, was far more firmly rooted in the urban communities of Northern Rhodesia than it was in the point of origin of the movies themselves.

At first sight, the Flemish teenagers described by Philippe Meers in the final essay in this collection would seem to provide evidence of the depth of Americanisation in present-day Europe. Meers makes clear the extent to which Hollywood's product dominates the choices available to the contemporary megaplex audience, and the extent to which American international distribution has reduced the viewing options available for most spectators in Europe and other First World markets, as well as in the US itself. His survey finds that young Belgian audiences display an overwhelming preference for Hollywood, perceiving it less as a national American cinema than the broad category of commercial mainstream cinema against which national cinemas are defined as stylistically and financially antithetical. Flemish teenagers make the same kinds of associations between Hollywood and 'quality' that the audiences of Subaruza were encouraged to make more than half a century earlier: 'quality' is a matter of budget, spectacle and star performance. By comparison, their horizons of expectation are much lower for Flemish film, although this also meant that, on occasion, the local product may produce unexpectedly high levels of satisfaction and pleasure.

Invoking Ien Ang's concepts of 'emotional' and 'empiricist realism', Meers argues that while Hollywood presents itself as exotically remote from everyday reality, its stylistic and discursive familiarity allows for a high level of spectatorial identification with its plausible fantasy.[54] This perception of 'American' culture as fantastic and therefore credible coincides with the observation of a German publisher of crime fiction that his readers found detective novels set in Germany either boring or incredible, and tourism had rendered the rest of Europe 'commonplace . . . Only America is left to us. It is the only place where the reality of things cannot be checked personally by most European readers. American crime is still credible'.[55]

Classical Hollywood cinema created an intensely self-referential world, much of the attraction of which lay precisely in its difference and distance from the world outside the cinema. Viewers were rewarded for their engagement with Hollywood's self-referential world by their pleasurable knowledge of a familiar but foreign territory, distanced from any potentially troubling relation to the 'real'. Instead, as Ruth Vasey has argued, Hollywood's very distance from verifiable experience enabled it,

> uniquely to define a cinematic world that offered audiences 'authentic' entertainment in terms of its own criteria of action, spectacle and eroticism . . . Operating according to

their own internally consistent laws and imperatives, and shaped by established industrial and distribution practices, Hollywood movies established themselves as the locus of an imaginative, experiential 'reality' that could only be *imitated* by filmmakers elsewhere.[56]

'Hollywood', the utopian place in which all 'American' movies were set, was a geographically free-floating signifier of American-ness, its own location on a map of America no more precisely defined than were the borders of Ruritania, Freedonia or any of its other mythical kingdoms. In the community or the privacy of their own spaces, viewers could appropriate aspects of its representation into their own material existence, creating their own imagined 'Americas'. Through Hollywood, 'Americanisation' became both a material reality and a discursive practice. The material reality of the movies' Americanisation took place through the distribution system constructed from 1916, which secured 80 per cent of the world's screens for the profit of American distribution companies. But the act of Americanisation took place in the space between the audience and the screen, in the transient act of consumption of the shadow images of cinema's Great Dark Room. That act might often have material consequences, in the increase in the foreign sales of American automobiles and typewriters, but the act of Americanisation was and is also itself almost untraceable, in part because of the circumstances of its enactment, and in part because of the elusive, relativistic quality of the 'America' that was Americanized. This relativistic quality was both a property of the movies' textual organisation and a condition of their reception. As such, it was liable to multiple variation, inflection and change, since, in the acquisitive imaginations of Hollywood's foreign audiences, not even the most ideologically predetermined artefact could avoid the processes of decontextualisation and reinterpretation.

## Notes

1 'What is Being Done for Motion Pictures', statement by Will H. Hays, London, 5 October 1923, p. 8, in Douglas Gomery (ed.), *The Will Hays Papers* (microfilm, Frederick, MD: University Publications of America, 1986), part 1, reel 12, frame 813 (hereafter Hays Papers).

2 Walter Lippmann, 'Empire: the Days of Our Nonage Are Over', in Lippmann, *Men of Destiny* (New York: Macmillan, 1927), pp. 215–19.

3 Anthony D. Smith, 'Towards a Global Culture?', in Mike Featherstone (ed.), *Global Culture: Nationalism, Globalization and Modernity: A Theory, Culture and Society Special Issue* (London: Sage, 1990), p. 179.

4 Mrs W., in interview with Charles Ambler, Kamwala, Lusaka, 5 July 1988.

5 Quoted in Charles Eckert, 'The Carole Lombard in Macy's Window', *Quarterly Review of Film Studies*, no. 3 (winter 1978), pp. 4–5.

6 Edward G. Lowry, 'Certain Factors and Considerations Affecting the European Market', internal MPPDA memo, 25 October 1928, in Andrew Higson and Richard Maltby (eds), *'Film Europe' and 'Film America': Cinema, Commerce and Cultural Exchange, 1925–1939* (Exeter: University of Exeter Press, 1999), p. 353.

7 Gary Gerstle argues that Americanism emerged 'as a political language, a set of words, phrases, and concepts that individuals used – either by choice or necessity – to articulate their political beliefs and press their political demands' in the 1920s and

1930s as an outgrowth of the Americanisation movement, the implementation of 'consumptionism', Fordism or the American Plan of industrial relations, and the national diffusion of 'American' cultural values through the mass media: 'The combined result of these forces . . . was an unprecedented national emphasis on pledging loyalty to American institutions, on defining what it meant to be an American, and on elaborating an American way of life.' Gary Gerstle, *Working-Class Americanism: The Politics of Labor in a Textile City, 1914–1960* (Cambridge: Cambridge University Press, 1989), p. 8.

8  Melvyn Stokes and Richard Maltby (eds), *American Movie Audiences: From the Turn of the Century to the Early Sound Era* (London: BFI, 1999); Melvyn Stokes and Richard Maltby (eds), *Identifying Hollywood's Audiences: Cultural Identity and the Movies* (London: BFI, 1999); Melvyn Stokes and Richard Maltby (eds), *Hollywood Spectatorship: Changing Perceptions of Cinema Audiences* (London: BFI, 2001).

9  Richard Slotkin, *Gunfighter Nation: The Myth of the Frontier in Twentieth-Century America* (New York: HarperCollins, 1993), p. 10 (emphasis in original).

10  Rick Altman, *The American Film Musical* (Bloomington: Indiana University Press, 1989), p. 340.

11  Sally Price discusses 'the plight of objects from around the world that . . . have been discovered, seized, commoditized, stripped of their social ties, redefined in new settings, and reconceptualized to fit into the economic, cultural, political and ideological needs of people from distant societies' in the construction of 'Primitive Art' as an aesthetic category, in *Primitive Art in Civilized Places* (Chicago: University of Chicago Press, 1989), p. 5. See also James Clifford, 'Histories of the Tribal and the Modern', and 'On Collecting Art and Culture', in *The Predicament of Culture: Twentieth-Century Ethnography, Literature, and Art* (Cambridge, MA: Harvard University Press, 1988), pp. 189–251.

12  In engaging in the dubious practice of auto-ethnography, I am not unmindful (as Will Hays often said) of Ariel Dorfman's analysis of childhood as underdevelopment, and his argument that 'due to its own self-image, its historic development and what it had learned about humankind during that development, America was able to project a universal category – childhood – onto alien cultures that were subjected politically and economically, and to seek in them infantile echoes, the yearning for redemption, innocence, and eternal life that, to one degree or another, are part of the human condition. American mass culture appealed to the child the audience would like to be, the child they remembered, the child they still felt themselves at times to be.' Ariel Dorfman, *The Empire's New Clothes: What the Lone Ranger, Barbar, and Other Innocent Heroes Do to Our Minds* (New York: Pantheon, 1983), p. 203.

13  I take my sense of the significance of accent from Michael Denning's adaptation of V. N. Voloshinov's concept of 'the social multiaccentuality of the ideological sign'. In discussing the 'mechanic accents' in late nineteenth-century American dime novels, Denning argues that their 'class accents can sometimes be detected in their production . . . but they are equally active in their reception, in the way readers accent their reading. This can be difficult to detect; thus it is essential to begin with an assumption of contradiction, of the multiaccentuality of all ideological signs. Otherwise, the constant attempt of the dominant culture to render them univocal, to make them speak in legitimate accents, will conceal the struggle, and thus the meaning of the ideological

document.' Michael Denning, *Mechanic Accents: Dime Novels and Working-Class Culture in America* (London: Verso, 1987), pp. 82–3.

14 Andrew Higson, 'The Concept of National Cinema', *Screen*, vol. 30, no. 4 (autumn 1999), p. 37.

15 Ibid., p. 44; Benedict Anderson, *Imagined Communities: Reflections on the Origin and Spread of Nationalism* (London: Verso, 1983).

16 Higson, 'The Concept of National Cinema', p. 37.

17 Ibid., p. 39.

18 Richard Kuisel, *Seducing the French: The Dilemma of Americanisation* (Berkeley: University of California Press, 1993), p. 237.

19 Dick Hebdidge, 'Towards a Cartography of Taste 1935–1962', in *Hiding in the Light* (London: Routledge, 1988), p. 52.

20 Maurice Thorez, General Secretary of the French Communist Party, 18 April 1948, quoted in Jean-Pierre Jeancolas, 'From the Blum-Byrnes Agreement to the GATT Affair', in Geoffrey Nowell-Smith and Steven Ricci (eds), *Hollywood and Europe: Economics, Culture, National Identity: 1945–95* (London: BFI, 1998), p. 51.

21 Anthony D. Smith discusses the extent to which the continental and explicitly ideological cultures of US and the Soviet Union challenged or transcended the narrow nationalisms that had prevailed, particularly in Europe, before World War II, but his discussion is primarily concerned with the post-war period of 'superpower' conflict. Zygmunt Bauman's discussion of national cultures and the 'stranger' suggests an interpretative framework in which American culture in the inter-war period might productively be viewed as differently Other than the Otherness of the national enemy. Smith, 'Towards a Global Culture?', pp. 171–91; Zygmunt Bauman, 'Modernity and Ambivalence', in Featherstone, *Global Culture*, pp. 143–69.

22 At its most extreme, among the European far right in the 1930s, the fear of 'Americanisation' overlapped with anti-Semitism in claims that 'American cinema is the property of a certain group of Israelite finance' which 'attempts to export the American spirit', and accusations of the debauching influence of 'judéo-negro-américaine' culture. John Trumpbour, *Selling Hollywood to the World: US and European Struggles for Mastery of the Global Film Industry, 1920–1950* (Cambridge: Cambridge University Press, 2002), p. 231. See also Richard Maltby and Ruth Vasey, ' "Temporary American Citizens": Cultural Anxieties and Industrial Strategies in the Americanisation of European Cinema', in *'Film Europe' and 'Film America'*, pp. 32–55.

23 Joseph Nye, *The Paradox of American Power: Why the World's Only Superpower Can't Go It Alone* (New York; Oxford University Press, 2002), p. 11; 'America in the very literal sense is truly the world-state . . . Our country represents the greatest single uniting of races, peoples and culture. Is it not possible that this very quality enabled America to express itself by the creation and development of the m[otion] p[icture]?' Will Hays, 'What's Right with America' speech, Philadelphia, 17 January 1938, Hays Papers, part 2, reel 19, frame 1169.

24 The archetypal statement of this position is Dwight MacDonald, 'Masscult and Midcult', in MacDonald, *Against the American Grain: Essays on the Effects of Mass Culture* (London: Gollancz, 1963), pp. 3–75.

25 According to Francis Stonor Saunders, the CIA's campaign was rationalised by the 'expansive conception of [America's] security requirements' contained in security

directive NSC 10/2 (June 1948), 'to include a world substantially made over in its own image'. Francis Stonor Saunders, *The Cultural Cold War: The CIA and the World of Arts and Letters* (New York: New Press, 2000), pp. 39, 101.

26 Malcolm Cowley, quoted in Saunders, *The Cultural Cold War*, p. 140.

27 Ellwood P. Cubberley, quoted in Roger Daniels, *Not Like Us: Immigrants and Minorities in America, 1890–1924* (Chicago: Ivan R. Dee, 1997), p. 91.

28 Will Hays, speech, New York, 1 November 1926, Motion Picture Producers and Distributors of America, Inc. Archive, 1926 Americanisation file.

29 C. Panunzio, quoted in Daniels, *Not Like Us*, p. 93.

30 Jack Valenti, 'Copyright & Creativity – The Jewel in America's Trade Crown', speech to the International Trademark Association, Santa Monica, California, 22 January 2001. Accessed from the Motion Picture Association of America website, http://www.mpaa.org/jack/

31 Quoted in Simon Dumenco, 'Stopping Spin Laden', *New York Magazine*, 12 November 2001. Accessed from http://www.newyorkmetro.com/nymetro/news/media/features/5379/index2.html

32 Quoted in Simon Dumenco, 'Stopping Spin Laden'.

33 Franklin Foer, quoted in 'Background Briefing: Culture Bombs', Australian Broadcasting Corporation National Radio broadcast, 7 July 2002. Accessed from http://www.abc.net.au/rn/talks/bbing/docs/bb_020707_culture.rtf

34 Quoted in 'Background Briefing: Culture Bombs'.

35 Charles Evans Hughes, 1924, quoted in Trumpbour, *Selling Hollywood to the World*, p. 29.

36 For an historical account imbued with the assumptions of American cultural imperialism, see David Puttnam with Neil Watson, *The Undeclared War: The Struggle for Control of the World's Film Industry* (London: HarperCollins, 1997).

37 Smith, 'Towards a Global Culture?', pp. 175–6. Robert McChesney's trenchant critique of the role of transnational corporations in 'The Media System Goes Global' suggests a significant redefinition of media imperialism, but examines questions of the media's political economy rather than reception. Robert W. McChesney, *Rich Media, Poor Democracy: Communication Politics in Dubious Times* (New York: New Press, 2000), pp. 78–118. A summary discussion of the debates around media and cultural imperialism can be found in James Curran and Myung-Jin Park, 'Beyond Globalization Theory', in James Curran and Myung-Jin Park (eds), *De-Westernizing Media Studies* (London: Routledge, 2000), pp. 3–18. Curran and Park argue for the continued importance of the nation state, most importantly because 'media systems are shaped not merely by national regulatory regimes and national audience preference, but by a complex ensemble of social relations that have taken shape in national contexts. It is precisely the historically grounded density of these relationships that tends to be excluded from simplified global accounts, in which theorists survey the universe while never straying far from the international airport,' p. 12. See also John Tomlinson, *Globalization and Culture* (Chicago: University of Chicago Press, 1999), and Ella Shohat and Robert Stam, *Unthinking Eurocentrism: Multiculturalism and the Media* (London: Routledge, 1994).

38 Higson, 'The Concept of National Cinema', pp. 45–6.

39 A. G. Atkinson, *Daily Express*, in *J. Walter Thompson Co. Newsletter* 183 (1 July 1927), p. 320, quoted in Maltby and Vasey, 'Temporary American Citizens', p. 34.

40  Recent examples of similar approaches to exhibition and reception history include
    Gregory A. Waller, *Main Street Amusements: Movies and Commercial Entertainment in a
    Southern City, 1896–1930* (Washington, DC: Smithsonian Institution Press, 1995), and
    Mark Jancovich and Lucy Faire with Sarah Stubbings, *The Place of the Audience:
    Cultural Geographies of Film Consumption* (London: BFI, 2003).

41  David Bordwell, Janet Staiger and Kristin Thompson, *The Classical Hollywood Cinema
    Film Style and Mode of Production to 1960* (London: Routledge and Kegan Paul, 1985),
    pp. 155–240; Richard Maltby, *Hollywood Cinema: Second Edition* (Oxford: Blackwell,
    2003), pp. 5–110.

42  Annette Kuhn discusses 'cinema memory' in *An Everyday Magic: Cinema and Cultural
    Memory* (London: I. B. Tauris, 2002): see in particular chapters 5, 'Growing Up With
    Cinema', and 9, 'Oh! Dreamland!'

43  H. S. Villard, Office of the Economic Adviser, Department of State, 'Foreign
    Restrictions on American Films', 25 March 1929, quoted in Trumpbour, *Selling
    Hollywood to the World*, p. 70.

44  Emily S. Rosenberg, *Spreading the American Dream: American Economic and Cultural
    Expansion, 1890–1945* (New York: Hill and Wang, 1982), pp. 87–107, 122; Owen D.
    Young, speech, July 1930, quoted in Frank Costigliola, *Awkward Dominion: American
    Political, Economic, and Cultural Relations with Europe, 1919–1933* (Ithaca, NY: Cornell
    University Press, 1984), p. 140.

45  Victoria de Grazia, 'Mass Culture and Sovereignty: The American Challenge to
    European Cinema, 1920–1960', *Journal of Modern History*, vol. 61 (March 1989), p. 60.

46  Young, quoted in Costigliola, *Awkward Dominion*, p. 153.

47  Rosenberg, *Spreading the American Dream*, p. 229.

48  Christine Frederick, *Selling Mrs. Consumer* (New York: The Business Bourse, 1929),
    p. 5.

49  Gary Cross, *An All-Consuming Century: Why Commercialism Won in Modern America*
    (New York: Columbia University Press, 2000), p. 1.

50  Ibid., p. 21.

51  Philip Rosen, 'Reformulating Hollywood As Global Cinema', paper at the Flinders
    Humanities Symposium on Hollywood as Global Cinema, Adelaide, 2002.

52  Ruth Vasey, *The World According to Hollywood, 1918–1939* (Exeter: University of Exeter
    Press, 1997), pp. 194–224; Maltby, *Hollywood Cinema*, pp. 471–90.

53  Editor's reply to a letter in the *Biz Bize* column of *Hollywood Dunyasi*, nd (c. 1945),
    quoted in Nezih Erdogan's chapter in this volume.

54  Ien Ang, *Watching 'Dallas': Soap Opera and the Melodramatic Imagination* (London:
    Methuen, 1985), p. 45.

55  Quoted in Klaus Kunkel, 'Ein artiger James Bond: Jerry Cotton und der Bastei-Verlag',
    in Jochen Vogt (ed.), *Der Kriminalroman: zur Theorie und Geschichte einer Gattung*
    (Munich: W. Fink, 1971), p. 564.

56  Ruth Vasey, 'Hollywood and Authenticity', paper at the German Historical Association
    Conference on 'Global Hollywood', Victoria, British Columbia, 2001.

# 1

# The Reception of American Films in France, c. 1910–20

Raphaëlle Costa de Beauregard and Melvyn Stokes

In a recent study of how Hollywood films first came to dominate the French market, Jens Ulff-Møller listed four crucial factors: the failure of the French film industry to develop the same kind of strong vertical integration as its American competitors; the more restrictive application of cinema law in France compared to the US; the aggressive nature of American export trade policy and legislation after World War I; and the active support of the American government during the 1920s in helping encourage the export of Hollywood films.[1] The first three factors had already been explored by numerous scholars.[2] Ulff-Møller's own work was dedicated to an examination of the fourth. Concentrating on economics, law, politics and diplomacy, these studies did not, however, directly address the key questions of how and why French audiences responded as favourably as they did to American films. The chapter which follows attempts to provide answers to these questions.

Any attempt to 'bring the audience back in' does, of course, require some discussion of the nature of the evidence available. Sadly, there is no French equivalent of Emilie Altenloh's groundbreaking *Sociology of the Cinema* (1914), which gave much detailed information on contemporary German cinemagoing.[3] In studying early French moviegoing, there are three principal sources of evidence. Newspapers catering to distinct sections of the reading public, such as *Le Temps* and *Le Figaro*, contain movie advertisements and, later, reviews. Trade journals such as *Ciné-Journal* and *Le Courrier Cinématographique*, directed mainly at film distributors and exhibitors, provide a second source of information, while specialist film journals such as the *Le Film* supply a third. Writers for these periodicals, such as Louis Delluc,[4] played a major role in the exploration of the reasons why French audiences had developed a taste for American films.[5] This chapter is based on the analysis of these varying sources.

It is by no means clear when American films first began to dominate the French market. Susan Hayward comments that it was partially because films originating in America 'had garnered the popular cinema market' that Charles Pathé switched in 1908 to making the more upmarket *film d'art*, based on productions by legitimate theatre and thus intended to appeal to a more middle-class audience.[6] Other scholars have suggested that it was during the course of World War I – the early stages of which saw the virtual collapse of the French film industry – that American cinema established its hegemony. Examining newspapers and journals such as *L'Illustration* and *Ciné-Journal*, however, indicates that the true beginnings of the popularity of American film in France was during the period between 1910 and 1913.

## Early French Cinema Audiences

Since French moving pictures were initially shown in vaudeville theatres, music halls (*caf'conc'*) and tents at local fairs, their spectators were mainly the working-class audiences drawn to such entertainments.[7] By 1906, however, film was playing an increasingly significant role in live theatres and halls devoted only to showing films were appearing in larger numbers. 'Every day a new movie theatre opens', commented the *Photo-Ciné-Gazette* in April 1907.[8] Writing a few months later on the situation in Paris, novelist and critic Rémy de Gourmont underlined cinema's growing ubiquity as an inexpensive form of entertainment:

> the biggest theaters have now opened their doors. The Chatelet, the Variétés, and the Gymnase all now include cinema programs, and one can queue up at the small boulevard cinemas that specialize in them. The price is still reasonable everywhere. For two francs, you can have an orchestra seat, and for a franc you can still get a seat which in the theater would cost five or six times as much.[9]

Nearly five years later, 'Yhcam' (a pseudonym) also emphasised cinema's appeal to the lower classes because of its cost and accessibility:

> The cinema has allowed a huge number of people to satisfy their taste for the theater, a taste which they already had, but which the meagerness of their means did not allow them to satisfy.
>
> Specifically, a person who could only go to the theater once on five francs can frequent the cinema five times, for the price of tickets is about five times less expensive.[10]

Jean-Jacques Meusy has commented on the appeal that the new cinema 'palaces' built after 1911 had for what was still an 'essentially working-class' clientele: 'wasn't it marvelous to be offered, for one franc or even less, entrance into a palace !'[11] In 1913, Louis Haugmard, a journalist working for a Catholic weekly paper, deplored the fact that 'many deconsecrated chapels are becoming cinema halls; and that is symbolic, if one realizes that, for an important segment of the working class, the cinema is already a "religion of the people" or, rather, "the irreligion of the future." '[12]

Meusy has estimated that there were approximately 180 cinemas existing in Paris in 1913. Of these, many were located in such outlying working-class arrondissements as the 13th, the 14th, the 18th, the 19th and the 20th.[13] The wealthier areas of western Paris had been much slower to acquire cinemas: the 16th acquired its first in December 1910 and the 8th only in 1913, when the Colisée opened on the Champs-Elysées.[14] Yet, starting around 1906, Charles Pathé – followed by Léon Gaumont and others – had begun to open cinemas on the grands boulevards in Paris and later in provincial cities. These new halls attracted a more middle-class clientele – a process further encouraged by the emergence of a new kind of film: the so-called film d'art. Articulating ambition in their very name, these films were intended to appeal to a new middle-class audience by consciously associating themselves with forms of cultural expression already accepted by bourgeois opinion as legitimate forms of art: literature, theatre and music. The new type of film was to be based usually on literary adaptations (or historical reconstructions). It was to have its roots in the theatre, involving established stage directors (especially from the Comédie Française), writers, actors and scenic designers. It was also to involve music: *L'assassinat du Duc de Guise* (1908), the pioneering model for this new type of film, was released together with a musical score specially composed by Camille Saint-Saëns.[15]

The appearance of *L'Assassinat du Duc de Guise* was the signal for an attempt, on the part of some representatives of the French periodical and newspaper press, to construct two different kinds of audience: the popular one ('la foule'), whose main aim was to be surprised and moved to tears of joy or sadness (often by family melodramas), and a more respectable, middle-class one that was thought to be able to appreciate more 'artistic' films. By 1910, the daily newspaper *Le Figaro*, catering for an upwardly mobile, mainly Paris-based readership, was making this distinction, at least implicitly. It printed only selective cinema programmes, recommending – usually with the description 'artistique' – films considered 'high culture' enough to be a suitable subject for intelligent conversation. More republican in its sentiments, the weekly *L'Illustration* celebrated – in its detailed account of *L'Assassinat* – the fact that this type of film was able to please 'crowds where the most humble and the most refined people are jumbled together'.[16]

In some respects, this strategy of appealing to a wider audience through a new type of film worked well. In December 1911, George Dureau, editor of the trade magazine *Ciné-Journal*, noted that 'the middle-bourgeoisie had become regular cinemagoers, attracted in particular by the various series of "artistic" films'.[17] Looking back from the perspective of 1935, however, one writer saw the movement for the acquisition and acculturation of cinema by the educated classes as the true beginning of the downfall of French cinema. 'People from the world of the Theatre and from the literary circles', Robert de Beauplan alleged,

> academicians such as Henri Lavedan, Le Bargy and a few others, had become aware that cinema was, or could be somewhat better than a mere vulgar entertainment and that it was destined to a higher career. They founded the 'Film d'Art'. That proceeded from an excellent intention . . . Alack! These would-be saviours of cinema, though quite unwittingly, did it a rather bad turn. They turned cinema into an imitator of theatre.[18]

Without the theatre's capacity for speech, actors in film d'art productions often used exaggerated actions and gestures. At other times, the films themselves seemed to offer only a succession of *tableaux vivants*.[19] They became little more, as Dada-ist poet Philippe Soupault later wrote, than 'the colorless mirror and mute echo of the theater'.[20]

The exaggerated acting in the most 'artistic' French films contrasted strongly with films originating in America, and may have aided the latters' growing prominence in France. 'Lately', observed Louis Feuillade, Gaumont's principal director, in April 1911, 'public taste has favored "films" in which one can see excellently trained actors perform naturally, simply, with neither bombast nor ridiculous pantomime'. Almost certainly, he was referring to the Vitagraph films that were then enthusing French audiences. 'The public wanted nothing but Vitagraph films', asserted Victorin Jasset six months later.[21] Jasset, a former stage manager who was now the main film director at the Eclair studio (where he produced *Nick Carter, roi de détectives* and other crime series), attempted to analyse the reasons for what he termed the 'infatuation' of the French moviegoing public with Vitagraph films. The latter, he believed, represented 'an absolutely new method' of film-making, based on the use of close-ups: 'Americans had noticed the effect of physical expression and gesture in close shots, and they made use of the overall [long] shot only when they needed to include characters who remained slightly more immobile'. Close-ups themselves required a very different form of acting to that which characterised most French cinema: in the Vitagraph films it 'was absolutely calm, to the point of exaggeration'.[22] Americans were also superior when it came to creating scenarios: 'they made films as simple and as naive as possible . . . trying as best they could to approximate real life, and often constructing an action in a straight line that ended in a bright, happy denouement'. Lastly, as Jasset perceptively noted, the Vitagraph company was experimenting with the origins of what would soon come to be known as the 'star' system: its group of actors 'included several performers that the public noticed immediately, became familiar with, and claimed as their own. The periodic return of these same performers was awaited and cheered.'[23]

Vitagraph was better known to French audiences than its American competitors, such as Biograph, Lubin, Selig and Edison, because it had built up a much more effective distribution system in Europe.[24] But the advertisements that appeared in *Ciné-Journal* from 1910 onwards suggested a species of 'family' resemblance between American films that underlined their difference from those produced in France or Italy. Showing a good understanding of popular taste, these ads downplayed 'educational' subjects and themes. They also offered photographs of male and female actors, focusing on their personal appeal to French moviegoers in preference to the general emphasis on new artistic achievement and the source of the film that were common in publicity for film d'art productions.

In drawing attention to the strengths of American productions, some of the advertisements implicitly commented on the weaknesses of their European counterparts. 'Why are the films of the great trademark Edison so well liked by the public?' asked one ad rhetorically in *Ciné-Journal* in September 1911. It answered its own question: 'Because they bring together the following qualities: Photographic perfection – Absolute fixity – Sensational scenarios – Natural acting – Interpretation by performers of the first rank'.[25] The fact that the stability of the images, interesting scenarios, acting that seemed 'natural' and employment of well-known actresses/actors were considered worth drawing attention to in Edison productions suggests that they were widely seen as lacking in films produced by Edison's French competitors.

In the same issue of *Ciné-Journal*, distributors for Vitagraph inserted a long advertisement for *La Bastille* (1911). Dealing with a major episode in French history, this film probably had a particular appeal for French audiences. The ad itself took the form of comments by six movie-theatre managers on the enthusiastic way in which the film had been received. The comments, of course, were intended to attract additional custom: the managers emphasised that they had full houses and that audiences were really enjoying the film itself. But the locations of the cinemas themselves suggested that this film in particular (and Vitagraph films generally) attracted French spectators from different social backgrounds. Most of the Paris cinemas cited were located either in or on the periphery of the working-class districts of the 18th and 20th arrondissements. Clearly, *La Bastille* appealed to working-class or *populaire* audiences, both in the capital and in provincial Marseilles. It also proved very successful, however, at the Brasserie Cinéma-Rochechouart

in Paris's middle-class 3rd arrondissement.[26] According to the theatre managers, there were two things in particular about the film that explained its impact on French audiences. One was the style of acting ('what I admire most, remarked the manager of the Royal Bio, 'is the marvellous acting of the Vitagraph performers'). The other was that, instead of offering a 'highbrow' historical reconstruction of the French Revolution (as a film d'art production would have done), La Bastille was deliberately designed to thrill its spectators by appealing to a gamut of emotions. 'There is not a spectator', commented the manager of the Cinéma Pigalle, 'who has not experienced genuine emotion in seeing this succession of tableaux, some tender, some moving to the point of anguish.'[27]

In May 1913, Louis Haugmard commented that most films shown in France had intertitles that were 'usually in good basic English'.[28] His remark probably pointed to the growing penetration of the French market by American films. That penetration was encouraged by the decision of Pathé Frères, also in 1913, to cut back on domestic film production in order to concentrate on distribution and exhibition. Yet the French film industry was still quite resilient in the years before the outbreak of war. Unlike Pathé, Gaumont actually increased production during this period and its leading director, Louis Feuillade, secured perhaps his greatest success up to that point with his crime series *Fantômas* (1913–14).[29] Moreover, the fact that many French cinemas offered a varied programme meant that American films still often constituted only part of that programme. For example, reviewing the opening night of a new, large Paris movie-theatre in late December 1913, *Le Courrier Cinématographique* commented that:

> The Lutetia Wagram presents the most beautiful films from every company, both French and foreign. Indeed, the program included an amusing *Léonce* from Gaumont,[30] a dramatic piece from Vitagraph, a documentary film, *L'Ecole maternelle de Stockholm*, from Literia-Film, as well as Pierre Veber's *Extra*, with Jacques Féraudy in the principal role.[31]

## French Audiences and American Film during World War I

While American films were becoming increasingly familiar to French filmgoers in the period 1910–13, it was during World War I that they attained a position of dominance in the French market. Once France entered the war, cinemas closed and film production halted. As hopes of a quick end to the war faded in late 1914, some movie theatres reopened and films began to be produced again from early 1915. For French film-makers, however, the war provided an inescapable backcloth to their work – unless, like Max Linder and Léonce Perret, they left for Hollywood. To help the war effort, they produced a succession of feature films either demonising the Germans or praising the courage and determination of the French. Unimpressed with these 'patriotic melodramas', audiences increasingly came to look to American films for entertainment.[32] By May 1916, the weekly volume of foreign (mostly American) film stock becoming available in France demonstrated the increasing dominance of American films in the French market. In 1917, American-made films finally 'passed the 50 percent mark in French exhibition'.[33]

The beginnings of this American 'invasion' would later be recalled in fairly dramatic terms. 'One day', Philippe Soupault declared,

> we saw great long bill-posters stretched along the sign-boards like serpents. At each corner of the street a man, his face covered with a red handkerchief, threatened the peaceful passers-by with a revolver. We heard galloping horses, chugging motors, screams and death-rattles. We dashed into the movie houses and realized that all was changed. The smile of Pearl White appeared on the screen, that almost ferocious smile announcing the upheaval of the new world.[34]

Soupault was referring to the start of *Les Mystères de New York*, a twenty-two-reel serial released in France between December 1915 and April 1916 and starring Pearl White as its heroine, Elaine. Made originally in Hollywood by expatriate French director Louis Gasnier for Pathé's semi-independent American affiliate, these films ironically established 'the prestige of American cinema' in France.[35]

The success that *Les Mystères* enjoyed with French audiences can be explained in several ways. As Soupault makes clear, the films' distributor in France – Pathé – promoted them energetically by means of an extensive advertising campaign. Even more important, perhaps, was the association of the serial with a pioneering French cultural product: the *ciné-roman*. Summarising the story of the films themselves, popular writer Pierre Decourcelle produced a novel that was itself serialised by the mass-circulation daily *Le Matin*, with each chapter coming out a week in advance of the comparable episode on film. This imaginative example of early trans-media co-operation created huge publicity for the films themselves.[36] There was also the appeal of crime dramas as a means of distraction from the ever-present reality of the war: Surrealist poet Robert Desnos would later declare that 'in our desire for escape and evasion, we rediscovered that privilege in the wake of Pearl White, in the touring cars of *Les Mystères de New York*, and the mock battles between bogus policemen and stupendous bandits'.[37]

Another crucial factor in the popularity of *Les Mystères* was Pearl White herself. Once a bareback rider in a circus and subsequently a stunt woman, the blonde, energetic White offered French viewers a new type of screen heroine. Her legion of French fans affectionately called her 'Quick Pearl' (*Perle Vite*). Louis Delluc, probably the most influential film critic in France between 1917, when he became editor-in-chief of *Le Film*, and his untimely death in 1924, described White as 'appetizing and dashing', a 'full-on heroine' who helped make 'the mishaps and ambiguous anxieties of these films' seem fascinating. 'Pearl White pleased me very much', Delluc confessed in 1919. 'It is understood that her films were idiotic or, what is worse, idiotically made. It was the energy and the zest. It was the health without ulterior motive.'[38] Delluc's enthusiasm was common among men, but it is also possible that White's active and sportive personality appealed to the French women who, according to the trade press, dominated cinema audiences during the war.[39]

If *Les Mystères de New York* showed French audiences what American cinema could do in terms of entertainment, Cecil B. DeMille's *The Cheat* opened the eyes of many to the artistic possibilities of the cinema itself. Delluc, by his own admission, had detested the cinema before the war: it was seeing *The Cheat* and Charlie Chaplin comedies that began his evolution from drama critic into film critic.[40] Other film critics, looking backward from the perspective of the 1920s, singled out *The Cheat* (*Forfaiture* in France) as the 'most striking' of the American films imported during the war.[41] According to Léon Moussinac, its arrival in France in 1916, 'initiated the greater French public's education about the cinema'.[42] In *The Cheat*, bored society lady Edith Ward (played by Fanny Ward) borrows from Arakau, a rich Japanese (Sessue Hayakawa) in return, it is implied, for the promise of sexual favours. When she fails to keep her side of the bargain, he literally brands her with a hot iron. Even though Edith is restored to her husband at the end of the film, and Arakau is criminalised, the fact that the film flirted with issues such as sexual immorality and miscegenation probably accounted for a good part of its popularity. However, as Colette pointed out in a review, *The Cheat* had other qualities that made it appealing, including high production values. French spectators accustomed to domestic films in which furniture, clothes and accessories were drab and lacking in style found themselves watching a film characterised by 'a beautiful luxuriating in lace, silk, furs' and 'millionaires who don't look as if they've rented their tuxedos by the week'. It also demonstrated 'what natural and well-designed lighting can add to cinematic fiction'.[43] Shot using the chiaroscuro lighting introduced by DeMille's cameraman, Alvyn Wyckoff, *The Cheat* was a new type of film characterised by a blend of light and shadow, as Colette shrewdly noted: screen characters were 'followed by their own shadows, their actual shadows, tragic or grotesque, of which until now the useless multiplicity of arc lamps has robbed us'. Finally, the film was helped by a new kind of screen acting: Colette (who had herself acted on stage) hailed Hayakawa as a 'genius' and praised Fanny Ward's ability to escape 'any sins of theatrical brusqueness or excess'.[44]

In its early days French cinema had practically invented two genres: the film comedy and the Western. According to Susan Hayward, it then 'fell victim . . . to its own export success and to the war'.[45] Both genres were effectively colonised by Americans, whose own products, particularly those featuring William S. Hart and Chaplin, began to dominate the French market during World War I. In attempting to explain the wide appeal of Chaplin ('*Charlot*') to French audiences, critics such as Delluc pointed to the mixture of comic genius and melancholy that distinguished his films – a melancholy that also characterised the work of Sessue Hayakawa ('I have never seen a cinema audience resist the enterprises of these two men').[46] 'He alone', asserted Louis Aragon of Chaplin, 'has sought the intimate sense of cinema and, endlessly persevering in his endeavours, he has drawn comedy towards the absurd and the tragic with equal inspiration.' Aragon's fellow-Surrealist Robert Desnos, writing a few years later, would assert that it had been 'four or five years after the man in the street' that the French avant-garde had 'discovered' Chaplin and taken him to their hearts.[47] The earlier comments by Delluc and Aragon suggest that Desnos was mistaken and that Charlot swiftly appealed to all sections of the French population, including the intellectual elite. As Jean Cocteau asserted in 1919, '[h]is films have no rivals . . . Chaplin is the modern Punch. He addresses all of us, everywhere.'[48]

William S. Hart, playing 'Rio Jim' in a series of Westerns, also had a wide-ranging appeal. Probably his first film to make a major impact on French audiences was *The Aryan* (1916). Released as *Pour sauver sa race*, it related the story of a gold prospector (Hart) who is cheated by a woman (Louise Glaum) and subsequently becomes an outlaw. Writing of the film's French reception, Delluc observed that:

> This film speaks to all hearts . . . I have seen it impress the most diverse audiences – in Marseille[s] before startled fishermen, in a small provincial village before timid and numbed peasants, enraptured. At the Belleville [a working-class cinema in the east of Paris run by the Communist Party], they cried; at the Colisée [on the Champs-Elysées in the heart of the socially exclusive 8th arrondissement], I saw ironists cease laughing and intellectuals, once completely refractory towards the cinema, now converted enthusiasts.[49]

To Delluc, Hart played 'Rio Jim' as 'the tragedian of the cinema'. In *The Cold Deck* (1917), for example, he displayed 'indifference, love, pity, arrogance, and ruin'. But, though he acted out a Sophoclean drama in the new, imaginative world created by Hollywood ('this stylised Far West'), audiences knew that he could always escape further suffering simply by riding away: 'It seems we breathe better when Rio Jim makes off on his horse across the valley.'[50]

Delluc and other commentators of the time tried to explain the success of American cinema in France as being also due to its artistic and technical superiority over French-made films. While arguing that Americans had not invented close-ups, Henry Fescourt and Jean-Louis Bouquet insisted that they *had* discovered 'how to use them rationally'. With close-ups, the camera could move from object to object, 'showing us only what was important to see'. By directing viewers' eyes either to particular objects or actor's faces, American film-makers were able to use close-ups to tell stories.[51] Yet the close-up as a technique required a new and different form of acting: abandoning techniques suitable for the stage, actors were obliged to scale down their gestures and try to convey thoughts or emotions by means of relatively small changes in facial expression. 'American actors', declared Emile Vuillermoz in 1916, 'take more time, perform more simply and "reduce," as suits them, their eyebrow wrinklings and smiles.' Such alterations made it possible for them to 'achieve remarkable effects of reality'.[52] As well as the close-up and a new style of acting, American cinema impressed French commentators most with its innovative editing. Conscious of the ways in which editing contributed to the narrative power of American films, observes Stuart Liebman, 'writers such as [Henri] Diamant-Berger pointed out how successive viewpoints on the action offered to a spectator presented gestures and expressions so legibly that the meaning of events became clearer and more vivid'.[53]

Delluc himself was so enthusiastic about American films that, by 1917, he was receiving letters denouncing him for being in Hollywood's pay.[54] Others later endeavoured to analyse the source of his fascination. Two, writing from the perspective of 1925, argued that he had been especially 'dazzled . . . by the "atmosphere," by the detail that cropped up, by the picturesqueness of the décor. What struck him was the drunken face of the cowboy, a pool of muddy water, a gray wall in front of which something happened.'[55] Certainly, in some of his writings, Delluc revealed a strong interest in what he called 'expressive details'. Yet he was not interested in them so much for their real qualities as for the ways in which the camera might reinscribe new meanings onto them. Delluc started from the assumption that French cinema as a whole – heavily influenced by the film d'art tradition – was too theatrical in orientation. Only American film-makers had begun to comprehend how nature could be reshaped in such a way as to add new meanings to filmic dramas.[56] From this conviction came the concept of *photogénie*, which Delluc may have conceived and certainly publicised. Despite its later influence – on French 'Impressionist' film-makers of the 1920s and critics of the 1940s and 1950s, including André Bazin – *photogénie* remains a rather hazy concept (certainly, Delluc himself never bothered to define it).[57] When he first began to use the term, however, towards the end of World War I, it was clear that the films he saw as photogenic were primarily American and not French.

Although Delluc in 1918 became the first French film reviewer to have a regular column in a daily, mass-circulation newspaper (*Paris-Midi*), he still did not believe himself to be a critic in the conventional sense. In October 1917, he informed the readership of *Le Film* (which he had edited since June) that he was 'neither heedless nor shrewd enough to assert the faults and failures of a spectacle . . . It is from the crowd actually that I gather the best impressions and the clearest judgements.' In a book published three years later, Delluc asserted that 'What the crowd thinks of a dramatic film . . . is an education.'[58] Delluc's view, that he was more concerned to describe audience reaction and response than just to write criticism, displayed a new respect for cinema as a popular art. In seeing himself as influenced by – and also representing – the wisdom of the crowd, Delluc was staking out a position very different from the dominant French view of the social psychology of the crowd. This had been laid out by sociologist Gustav Le Bon in his 1895 book *The Crowd: A Study of the Popular Mind*. To Le Bon, the crowd (*la foule*) was an irrational threat to social order. Driven solely by emotional appeals, it was incapable of thought and could only be appealed to on the basis of unconscious motivations (Le Bon himself believed that using images was the most effective means of doing this).[59] Delluc accepted that an appreciation of film did not require much in the way of thought. Indeed, he argued that 'one of the most miraculous things' about cinema was its ability to touch everyone in its audiences 'without demanding the cerebral preparation of a book or music'. But he also saw it as an international art capable of transcending boundaries of nation and social background.[60]

Because Delluc believed he could learn much from audiences, there are many comments *upon* audiences in his writings. An article he wrote for *Paris-Midi* in August 1918 gives fascinating glimpses of moviegoing in France in the last stages of World War I, and of the penetration of American films into the furthest reaches of the French market. At Aurillac, in the south of France, for example, Delluc joined a provincial audience at a Saturday evening show in the town's only cinema, carrying away with him memories of 'Convalescents, billeted soldiers, respectable families, respectable young girls, the smoke from pipes, the ritornellos of an untuned piano, all in a deep, dark, cold cinema with *Le Courrier de Washington* [*Pearl of the Army*, 1916, a Pearl White serial] on the marquee.'[61] Consistent with his view that the appeal of film transcended all boundaries, including those of class, Delluc noted that '[t]he remarkable American films are celebrated' by the 'faithful and elegant clientele' of the cinemas of western Paris. At the same time, he was rather irritated (if also amused) by the noisy behaviour of upper-class Parisian audiences. The moviegoers he liked best, in fact, were the more lower-class ones from the city's outskirts [*faubourgs*], whom he praised not only for 'their silence and attention but also because of their acuteness, taste, and insight'. The Parisian movie-house he attended most regularly was 'a little cinema [near Gare de l'Est] frequented pell-mell by mechanics, pimps, laborers, and women warehouse packers'. Delluc was impressed that this working-class audience was delighted by the 'elegant subtleties' of the first Triangle films – just as a very similar audience (made up of men 'in peaked caps' and women 'without hats') in the extreme south of the city greeted with great respect Thomas Ince's 'complex, inspired' film *Civilization's Child* (1916).[62]

## Conclusion

By early 1920, in the aftermath of the war and the peace, French newspapers such as *Le Temps* and *Le Figaro* were showing an increasing interest in most things American. Perhaps reflecting the growing number of American residents in Paris, a comedy called *Les Américains chez nous* opened at the Odeon theatre on 8 January.[63] In musical terms, many French had already gone 'jazz mad', and the Casino de Paris scored a 'runaway success' in 1920 with a jazz revue.[64] Other kinds of entertainment had been 'Americanised' in varying ways: the vaudeville programme at the Marivaux theatre in

Paris on 2 January included American films (a Harry Carey Western and a Chaplin comedy) and performers with mainly American-style names.[65] By this point also, American cinema itself had achieved the hegemony over the French market that it would only lose, briefly, during World War II. That hegemony had been achieved for a variety of reasons, including the effects of the outbreak of World War I on the French film industry. A major part of the explanation, however, also has to do with the enthusiasm with which French audiences and critics received American films.

Aided by a simpler, less theatrical style of acting, the use of close-ups, better scenarios, and the origins of what would become the star system, American-produced films were already appealing to many French spectators before 1914. That appeal grew markedly during World War I, when technical changes (including new forms of lighting), innovative editing, high production values and the arrival of new and impressive stars (such as Pearl White, Sessue Hayakawa, Charlie Chaplin and William S. Hart) helped Hollywood first establish – and then reinforce – its dominant hold over French movie-going.

## Notes

1  Jens Ulff-Møller, *Hollywood's Film Wars with France: Film-Trade Diplomacy and the Emergence of the French Film Quota Policy* (Rochester, NY: University of Rochester Press, 2001), pp. xiii–xiv.

2  Paul Leglise, *Histoire de la politique du cinéma français: le cinéma et la IIIe Republique* (Paris: Pierre Lherminier, 1970); Kristin Thompson, *Exporting Entertainment: America in the World Film Market 1907–1934* (London: BFI, 1985); Jean-Pierre Jeancolas, 'L'arrangement: Blum–Byrnes á l'epreuve des faits . . .', *1895*, no. 12 (1992), pp. 3–49; Ian Jarvie, *Hollywood's Overseas Campaign: The North Atlantic Movie Trade, 1920–1950* (Cambridge: Cambridge University Press, 1992); Jacques Portes, *De la scène à l'écran: Naissance de la culture de masse aux États-Unis* (Paris: Belin, 1997); Andrew Higson and Richard Maltby (eds), *'Film Europe' and 'Film America': Cinema, Commerce and Cultural Exchange, 1920–1939* (Exeter: University of Exeter Press, 1999).

3  Emilie Altenloh, *Zur Soziologie des Kino: Die Kino-Unternehmung und die sozialen Schichten ihrer Besucher* (Leipzig: Spamersche Buckdrukerei, 1914).

4  Eugene C. McCreary, 'Louis Delluc, Film Theorist, Critic, and Prophet', *Cinema Journal*, vol. 16, no 1 (1976), pp. 14–35; Richard Abel, 'Louis Delluc: The Critic as Cinéaste', *Quarterly Review of Film Studies*, no. 1 (May 1976), pp. 205–44.

5  The tradition of French audiences preferring American cinema from the days of early cinema onwards would later be maintained by French 'auteur' critics of the 1960s and 1970s, who preferred to write about American films. See, for example, 'John Ford's *Young Mr Lincoln*: A Collective Text by the Editors of *Cahiers du Cinéma*', trans. Helen Lackner and Diana Matias, *Screen*, vol. 13, no. 3 (autumn 1972), pp. 5–44.

6  Susan Hayward, *French National Cinema* (Routledge: London, 1993), p. 50.

7  The appeal of cinema to society people was heavily undermined in May 1897 when a fire at the Charity Bazaar in Paris killed around 125 people, mainly drawn from the upper classes. Kristin Thompson and David Bordwell, *Film History: An Introduction* (New York: McGraw Hill, 1994), p. 15.

8  *Photo-Ciné-Gazette*, 1 April 1907, quoted in Vanessa R. Schwartz, *Spectacular Realities: Early Mass Culture in 'Fin-de'Siècle' Paris* (Berkeley: University of California Press, 1998), p. 195.

9 Rémy de Gourmont, *Mercure de France* (1 September 1907), reprinted in Richard Abel (ed.), *French Film Theory and Criticism: A History/Anthology 1907–1938, Vol. I: 1907–1929* (Princeton: Princeton University Press, 1988), p. 49.

10 Yhcam, 'La Cinématographie', in *Ciné-Journal* (20 April 1912), reprinted in Abel, *French Film Theory*, p. 77. Yhcam saw this as 'perhaps the sole reason . . . why the theaters are being abandoned in favor of the cinema'. Ibid.

11 Jean-Jacques Meusy, 'Palaces and Holes in the Wall: Conditions of Exhibition in Paris on the Eve of World War I', *The Velvet Light Trap*, no. 37 (spring 1996), p. 83.

12 Louis Haugmard, 'L"Esthétique" du cinématographe' (25 May 1913), reprinted in Abel, *French Film Theory*, p. 85. While Haugmard took a generally critical view of movie-going, he also recognised that it was one of the very small number of ways in which working-class families could go out together during the week. Ibid., pp. 15–16.

13 Meusy, 'Palaces and Holes in the Wall', pp. 81–2. F. Laurent published two articles in *Le Cinéma* in May–June 1912 on working-class cinemas in and around Paris. Abel, *French Film Theory*, pp. 15, 30 n. 76.

14 Meusy, 'Palaces and Holes in the Wall', pp. 82–3.

15 Russell Lack, *Twenty Four Frames Under: A Buried History of Film Music* (London: Quartet Books, 1997), pp. 28–9; Martin Miller Marks, *Music and the Silent Film: Contexts and Case Studies 1895–1924* (New York: Oxford University Press, 1997), pp. 50–61.

16 Henri Lavedan 'de l'Academie Française', '*L'Assassinat du Duc de Guise*, Drame cinématographique en six tableaux', *L'Illustration*, 21 November 1908.

17 Abel, *French Film Theory*, pp. 15, 30 n. 75.

18 Robert de Beauplan, 'Destin du cinéma', *L'Illustration*, 9 November 1935.

19 On actors assuming fixed poses in *L'Assassinat du Duc de Guise*, for example, see Ben Brewster and Lea Jacobs, *Theatre to Cinema: Stage Pictorialism and the Early Feature Film* (Oxford: Oxford University Press, 1997), pp. 48–9, 103.

20 Philippe Soupault, 'Note 1 sur le cinéma' (January 1918), reprinted in Abel, *French Film Theory*, p. 142

21 Louis Feuillade, 'Scènes de la vie telle qu'elle est' (22 April 1911); Victorin Jasset, 'Etude sur le mise-en-scène en cinématographie' (21 October 1911); both reprinted in Abel, *French Film Theory*, pp. 54, 57. The Vitagraph pictures may have reflected a more general trend in film acting in the US. Roberta E. Pearson has suggested that D. W. Griffith's Biograph movies of this period were characterised by the transformation from a demonstrative 'histrionic' style of acting to a more restrained and realistic 'verisimilar' style. Pearson, *Eloquent Gestures: The Transformation of Performance Style in the Griffith Biograph Films* (Berkeley: University of California Press, 1992).

22 Ibid., p. 57. 'Yhcam' repeated Jasset's points about acting style and close-ups six months later: 'In order to produce the maximum effect, while practicing a restraint which thwarts broad gestures, the Vitagraph actors have had to work especially on the play of facial features; and in order that their facial expressions could be seen clearly by the spectators (in all corners of the hall), the director has had to project the actors in close shots as often as possible'. Yhcam, 'La Cinématographie', *Ciné-Journal* (20 April 1912), reprinted in Abel, *French Film Theory*, p. 72.

23 Jasset, 'Etude sur le mise-en-scène en cinématographie', p. 57.

24 Eileen Bowser, *The Transformation of Cinema 1907–1915* (New York: Scribner's, 1990), p. 105.

25 *Ciné-Journal*, no. 160 (16 September 1911).

26 Ibid.; Meusy, 'Palaces and Holes in the Wall', p. 82.

27 *Ciné-Journal*, no. 160 (16 September 1911).

28 Haugmard, 'L'"Esthétique" du cinématographe', p. 83.

29 Thompson and Bordwell, *Film History*, pp. 60–2; Hayward, *French National Cinema*, pp. 92–3.

30 The 'Léonce' comedies featured and were directed by Léonce Perret. Starting as a comic actor, Perret also directed for Gaumont a number of serious films during this period.

31 Quoted in Meusy, 'Palaces and Holes in the Wall', p. 86.

32 Thompson and Bordwell, *Film History*, p. 62; Hayward, *French Cinema*, pp. 91, 101–2.

33 Richard Abel, 'Guarding the Borders in Early Cinema: The Shifting Ground of French-American Relations', in John Fullerton (ed.), *Celebrating 1895: The Centenary of Cinema* (London: John Libbey, 1998), pp. 50, 54 n. 34; Thompson and Bordwell, *Film History*, p. 63.

34 Philippe Soupault, 'The "USA" Cinema', *Broom*, vol. 5 (September 1923), pp. 65–6.

35 Gilles Delluc, *Louis Delluc 1890–1924: L'éveilleur du cinéma français au temps des années folles* (Paris: Pilote 24 Edition, 2002), p. 158.

36 Abel, *French Film Theory*, pp. 96, 117 n. 12. On the ciné-roman, see Alain and Odette Virmaux, *Le Ciné-Roman: Un genre nouveau* (Paris: Edilig, 1983).

37 Robert Desnos, '*Fantômas, Les Vampires, Les Mystères de New York*' (26 February 1927), reprinted in Abel, *French Film Theory*, p. 399.

38 Delluc, *Louis Delluc*, pp. 158–9.

39 Abel, 'Guarding the Borders in Early Cinema', p. 52.

40 Stuart Liebman, 'French Film Theory, 1910–1921', *Quarterly Review of Film Studies*, vol. 8, no. 1 (1983), p. 8; McCreary, 'Louis Delluc, Film Theorist, Critic, and Prophet', p. 29.

41 Henry Fescourt and Jean-Louis Bouquet, *L'Idée et l'écran: Opinions sur le cinéma* (1925), reprinted in Abel, *French Film Theory*, p. 374; cf. ibid., p. 371.

42 Léon Moussinac, 'Cinématographie: Le Lys brisé [*Broken Blossoms*]' (I February 1921), reprinted in Abel, *French Film Theory*, p. 230.

43 Colette, 'Cinéma: *Forfaiture*' (7 August 1916), reprinted in Alain and Odette Virmaux, *Colette at the Movies: Criticism and Screenplays* (New York: Frederick Ungar, 1980), p. 19.

44 Delluc, *Louis Delluc*, p. 171; Colette, 'Cinéma: *Forfaiture*', p. 19. Colette noted in the same review that France 'will have something to worry about and suffer from after the war because of the progress the American cinema is making'. Ibid., p. 20.

45 Hayward, *French National Cinema*, p. 91.

46 Delluc, 'La Beauté au cinéma' (6 August 1917), reprinted in Abel, *French Film Theory*, p. 139. Cf. Elie Faure, 'De la cinéplastique' (1922), ibid., p. 262.

47 Louis Aragon, 'Du Décor' (15 September 1918), reprinted in Abel, *French Film Theory*, p. 167; Robert Desnos, 'Cinéma d'avant-garde' (December 1929), ibid., p. 430. On this point, also see Soupault, 'The "USA" Cinema', pp. 67–8.

48 Jean Cocteau, 'Carte blanche' (April/May 1919), reprinted in Abel, *French Film Theory*, p. 173.

49 Louis Delluc, 'D'Oreste à Rio Jim' (9 December 1921), reprinted in Abel, *French Film Theory*, p. 257.

50 Louis Delluc, 'Cinéma: *Grand Frère*' (February 1919), reprinted in Abel, *French Film Theory*, pp. 171–2.

51 Fescourt and Bouquest, *L'Idée et l'écran*, reprinted in Abel, *French Film Theory*, pp. 374–5.

52 Emile Vuillermoz, 'Devant l'écran' (29 November 1916), reprinted in Abel, *French Film Theory*, p. 132. On French enthusiasm for the way American films broke with the theatrical tradition, also see John Trumpbour, *Selling Hollywood to the World: US and European Struggles for Mastery of the Global Film Industry, 1920–1950* (Cambridge: Cambridge University Press, 2002), p. 242.

53 Liebman, 'French Film Theory, 1910–1921', p. 17.

54 McCreary, 'Louis Delluc, Film Theorist, Critic, and Prophet', p. 15.

55 Fescourt and Bouquet, *L'Idée et l'écran*, reprinted in Abel, *French Film Theory*, p. 375.

56 Delluc, 'D'Orestes à Rio Jim', reprinted in Abel, *French Film Theory*, pp. 255–6.

57 'I would describe as photogenic any aspect of things, beings, or souls whose moral character is enhanced by filmic reproduction', declared Jean Epstein in 1924, going on to specify that 'only mobile aspects of the world, of things and souls, may see their moral value increased' in this way. Epstein, 'De quelques conditions de la photogénie' (15 August 1924), reprinted in Abel, *French Film Theory*, pp. 314–15; cf. Thompson and Bordwell, *Film History*, p. 92.

58 Louis Delluc, 'Abel Gance après *La Zone de la mort*', *Le Film* (22 October 1917); Louis Delluc, *Photogénie* (Paris: de Brunoff, 1920); both cited in Abel, *French Film Theory*, p. 101.

59 Gustav Le Bon, *The Crowd: A Study of the Popular Mind* (London: T. F. Unwin, 1897 [first published 1895]).

60 Louis Delluc, 'La Foule', *Paris-Midi* (24 August 1918), reprinted in Abel, *French Film Theory*, p. 162; McCreary, 'Louis Delluc, Film Theorist, Critic, and Prophet', p. 17.

61 Delluc, 'La Foule', reprinted in Abel, *French Film Theory*, p. 161. The programme also included a British film based on Rudyard Kipling's novel, *The Light That Failed*.

62 Delluc, 'La Foule', reprinted in Abel, *French Film Theory*, pp. 159–60, 163. Since Delluc specifically mentioned Ince, the film he probably had in mind here was *Civilization* (1916). On the other hand, he *may* have been referring to another American film, *Civilization's Child* (1916), directed by Charles Giblyn.

63 *Le Temps*, 8 January 1920.

64 Alistair Horne, *Seven Ages of Paris* (London: Macmillan, 2002), p. 379.

65 *Le Figaro*, 2 January 1920. While these entertainers may not, in fact, have been American, the fact that they opted to appear with Americanised stage names is itself a comment on the cultural prestige of the United States at this time.

# 2
# 'A Great American Sensation': Thomas Ince's *Civilization* at the Palladium, Southampton, 1917

Michael Hammond

During the Great War cinema culture in Britain, as in so many other nations, experienced the beginnings of a century-long (and continuing) domination by US-made films. In fact, the war years were part of a longer transitional period in British cinema culture (1911–20), in which the number of US films on British screens steadily increased, with a commensurate decrease in films from other nations.[1] This burgeoning dominance was also evident in subsidiary forms of cinema culture such as fan and trade magazines. By 1915 American film stars were topping most of the popularity polls in fan magazines such as *Pictures and the Picturegoer* and *Picture Palace News*. Pre-publicity for films made in Hollywood made up a considerable percentage of the articles in British fan magazines, while the two major London-based trade journals *The Bioscope* and *Kinematograph Weekly* sold much, if not most, of their advertising space to US-based distribution companies. Not surprisingly, a considerable amount of their editorial comment was given over to the subject of American predominance, and much of it held up US production and exhibition practices as a model to be followed, at the same time as expressing concern about the fate of British production in the face of this influx of American product.

From the perspective of exhibition and reception, British film culture after 1914 consisted of a heterogeneous mix of national cinemas, and production-led histories are unable adequately to account for this. A more complete history of Hollywood cinema outside the borders of the United States, and in Britain specifically, requires a detailed consideration of transnational reception. While such an exhaustive study is not possible here, some examples of the development of cinema culture in Britain at this time can provide a sense of the complexity of the factors at work in the transnational history of Hollywood cinema in Britain. This article seeks to contribute to that history through a specific focus on the reception of one film, Thomas Ince's *Civilization*, in one British city, Southampton.

In 1917, British film exhibitors faced significant changes to the way they conducted their business. In cities and towns where a large number of cinemas were clustered in and around the town centre, competition was considerable.[2] The introduction of the Entertainments Tax in 1916 had had the effect of reducing the frequency of attendance by working-class audiences, while better-paid audiences chose to purchase cheaper-priced tickets, resulting in an overall decline in revenue. At the same time, the shift from the open market system of acquiring films to the exclusives system, which presaged block booking, was having a significant impact on the way that exhibitors were able to attract and maintain their audiences. Exhibitors generally changed their programme every three days and sometimes held special programmes on Sunday. While there was a great demand for product, there was a tension between the need for flexibility on types of films and the desire for 'exclusives', or first-run films. The decline of the open market was exacerbated by the need for sure-fire box-office hits, which would not have prohibitive advertising costs and could generate sales of ephemera such as postcards. For example, adventure serials and Chaplin films were highly desired products throughout the war. An additional factor was the relationship between the exhibitor and the local community. Smaller exhibitors depended on a regular local clientele while the larger cinemas located on the high street competed with each other for the urban 'passing trade'. In Southampton, the main embarkation point for the Western Front, this was made particularly acute not only by the influx of soldiers, but also by the women who had taken on clerical and factory jobs vacated by men in service. This 'new' audience experienced a considerable increase in disposable income and leisure time. In this regard, Southampton stands as a plausible example that acts as a general indicator of these shifts nationwide.

As an overarching day-to-day reality in the public imagination, the war was central to the development of cinema culture in Britain, and specifically to the rise to dominance of American product. This was true not only in terms of the production-led theory that a national industry was starved though the privations of war and the conservatism of British financial institutions in financing British film ventures. Exhibitors were able to capitalise on, as well as gauge, audience interest in war subjects, actuality or fiction, in a number of ways. Although the war was a cause for concern about the 'appropriateness' of cinema during the first few weeks of August 1914, exhibitors quickly realised that the war offered an opportunity for inculcating the cinema into the social fabric of the community through patriotic front-of-house displays, newsreels from the front and charity events for soldiers and Belgian refugees. As the war continued, exhibitors also realised that cinema could be presented as a viable part of the war effort, as both a means of information and education and a rejuvenating leisure form. It was as the latter that the US-based product began to take hold because of its popularity as well as its availability. Exhibitors took advantage of the uplift strategies of US film companies through the development of the feature and the 'super-films' such as *The Birth of a Nation* (1915) and *Intolerance* (1916), mixing this with the comedies and dramas of a less lofty kind to counteract both reformers' concerns and an increasing 'war-weariness'. Audiences grew increasingly tired of war films, fiction or actuality, as the war dragged on and US-based films offered a popular alternative.

An appropriate model for understanding this as a phenomenon of transnational reception can be derived from the work of William Uricchio and Roberta Pearson. In their explanation of the production strategy of the Vitagraph company between 1908 and 1910 Uricchio and Pearson point to

> the Film Industry's desire to ally itself with dominant social formations in creating consensual values. The reception of the films might be interpreted in terms of appeals to the assimilationist and upwardly mobile tendencies of the workers and immigrants alleged to have constituted the bulk of the nickelodeon audience.[3]

In a cinema culture where the majority of the films screened are US-based it is crucial to expand or modify their model. What happens when these desires to 'ally' with 'dominant formations' cross the Atlantic? What kinds of differences are there in the dominant social formations in Britain as opposed to the US? As I will show in this study, these differences are inscribed primarily at the levels of distribution and exhibition, where the advertising campaign for *Civilization* (originally in many respects a pacifist film) was tailored specifically for a British audience, and the actual film edited in order to enable interpretations which were more in keeping with the war effort.

Raymond Bartlett for Triangle Kay-Be oversaw the editorial changes and the national advertising campaign for *Civilization*. British distributors and exhibitors, tailoring it to their specific local audiences, made further changes to the original advertising. These changes were an attempt to re-position the film's pacifist message alongside the dominant public language that cast the war as a moral crusade. The film's reception was characterised by a combination of these changes at the level of the text and of the advertising and exhibition strategies at the level of exhibition. In order to bring to light the factors at play during this crucial period of the rising dominance of Hollywood films, this chapter is divided into three parts. The first provides a fictitious account of a young single woman's experience of the première of the film, in order to set up the reception context for the film and outline the textual features which are then picked up in the next two parts. The second part describes the advertising strategies of the Palladium in order to illustrate the way in which exhibitors worked to bring the publicity provided by a US firm into line with their overall image within the community. The final section maps out the probable interpretations available to audiences based on the wider-reaching issues that were at play during the release of the film.

## The Première at the Palladium

It is Friday, 31 August 1917. Mabel, a young woman of eighteen, goes to the cinema with her new boyfriend, Walter, also eighteen. She lives with her parents in the suburb of Portswood, a little less than a mile north of Southampton town centre. She has a job as a shop assistant at Tyrell and Green's, a department store in Southampton. Walter works for the railway, transporting the wounded from the docks to the medical trains and unloading them at Netley hospital, the third largest military hospital in Britain at the time. Walter's job brings him in direct contact with the broken bodies from the front and he is under little illusion about the brutal effects of modern war. The film they go to see is Thomas Ince's *Civilization*. The cinema is the Palladium, which is just within walking distance from her house. The picture has been advertised as costing more than $1 million and involving 40,000 people and an array of military spectacle. Mabel's expectations of the evening are numerous. According to the advertisement in the *Southern Daily Echo*, there is the chance to view a spectacle of horrific battle scenes and the re-enactment of the sinking of a liner by torpedo from a submarine. Apart from the experience of the film itself, there is also the opportunity to meet friends. Given the coded nature of courtship, the chance to be alone in the dark with her new beau is a source of anxiety as well anticipation, and there are also the excitements of being out beyond the fetters of family and of forming part of an audience. On the whole, cinema offers Mabel her most accessible form of public entertainment. Her father, who owns a greengrocer's on Portswood high street not far from the Palladium, does not approve of her attending the music hall unless he accompanies her. In any case, both the music hall and the theatre are too expensive to be anything other than a rare treat. Normally, Mabel goes to the cinema with her girlfriends, but this is a special event: both the pre-mière of a new super-film and the chance to 'court'. The programme has other attrac-tions: the live music (she knew the pianist at school), the newsreel and the comedy short, and she has chosen the Palladium as much because of its location (it is close by and where she regularly goes) as because of the programme's content. That said, there has been a great deal of advertising for this film and her father had thought it would be a good film for her to see.

Walter comes to collect her at her house. As they approach the cinema there are pos-ters under the awning covering the entrance advertising *Civilization* spelled the American way, as the exhibitor had ordered his full-colour poster from the distributor the Transatlantic Film Company. Walter booked their tickets the previous evening. As they enter the foyer they are greeted with a breeze from the ceiling fans and the pleasant smell of oranges. Walter buys them one each to eat during the performance. The cinema is filled with people. Some of them she knows and there is the anxious thrill of being seen with her boyfriend. There are a number of children at the film who contribute to the general atmosphere of noisiness. After buying their tickets, the couple take their seats towards the back and the programme begins. She recognises a woman with her older children as one of the patrons of Tyrell and Green's and notes that she has never seen them at the cinema before. The small four-piece orchestra begins to play and then the lights dim. The newsreel is greeted with interest, particularly the information on the war news and the pictures of the American troops who have recently become involved. There are also the usual shots of the British Army. The thought crosses her mind that her uncle Tom is 'somewhere in France' and, as usual, she looks to see if she can see him in the footage of soldiers marching past. There are some fairly boisterous lads two rows behind them who have already been told to quieten down by the usher during the comedy short.

The main feature begins and the music starts just after the image is shown. The opening titles are sombre and religious in tone and include a drawing of a church win-dow with light streaming through. It reminds her of the kind of slide shows she had seen as a child at some church evenings. The opening scenes are of a peaceful rural set-ting and the farmers are dressed in a kind of peasant costume. The Emperor, who declares war, looks like the Kaiser. The hero, Count Ferdinand, is a friend and trusted aid to the Emperor, which is somewhat confusing. The hero's girlfriend, Katheryn Haldeman, joins a secret peace society that is marked by a Christian cross on her under-clothes. She tries to persuade Ferdinand, the captain of a submarine, not to go on his mission and reveals her commitment to peace. He leaves, but when he receives an order to sink a liner that has women and children on it, he refuses. He then reveals the cross on his undershirt to his men, and sinks the submarine. As it goes down he has a vision of the chaos on the ship, the scramble for lifeboats while it is sinking and the loss of women and children. This vision reminds Mabel of the *Lusitania* and the general fear of German submarines. She also thinks of the sinking of the *Titanic*, on which her best friend's father worked and was lost. Earlier there have been scenes of soldiers fighting which are pretty gruesome and there are some very sad scenes of families having to give up their sons to rough and brutal soldiers in German uniforms. For Walter these scenes have little impact and seem more affected than real.

Ferdinand is rescued, but mortally injured. The Emperor's doctors are called in. While unconscious, he has a dream and is taken through a kind of hell. There are a great many tortured and naked men writhing and/or pushing boulders up hills. It looks like a scene from one of the pictures in Mabel's illustrated Bible. Christ appears and moves into Ferdinand's body. He awakens, resuscitated by the doctors, and proceeds to preach peace. This makes the Emperor angry, and Ferdinand is brought to trial and sentenced to death. A great crowd of women on the march for peace descends on the city and his girlfriend leads the petition for the release of the hero. The Empress Eugenie is moved by the call for peace and begs for Ferdinand to be spared, but it is too late, for he has died in prison. The Emperor visits the cell. Christ arises out of the hero's body and takes the Emperor (also in spirit form) by the hand. He is first taken to the battlefield and shown the horrors of war. There are more scenes of death and destruction in the city as he sees refugees moving with their belongings on their backs, women weeping over their husband's dead bodies and lost children crying. Walter and Mabel had been discussing the war on their walk to the cinema. Walter was careful not to be explicit about the things that he sees everyday in his job but Mabel is not completely unaware of the condition of the wounded as she too has seen the medical trains coming from the docks. The silence of the trains is in marked contrast to the newspaper accounts of the wounded singing and cheering together on the trains. In fact, both are aware that Walter is now of conscription age and that he may be at the front in a year's time. The scenes of the film, therefore, are taken by both to be dramatic rather than realistic.

The Emperor realises what he has brought upon his people and Christ shows him the book of judgment. He is horrified to learn that his page is 'stained with the blood of his people'. The Emperor is then returned to his world where he declares peace. One scene at the end stands out. As the soldiers return home, there is a scene where a woman tries to console a grieving widow but cannot contain her excitement as she sees her own husband returning alive. This scene reinforces the impression of dramatic license for both Mabel and Walter. Mabel has friends who have relatives at the front and her uncle's return last December was quiet and solitary. Walter has seen relatives waiting at the station for their wounded son or brother or husband to arrive but this is the exception rather than the rule. Both have the overall experience of the war as a consistent and ominous background to their lives marked by private anguish rather than public celebration.

The film ends and Mabel and Walter file out. The noise during the film was lower than normal but there was still a good deal of talking among the lads behind, particularly when the Emperor, a thinly disguised representation of the Kaiser, was on the screen. Walter had whispered 'suffragette' during the peace-marching scene and Mabel had been reminded of a terse discussion she had had with her father about the right of women to vote and she wondered if Walter had felt the same. There had been a bit of sporadic irreverence during the Christ scenes as well as during the titles with the church windows. Overall the film was very impressive and Mabel was glad she had seen it. The film had reminded them both of the war in ways which they found less entertaining and more 'educational' or, to put it more bluntly, contrived. Nevertheless both feel a duty to outwardly applaud the film's patriotic, albeit somewhat oblique, message. Inwardly, Mabel wonders if she should raise the issue of women's suffrage with Walter, while Walter wonders whether he should relay some of his own experiences with the medical trains to compare with the overly dramatised scenes of the film. Both decide it best to concentrate on other subjects altogether and look forward to the Chaplin comedy that would be shown the following week.

## High Class at the Palladium

The Palladium opened on 17 February 1913 and was one of the first purpose-built cinemas in the town. It was a combined business venture of H. J. Hood, a local entrepreneur, and Sydney Bacon, managing director of Sydney Bacon's Pictures Circuit, based in London. The Palladium was not part of this circuit, but Bacon's probable position in the partnership was to bring the conveniences and contacts that his circuit had developed to the Palladium to ensure that exclusives were acquired as first runs in the town.[4] Located in Portswood, adjacent to the affluent area of Highfield, the Palladium aimed to attract a regular clientele through specific programming, advertising and house management strategies, which emphasised the cinema's 'high-class' quality of films, projection and décor and its educational value to the community. A year after it opened, the town's planning committee recognised the cinema as a public educational resource when it decided to build a branch library on the site next to it.[5]

The first move towards establishing a respectable reputation with the community was the opening of the cinema by the Mayor, Mr Henry Bowyer, who described it as 'the prettiest picture palace south of London'. The décor was in the Wedgewood style, with blue and white walls, ornamental features and matching plush seats. The cinema held 650 seats: 150 balcony and 500 stalls. Seats cost sixpence, ninepence and one shilling and twopence, with a threepence charge for booking. Little touches of showmanship by the first house manager, a Mr Urqhuart, were even noted in the national trade press:

> the installation has now been completed of a patent multi-bladed electric fan, capable of changing the atmosphere of the hall nine times in an hour. One of the films to be screened at the Palladium is 'The Story of the Willow Pattern'. One of the tips which Mr Urquhart has picked up during his travels in the East is that of perfuming the curtains and this practice is regularly pursued at the Palladium and helps to keep the hall fresh.[6]

These techniques were a form of address that anticipated a type of audience who would respond to the assurances of a comfortable and healthy environment particularly during the difficult summer season.[7]

From its opening, the adverts for the Palladium were prominently displayed on the front page of the *Southern Daily Echo*, usually in the centre. Rather than advertise in either the entertainment weekly *What's On in Southampton* or the *Southampton and District Pictorial*, the Palladium's exclusive use of the *Southern Daily Echo* indicates both its appeal to a specific regular suburban clientele and its attempt to impart a sense of the exclusive nature of the cinema. As the paper was a daily, the change of programme was advertised regularly and allowed for the kind of publicity build-up, or 'booming', that was required for prestige features which were a mainstay in the Palladium's programming policy.

Although the advertising methods of the manager and directors indicate a specific clientele, the location of the Palladium at Portswood suggests that the appeal was not simply to the inhabitants of the immediate area. Located directly across from the tram depot, the cinema was accessible from all parts of the town. Its proximity to Highfield directly to the north was matched by the easy walking distance (about half a mile) to the working-class district of Northam, home to many of the local men who worked on the liners, to the south. The Palladium probably also attracted people from the nearby Basset and Shirley areas where stewards and other crew for the liners lived. This diversity of the cinema's catchment area was reflected in the stratification of its seats and prices, suggesting that it managed to attract both working-class and middle-class film-goers.[8] It also set up the conditions for the successful exhibition of super-films such as *Civilization*, because it was accessible to a wider range of audiences, and could therefore support the kind of lengthy runs (usually a week) that the distributors of these films demanded.

The Palladium distinguished its programme by offering features of 'high standards and distinct educational values'.[9] From its opening, it cultivated a reputation as a house for first-run prestige features. In January 1914, it ran *Antony and Cleopatra* for a week. Subsequent exhibitions of *Quo Vadis?* and Hepworth's *David Copperfield* indicated a distinct appeal to a reading public. The *Kinematograph Year Book* for that year could have been referring to the Palladium and its close proximity to the lending library when it noted the turn to this type of feature:

> A curious fact was made known at the beginning of the year, namely that the kinematograph fostered a taste for book reading. With the advent of 'Les Miserables', 'David Copperfield', 'Quo Vadis?', 'Antony and Cleopatra', 'Last Days of Pompeii', 'The Three Musketeers', 'The House of Temperley', and other films founded upon well known novels, the lucky publishers admitted that a tremendous demand had been created for their works. Librarians, too, experienced an extraordinary demand for certain works because films founded on them were being shown in their district. This seems to contradict the assertion so frequently made use of in press and pulpit that the picture theatre had destroyed the utility of public libraries.[10]

During the early months of the war the programme featured such a significant number of these literary adaptations that *The Bioscope* reported it as a good method of maintaining audiences during the uncertain climate of wartime:

> Portswood Palladium does not appear to have suffered on account of the war. On my last visit I found the hall filled and Mr W. T. Bartlett, the manager, assured me that the attendances had been exceedingly well maintained. Book plays are great favourites with Palladium audiences. The picture dramatisations of Dickens' 'Old Curiosity Shop' and Jules Verne's 'Children of Captain Grant' formed the features for this week . . .[11]

The Palladium's reputation as a 'high class' cinema was predicated on a combination of the type of films screened, the presentation and décor of the hall and the high-profile social events that were held there. Prior to the outbreak of war the cinema had played host to special events. During the war, Bartlett built upon this policy by holding special screenings for soldiers and Belgian refugees.[12]

The Palladium's reputation for exclusive and educational entertainment explains why more controversial films such as Lois Weber's *Where Are My Children?* (1915) were able to play only at the Palladium. *Where Are My Children?* opened on 2 December 1916 and was advertised as for adults only. This film concerned birth control and abortion and was sponsored by the National Council of Public Morals (NCPM). It was not intended for commercial release in Britain but for special educational screenings. Annette Kuhn has shown that the relationship between the NCPM and the industry around this film served to further the quite different interests of both. In 1916 the industry was eager to associate the cinema with social and moral education, and keen to acquire the endorsement of the NCPM to head off the threat of state censorship. The NCPM, in turn, was concerned with the use of cinema as an educational medium, and was also undertaking research for what would become the Report of the Cinema Commission, published in 1917. Cinemas such as the Palladium, with high profiles of 'educational and high class programmes' and an ostensibly more educated clientele, were the exception in a policy of screening *Where Are My Children?* in theatres and town halls associated with public lectures and educational events, rather than in commercial cinemas. This gives some indication of the profile in the town that the Palladium enjoyed.

This reputation had been gained by the management's consistent practice of catering to their local clientele. At the same time, however, the Palladium's easy access to the centre of the town suggests that the audience constituency was wider than the local area. The screening of *Where Are My Children?* indicates the flexibility enjoyed by the managers, who were able to appeal to specific audiences at given times. While they normally emphasised feature films, this was not the only means of maintaining their audiences: Chaplin films, for example, were introduced as a part of the programme during the summer of 1915 and these and other comedy films continued to be shown at the Palladium with some regularity throughout the war.

The way that the Palladium attempted to benefit from the Chaplin phenomenon offers an insight into the nature of the competitive environment of local cinema exhibition at the time, and reveals that 'uplift' was a convenient advertising tag as much as a committed policy. Chaplin films had been running in Southampton since the summer of 1914, with *Between Showers* (US release: 28 February 1914) appearing on 18 July at the palace music hall as part of their Sunday evening 'first-time screened' film programme.[13] Throughout the winter and spring of 1915 Chaplin's popularity had grown. The summer of that year is generally considered 'Chaplin's summer', when he achieved the international superstar status that he enjoyed for the next two decades. In January 1914 he had moved from the Keystone studios to Essanay, and such was the popularity of Chaplin films that, in September, Essanay sought to benefit by introducing an exclusive arrangement for exhibitors including those in Britain. In order to obtain a Chaplin film they were obliged also to rent three other Essanay subjects. This form of block booking ran counter to the open market system that was the standard means of acquiring films in Britain.[14] The Palladium had been fairly late in picking up on Chaplin, only screening re-run Keystones in March of 1915 and then one or two per month from June. This was sporadic compared to other cinemas, large and small, which had been showing Chaplin Keystones since July 1914.[15] It was not until the early part of 1916 that the Palladium began showing Chaplin films with regularity and then, to avoid the controlling Essanay policy, they ran re-released Keystones under changed titles.[16] This can be understood as an attempt to maximise audiences by appealing to 'lower-taste sensibilities' through slapstick, but it is more likely that Chaplin's name was proving a considerable draw generally and one that managers H. J. Hood and Sidney Bacon could not afford to ignore.

This is an important illustration of how the geography and demographics of medium- to large-size towns and cities in Britain presented diverse problems and opportunities to local exhibitors. In the US, the outlying suburban areas were dependent upon a regular clientele and those theatres were more likely to support the feature.[17] The Palladium was able to mix its programme and cater to both regular patrons and a floating clientele. The increasing use of Chaplin films suggests that both types of audience were necessary for profitable business, particularly considering the large number of cinemas in the town. Such an appeal to a heterogeneous constituency, and its emphasis on 'uplifting' programming, made the Palladium a viable cinema for the exhibition of the super-films such as *Intolerance*, *Civilization* or Selig's *The Garden of Allah* (1918), films which could only be obtained for the longer run of six days. Some exhibitors tried these super-films out with varying degrees of success. Mr D. Stratton, the manager of the Palace in Runcorn, wrote to the Selig company in April 1918 concerning his screening of *The Garden of Allah*: 'You forgot that all shows are not continuous and that seven reels while suiting city halls becomes a stumbling block to suburban halls. We outsiders must give a varied programme'.[18] The Palladium, on the other hand, was consistently able to run the super-films because of its mix of programming and its reputation for respectability. That reputation helped to build a particular set of expectations for its regular clientele, and these expectations in turn informed the reception of Ince's super-film in Britain.

## 'Civilisation; What Every True Briton is Fighting For'

Thomas Ince's film *Civilization* had enjoyed a successful first run in the United States. The film had been premièred on 2 June 1916 at the Criterion Theatre in New York and had run for five months. The critical reception was enthusiastic. The picture generated acknowledgment from the Wilson administration for its message of peace and the spectacle of the battle scenes was highly praised. The film dealt with its subject matter in a way which gave space to contentious issues, such as the pacifist movement and the sinking of commercial liners by submarines, but then displaced them by setting them in a rural, distinctly Germanic fictitious nation. The blame for the belligerence is placed on the Emperor, and divine intervention in the embodiment of Christ implies forgiveness, the attitude necessary to the cessation of hostilities. In this way the call for peace lined up with Wilson's apparent proposal for 'taking the United States into the World War early in 1916 on the basis of a "clean peace" without offering any spoils to the Entente participants . . .'[19] Most critics responded to the film's ambiguous allegory with positive reviews although one critic from *Photoplay*, articulating the suspicion of an isolationist, wrote in August: 'What keeps this from being a master film? Absence of intimacy, not our people, not our war'.[20]

The British advertising campaign for the film began in earnest in the trade press in January 1917. Articles in *The Bioscope* and *Kinematograph Weekly* reflected the impact of the advertising campaign for *The Birth of a Nation*, emphasising spectacle and downplaying the pacifist message. *The Bioscope* featured an interview with the film's publicist, Raymond Bartlett. Asked about the changes made for the British market, Bartlett explained that 'it has been considerably modified. The full English title is "Civilisation; What Every True Briton is Fighting For" '.[21] Both journal articles focused on the 'realistic battle scenes', with the *Kinematograph Weekly* stating that it was a 'great American sensation' which is 'no maudlin, sickly attempt to preach a moral, but a strong series of extraordinary scenes showing in all its vividness and reality the horror of war, including fierce fighting on land and sea'. There were also 'many domestic scenes and pictures of family life . . . and other strong touches by the producer [to] relieve . . . the terrible scenes of warfare'.[22]

The film was screened for the trade at Marble Arch on 5 February. The critical reception of the trade show was enthusiastic, but not without some reservations. In an article subtitled 'The War Through Neutral Spectacles', *The Bioscope* expressed concern for what they termed 'excessive sentimentality' for the Germans. Throughout this review it was assumed that the Teutonic world created by the film was in fact Germany and the Emperor was meant to represent the Kaiser. The *Kinematograph* reviewer also referred to the liner sinking sequence as 'an attempt to realise the awful destruction of the "Lusitania" '.[23] *The Bioscope* found it necessary to comment on this scene in some detail:

> The sinking of the liner is an instance of the producer's anxiety to include every aspect
> of the war, for as it is only suggested as the outcome of the commander's imagination,
> the story provides a legitimate reason for its insertion. That it is a scene conjured up by
> the brain of a German officer, no doubt accounts for the state of wild panic, and which,
> we are proud to believe, is not in accordance with authenticated fact.[24]

The reviewer's nationalistic sensibilities consequently led him to deny that the scenes of panic presented in Ince's film were modelled on what actually happened on the Cunard liner *Lusitania* in May 1915. They could only exist in the tortured imagination of the German officer.

In many of the publicity efforts on the film's behalf, there were complexities and degrees of ambivalence. Part of the advertising campaign focused on patriotism. The original two-page fold-out advertisement for the film in the British trade press was modified by the added words 'What Every True Briton is Fighting For'. (The 'z' in 'civilization' remains.) But the advertisement also contains a visual metaphor for pacifism: there is a depiction of the sun in the left-hand corner and, directly underneath, a torch of enlightenment with Ince's picture in the flame. Both are shining on the globe on top of which a battle is taking place. This is not referred to in the text of the advertisement, where the only phrase that comes close to articulating pacifist sentiment describes *Civilization* as 'A Picture of modern warfare that thrills and appals'.

The earlier, ambivalent advertising rhetoric was reproduced for the local première of the film at the Palladium on 25 August, but with some changes. The 'z' in the film's title had been replaced by the anglicising 's' but the tag line 'What Every True Briton is Fighting For' had been dropped. While the catchword in the majority of the advertisements was 'stupendous', which emphasised its super-film status, the large crowds and the amount of money it took to produce, the reference to the appalling nature of the images remained. The advertising campaign began a fortnight prior to the screening. A pre-review article entitled 'Super-film at the Palladium' stated that it was considered 'by many an expert in cinematography . . . cinema spectacle beyond compare. In it one is brought face to face with the grimmest reality of all ages, namely the last three years.'[25] The reference to the reality of the depiction of war had a resonance in Britain at this time, following as it did the screenings of *The Battle of the Somme* during the previous year and, earlier in 1917, of *The Battle of the Ancre and the Advance of the Tanks*. Both of these films played their first runs at the Palladium. The impact of these films and their intersection with the experience of loss in British lives had by this time become a significant aspect of adult cinemagoers' realm of experience.

By February 1917 there is clear evidence that the appeal of official war pictures was fading. Indication of this is revealed in *The Bioscope*'s regular column 'The Scottish Section':

> I am not very sure if what I have to write about the Battle of the Ancre film will not be considered a breach of the Defence of the Realm Act but the fact remains that, as a draw 'The Tanks' have not been a success on their first run. It may be from the fact that so many houses, city and suburban were showing them, and it may be that the public are fed up with war pictures, but the fact remains that after two days their drawing powers ceased and on Thursday and Friday some houses took them off altogether.[26]

Broad speculation at the time suggested that people had become tired of these films. There may be a more specific reason. The official films such as *The Battle of the Ancre*, which followed *The Battle of the Somme* in subsequent months, have a marked absence of the kind of explicit footage exhibited by the attack in the *Somme* film. The restrictions of actuality and the mode of address produced films which contrasted sharply with the protagonist-centred fiction films dominating cinema programmes. The expectation of the kind of experience afforded by the official films by February 1917 had changed from tragic/heroic depictions of moments of death to the endless parade of the machinery of modern warfare.

At the beginning of the war there had been a flood of British fictional war films, but as casualty figures mounted such films were considered inappropriate. As early as April 1915 the Regent cinema, in the Southampton suburb of Shirley, advertised a film entitled *The Massacre of the 4th Cavalry* with the added phrase 'Nothing to offend the most sensitive'. Two-reel war films with a message fell from favour with audiences generally, but the war as a setting for adventure in serials such as *Pearl of the Army* (Pathé, 1916), and later comedies such as *The Better 'Ole* (UK, George Pearson, 1918) and Chaplin's *Shoulder Arms* (1918) fared better. Generally, films that displaced the war onto other historical periods or took place during an indeterminate war with Teutonic-looking enemies continued to enjoy popularity.

If the public were tiring of the official films, there was still a good deal of mileage in the spectacle of war as it was expressed in the super-films, notably *The Birth of a Nation* and *Civilization*. On the night of 25 August 1917 there was standing room only for the première of *Civilization* at the Palladium. The review of the evening stated that it had attracted big crowds and that the film is 'undoubtedly one of the most astounding pictures of modern warfare which has been produced, showing as it does, all the phases of war'.[27] The review echoes the tone of the trade press by foregrounding the spectacle of the battle scenes and the counterbalance of the human story, the actions of one man helped by 'the women', the return of men to families and the grief of those who have

lost loved ones. It also assumes that the characters are German and that the peace message is a lesson for Germans to learn. Finally, there is a convergence of educational and
entertainment discourses in its final statement, that 'Civilization is a truly stupendous
spectacle and one which brings home the horrors of war.' 'Bringing the horrors of war
home' had been a phrase commonly used by reviewers of the official war films. The fact
that the film's publicity constructed it as a prestige production and focused on spectacle as 'stupendous and instructive' served to de-emphasise the potentially moralising
tone (some of which had been removed in the version shown in Britain[28]) and, more
specifically, the sensitive issue of pacifism.

The film's depiction of war in all its phases, the sinking of the liner, the 'co-operation
of the women' and the homecoming scenes all had a resonance for the Palladium audience. The sinking of merchant ships was a continuous threat to the community overall.
Although the *Lusitania* herself had not been based in Southampton, the re-enactment
of the sinking held obvious significance for this kind of audience. The *Titanic* had sunk
five years earlier and the town was still in the process of erecting monuments to those
who had lost their lives in her (no less than 125 children from the Northam primary
school had lost a family member on the *Titanic*).

On 28 August 1917, three days after the première of *Civilisation*, the *Echo* ran a letter from the Reverend Frank Blandford, pastor of Bitterne Congregational Church.
Blandford was 'considerably impressed' by his visit to the Palladium. 'It is splendid', he
writes,

> The picture is brilliantly conceived and brilliantly executed. Among its outstanding
> features . . . [are] the contrast between the method of autocracy and the method of
> democracy, a contrast which is frequently brought out . . . The frequent emphasis on
> spiritual values, the suitable and pointed language of the narrative, the prominent part
> played by the 'Mothers of Men' in an anti-war crusade – these points and many others
> give a great teaching and inspiring power to a most splendid film.[29]

His reference to 'Mothers of Men' is significant as it is connected to the film's message
as anti-war but not pacifist. The distinction between the two suggests an active interpretation of the film's profound ambiguity around this issue. The pacifist movement in
the United States and in Britain had come under criticism from conservative pro-war
groups and by government edict in both countries. Susan Zeiger has pointed out the
way in which competing constructions of motherhood in the US had equated the
'patriotic' mother with selfless sacrifice as a positive image while the pacifist mother was
condemned as 'feminist', selfish and exerting an overprotective and unhealthy control
over her sons.[30] Sharon Ouditt has noted that the use of a maternalist discourse by
suffragist pacifists in Britain caused difficulties in their attempt to 'catalyse large-scale
political reorganisation . . . They used the image, though, as a literary and political
device. World politics seen through the eyes of maternalism, is defamiliarised . . . leaving the way clear for a less barbaric, more egalitarian system to emerge' – one equivalent to that articulated in the pacifist message of *Civilization*.[31]

The national attention received by British suffragist pacifists was generally derogatory
in the press. However, members of the National Union of Women's Suffrage Societies
(NUWSS) such as Catherine Marshall and Helena Swanick were involved in pacifist

organisations such as the No-Conscription Fellowship and the Union of Democratic Control. Both organisations brought together suffragists and figures such as Ramsay MacDonald and Bertrand Russell. Since 1911 the NUWSS had been aware of the need to contact trade unions for support and had contacted the Independent Labour Party in Southampton. The NUWSS's relation to the unions in the local area was complicated by the organisation's own rift between those demanding the vote for women (or, at least, middle-class women with property) and the adultists, or advocates of universal suffrage. During the war, the position of the suffragists was still further complicated by the general support for the war and the work generated by the war effort. Southampton at this time was a focus for debates and disputes on conditions of service for women in jobs normally done by men. The scenes of women on the march in the film, when seen against this background, were potentially explosive. Yet their impact was no doubt mitigated by the way in which the cinema itself was identified as a site for entertainment. The screening of the film at the Palladium created specific expectations of the public space of this particular cinema and functioned to prompt certain performative response codes and to reinforce accepted social codes of behaviour. The added understanding that the film was an American production provided a further distance from which the images of Germans learning to become peaceful could be read and interpreted.

## Conclusion

Let us now return briefly to our fictitious cinemagoer and her boyfriend. Mabel had access to the local reception of the film both in the press and by word of mouth. She was able to go to the cinema weekly, if not more often, and her experience of the film *Civilization* was part of a much broader experience of cinemagoing. This experience was characterised as a space where courting, for example, was sanctioned by both the prestige of the cinema and the educational character of the film. Her experience of working in the centre of Southampton in 1916–17 ensured that she witnessed the public impact of the war through the sight of the wounded and convalescing, while other effects, such as those resulting from her uncle's service, would have had more individual resonances. For Walter this would have been more immediate, although patriotic propriety would probably have prevented explicit discussion of the condition of the wounded he was loading every day.[32] The personal context for Mabel's reception of *Civilization* was, therefore, somewhat different than Walter's but with the subject matter of the film being both dutiful, in the sense that it purported to be an important moral message concerning the war, as well as a reminder of the true horrors of war, probably gave little reason to discuss these openly. The fact that all this was tied up with the ritual of courting intensified this effect. Both of these impressions illustrate one means of interpretation that contrasts with Reverend Blandford's, not only because of the obvious differences in their backgrounds, gender and age, but also because of the different social forces governing public discourse in Blandford's case and the personal realm in the case of Mabel and Walter. Rather than argue for an infinite number of possible readings, I have tried to mark out the way in which the film and its advertising interacted with the prevailing conditions of reception within a particular local area to encourage specific public and private responses.

The strategies of the cinema exhibitor indicate the local complexities of film culture and impact on Mabel's and Walter's experience. Hood, Bacon and their managers worked to incorporate their cinema into the local suburban community with methods designed to highlight its benevolent social function. By mixing their programme between a variety of short films, prestige features and super-films they were able simultaneously to extend their audience constituency and maintain a reputation for 'high-class programmes' that were educational and entertaining; hence Mabel's father could feel more comfortable both with the film and the venue. The role of US films, exemplified by the use of Chaplin films, was central to this, not only in terms of the number of films available compared to British product but also through the type of films on offer. The Palladium secured first runs of the Chaplin Mutuals and the First National 'million dollar Chaplins' from late 1917 until the end of the war and beyond. The fact that they showed very few Chaplin Essanays is arguably due to their rejection of the block booking policy of Essanay in order to maintain maximum flexibility in programming and therefore maintain their reputation in the local area. However, the move away from the sombre subject matter of the war is evident in the Palladium's programming of more comedy and adventure serials in the last two years of the war. By speculating on the thoughts of the two fictitious characters Mabel and Walter I have tried to illustrate the nature of 'war-weariness'. Hood and Bacon were not unaware of this growing public attitude and it is clear that the Palladium, along with the general national trend in programming in the later years of the war, attempted to position their venue accordingly.

The war amplified the shifting perception of cinema's social function from being a source of informative education to providing diverting, and regenerating, entertainment. Mabel and Walter would understandably be looking for a place of entertainment to set a good tone for their evening. The super-films such as the reconfigured *Civilization*, a 'great American sensation' in the words of *Kinematograph Weekly*, offered thrilling yet educational spectacle, where educational meant a convergence between the spectacle of war and concurrence with the dominant patriotic discourse. As we have seen, the Palladium was able effectively to negotiate between uplift and thrill in its programming, house management and advertising strategies so that both Chaplin and *Civilization* could be seen, with only slight latitude, as respectable and compatible with the war effort. Mabel and Walter could therefore be assured of a socially sanctioned date by attending the film at the Palladium even though it may not have been their first choice of entertainment. The audience expectations encouraged by these strategies enhanced the interpretation of *Civilization* as significantly as the editorial changes imposed on the film nationally, and highlight the important role the exhibition sector played in the transnational reception, and dominance, of US cinema on British screens.

## Notes

1 The percentage of British films for this period actually slightly increases.

2 Southampton listed sixteen cinemas in 1917 for a population of 110,000. This is not unusual for a mid-size town like Southampton and even smaller towns such as Carlisle, which had a population of around 50,000, had thirteen fixed-site cinemas during this period.

3 William Uricchio and Roberta E. Pearson, *Reframing Culture: The Case of the Vitagraph Quality Films* (Princeton: Princeton University Press, 1993), p. 6.

4 Sydney Bacon's Picture Circuit is listed in the *Kinematograph Year Book, Film Diary and Directory* for 1914 and 1915. The circuit consisted of five cinemas: the Electra Palace in

London, the Olympia in Newcastle, the Public Hall and Her Majesty's Theatre, both in Carlisle, and the Public Hall in Kent. The Palladium does not appear as a part of the circuit, which suggests that Bacon was a silent partner.

5  Sir Sidney Kimber, *Thirty-Eight Years of Public Life, 1910–1948* (Southampton: privately published, 1949), pp. 20–1.

6  'The Southampton Shows', *The Bioscope*, 4 June 1914, p. 1054.

7  The summer season in Britain was difficult for exhibitors because of the warm weather and the competition from summer fairs and other outside activities.

8  Nicholas Hiley, 'The British Cinema Auditorium', in Karel Dibbets and Bert Hogenkamp (eds), *Film and The First World War* (Amsterdam: Amsterdam University Press, 1995), pp. 160–8.

9  'Cinema Notes', *Southern Daily Echo*, 15 January 1914, p. 4.

10  'A Retrospect of the Year', *Kinematograph Year Book*, 1915, p. 19.

11  'Southampton Shows', *The Bioscope*, 8 October 1914, p. 166.

12  'Southampton Shows', *The Bioscope*, 13 August 1914, p. 643.

13  The Palace had been able to secure exclusive 'first-time screened' films for Sunday evening performances probably because it was a part of the MacNaughton's Music Hall Circuit. Films were booked for the circuit as a whole through well-established relationships with renters. It was also common practice for exhibitors to work through the same renter and therefore share programmes. As the Alexandra, the larger high-street cinema located a short distance from the Palace, screened Keystones regularly at this time, it is possible that such an arrangement was made between the two.

14  Kristin Thompson, *Exporting Entertainment: American in the World Film Market 1907–1934* (London: BFI, 1985), p. 82.

15  As an indicator of the kind of market saturation for Chaplin films in Southampton between 1914 and 1918, I have found only a two-week period between mid-March and early April 1916 when it was not possible to see a Chaplin film at one of the cinemas. The general tendency was that most cinemas showed at least one Chaplin programme per month and some, like the Carlton, advertised 'A Chaplin on every programme'.

16  In fact the Palladium ran very few Essanay Chaplins, but did secure an exclusive run of the Mutual Chaplins in 1917. Interestingly, this coincides with Chaplin's increasing control over his films and his development of the mixture of pathos and humour which would characterise his later work, and is arguably the focal point of the elevation of Chaplin to the status of artist in the critical discourse of the period.

17  Richard Koszarski, *An Evening's Entertainment: The Age of the Silent Feature Picture, 1915–1928* (Berkeley: University of California Press, 1990), p. 163. Koszarski quotes Horace Plimpton, Edison's production manager, arguing that 'the theatres in residential sections are more likely to do better with long films because families are able, or more apt, to make an evening's entertainment out of their visit, whereas those catering to more transient trade are better off with more and shorter subjects.' ('How Long Should Films Be?', *New York Dramatic Mirror*, 24 February 1915, p. 22). According to Koszarski, US picture palaces eventually adopted a policy of showing features and shorts on a variety programme (p. 164). The Palladium showed significant foresight by adopting such a policy by 1914. Nevertheless, in Britain, as Stratton's letter shows, while the solution was eventually the same the sets of problems for exhibitors differed significantly from those in the US as outlined by Plimpton.

18 AMPAS, Selig Collection, Folder 55.

19 Charles A. Beard, 'A Frenchman in America', *The New Republic*, vol. 51, no. 653 (8 June 1927), pp. 75–6. Beard's reference is to the House-Grey Memorandum of February 1916, through which Wilson made a 'probable' commitment to a US entry into the war if the Germans declined to attend a peace conference he proposed to call.

20 *Photoplay Journal*, August 1916, p. 135. I would like to thank Kevin Brownlow for his generosity in sharing his notes. Of course any factual errors or misinterpretations are entirely my own.

21 'Civilisation. Great Spectacular Film to be seen in England. Interview With Mr R. K. Bartlett', *The Bioscope*, 25 January 1917, p. 307.

22 'Thomas H. Ince's "Civilisation", Coming Great American Sensation That is Said to Eclipse Anything Before Shown', *Kinematograph and Lantern Weekly*, 25 January 1917, p. 32.

23 'Civilisation: A Stupendous Production', *Kinematograph and Lantern Weekly*, 8 February 1917, p. 25.

24 'A Great Spectacular Triumph. Civilisation – The Supreme Art of Thomas H. Ince – The War Through Neutral Spectacles', *The Bioscope*, 8 February 1917, pp. 544–5.

25 'Civilisation: Super-film at the Palladium', *Southern Daily Echo*, 25 August 1917, p. 2.

26 'The Scottish Section', *The Bioscope*, 15 February 1917, p. 737.

27 'The Palladium', *Southern Daily Echo*, 28 August 1917, p. 2.

28 Kevin Brownlow describes the changes to the film for the British market as follows: 'Away went the introductory subtitle: "Can we call ourselves civilized when we shut our eyes against the command of the Prince of Peace – 'Love thy Neighbor as thyself?'" Luther Rolfe was spared any change of name – his own sounded German enough – but he was transformed into a socialist'. The King, unsurprisingly, was changed into an Emperor. 'The similarity of the fictitious country Wredpryd to Germany', notes Brownlow, 'caused this British version to run into trouble. How could Christ – hardly ever shown on the screen in England – appear to British audiences in the guise of a German officer? The emphasis was hurriedly altered; Count Ferdinand's body returned to earth merely *animated* by the spirit of Christ.' Additional recruiting scenes were also shot 'to ensure the film's acceptance in Britain'. Brownlow, *The War, The West and The Wilderness* (London: Secker & Warburg, 1979), p. 77.

29 'Topics of the Hour', *Southern Daily Echo*, 28 August 1917, p. 3.

30 Susan Zeiger, 'She didn't raise her boy to be a slacker: motherhood, conscription, and the culture of the First World War', *Feminist Studies*, vol. 2 (spring 1996), pp. 6–39.

31 Sharon Ouditt, *Fighting Forces: Writing Women, Identity and Ideology in the First World War* (London: Routledge, 1994), pp. 139–40.

32 The Red Cross and the Military made considerable efforts to hide the convalescing soldiers from public display. However, the enormous number of casualties meant that on average two full trains per day were loaded at Southampton docks and were taken to Netley hospital and it was possible either through direct witness or by word of mouth to get a sense of the severity of the situation. For a detailed account of the embarkation of the wounded from Southampton to Netley hospital see Philip Hoare, *Spike Island: The Memory of a Military Hospital* (London: Fourth Estate, 2001), pp. 175–95.

# 3

# A Balanced Show: the Australian Picture Theatre Manager at Work in 1922

Anne Bittner

On Saturday, 22 April 1922 a typical evening's entertainment was offered to the patrons of the York picture theatre, in Adelaide, the state capital of South Australia. It consisted of music, films and stage presentations – the same type of programme that was being offered in one or more picture theatre in every central business district of every state capital in Australia on a regular basis, and occasionally at suburban and country picture theatres as well. This type of programme was one of a range of entertainments found in the amusements column of any metropolitan daily newspaper, which otherwise included classical drama, melodrama, musicals, pantomimes, variety, vaudeville, films, concerts and dancing.[1] The documentary evidence of this event consists of a programme describing its contents, a brief review and newspaper advertisements contained in the scrapbook of Babs St Clair, who was one of the participants.

Programmes, which were handed to patrons as they entered the picture theatre, can

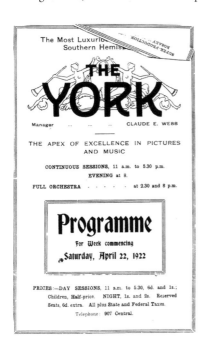

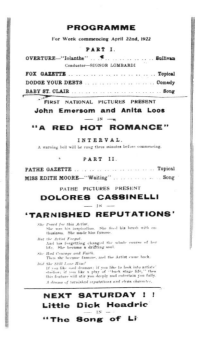

now be found in libraries, private collections and scrapbooks. Usually made of poor-quality paper, now fragile and yellow, not many of them remain because they were as ephemeral as tram tickets – an ordinary part of the experience of everyday life to be discarded after use. As textual documents, they can be read, handled and subjected to literary analysis. The meanings assigned to them by the use of such methods would, however, be associated with the cultural baggage of the modern reader unless, as Janet Staiger argues, that reader 'seeks to understand textual interpretations as they are produced historically'.[2] The programme document needs to be placed within the 'complex cultural, social, and political context' of the event of going to the picture theatre to see a show in 1922, a context that structured how the various participants in this event behaved.[3] Then the focus of interpretation shifts from the cultural object to the relationships between the participants in this cultural event: the performers, the theatre management and the spectators, the 'specific groups' to which Staiger refers.

This case study uses the programme document and other material from scrapbooks, autobiographies, management manuals and trade journals as aids in exploring the relationships between these three groups of people in order to elicit reasons for its existence and the meaning it had for the audience.

## The Picture Theatre Manager and his Patrons

When the programme is regarded as a marketing and promotional tool, clear indications are given of management's perception of the York theatre's niche in the marketplace and, therefore, the audience to which it catered. The front page is concerned with the practicalities of date, time and price. At two shillings for the best seat at an evening performance, this was top of the range for picture theatre admissions but bottom of the range for legitimate theatre. Further evidence of this superior niche in the picture theatre industry is given by the fact that the York management did not sully the programme with advertisements for local goods and services, as did many other picture theatres. It was also given to patrons free of charge. Thus the York did not use the programme as a source of income but solely as a medium for advertising its services to its patrons.

In addition, management actively sought repeat business through the provision of a form at the bottom of the inside front page of the programme offering to 'mail you this programme regularly if you will fill out this blank and hand to the doorman on leaving'. Return business was the goal of all picture theatre managers and the subject of picture theatre management manuals. The York's manager, Claude E. Webb, demonstrated his awareness of this business precept in the following extract of an interview in the trade journal *Everyones*:

> [T]heatre-goers are not merely casual: they, as a matter of fact, are always with us, and a big majority of them are in the habit of visiting the legitimate or picture house at least once a week. Naturally, the patron who has been a regular attendant for years, looks for an improved service – and he is the man to be considered.[4]

Webb, who was one of more than 900 picture theatre managers in Australia at this time, had been considerate of Adelaide spectators for five years in his capacity as manager of the Pavilion theatre, a second-run house, before taking up his current appointment.[5] Built in 1912 and commonly known as the 'Pav', it was one of the Union theatre chain, showing films on a 'continuous' basis: continuous screening from morning to evening without any live performances. Before moving to Adelaide, Webb had been manager of the Lyric theatre, Sydney, also a Union house.

Like the Pavilion, the York was a purpose-built cinema of 2,000 seats with 'eight storeys of office space above a vestibule-foyer' which had opened on 5 November 1921. It was designed to sit quietly in a business environment: no garish marquee was in evidence to mark the difference in purpose between this and any other building in the street.[6] The Greater Wondergraph Company owned the York and the Wondergraph, which had been purpose-built in 1913 to seat 1,800, and operated both houses independently of any of the picture theatre chains which were building up at that stage around Australia. They were in competition with five other film exhibition venues in Adelaide: West's Olympia, the only non-independent house, the Grand, the Pavilion, the Empire and the Theatre Royal which, although built as a theatre in 1868, was then showing films before reverting to its original purpose in 1923. Webb was an experienced showman, and was careful to select an appropriate market niche for the York. As the *Everyones* article says:

> Mr Webb has everything to recommend him for the proud position he now holds, for he is an experienced pressman, a first-class organiser, and possesses any amount of initiative. Add to this a commanding personality, and you see Claude Webb as a legion of friends know him.[7]

When considering programming strategies for his regular patrons in 1922 at the York theatre, however, Webb had to work under one major constraint. As a small independent exhibitor, he could not depend on a continuous supply of quality films, because of the way in which films were distributed. Before World War I, London had been the international exchange through which practically all film distribution occurred, so Australia received both British and American films. When shipping was disrupted during the war, America began shipping product directly to Australia. Kristin Thompson suggests that whereas 'the American share of the British market reached a maximum of about 90% by the 20s, in Australasia the estimate invariably given was 95%'.[8] These American films were distributed to exhibitors through film exchanges under a contract system of blind and block booking. The exhibitor had very little, if any, control over the films he received; he simply had to take what he was sent. Consequently, his programming strategies had to be sufficiently flexible to package films of questionable quality as attractively as possible in order to retain his patrons.

At the same time, the preponderance of American films depicting the American way of life together with American values and attitudes was of great concern to the moral lobbyists. This group, consisting of 'club women, empire loyalists, clergy, educationalists, and sections of the press'[9] was convinced that Australian youth was being corrupted by exposure to 'this prurient rubbish'.[10] They were concerned that 'no country can afford to allow the moral sense of its future fathers and mothers to be thus sapped or injured'.[11] They feared the erosion of the British culture containing values and attitudes which had helped to shape the British Empire. Australia's strong political, economic and cultural ties with Britain were evident in the newsreel *Home Gazette*, devoted to footage of events in Britain distributed by Pathé since 1913.[12] The fear of cultural takeover through exposure to foreign films with different cultural norms was a constant topic of discussion in trade papers and newspapers in the 1920s and became an underlying theme of the Royal Commission on the Moving Picture Industry, which reported in 1928. Among the witnesses from Adelaide were representatives from the Young Women's Christian Association, Women Police, Returned Sailors and Soldiers' Imperial League, the State Censors Board, the Education Department, and Methodist Foreign Missions, as well as local picture theatre exhibitors.

In 1922, some responsibility for preserving Australian moral standards was taken by the systems of film censorship in place at both federal and state level. No American films could be exhibited without the approval of the Commonwealth Censorship Board which began its work in 1917. Films to be shown in Adelaide were also subject to censorship by the South Australian State Censorship Board. For its programme to comply with the regulations, the York management had to provide the inspector of public places of entertainment with a copy of the programme, together with a brief description of each item on it, at least six hours prior to the first screening. There was a penalty of £20 for the first breach of the regulations and a further penalty of £2 per day if the offending film continued to be screened.[13] Ultimately, however, the responsibility for providing respectable entertainment rested with the exhibitor, and it was his job to create attractive programmes for his local audience from block-booked sight-unseen imported films.

On this occasion, Webb's task was to present two American feature films to his Australian audience in a manner which was acceptable to them. In addition to the official approval which was obviously obtained for this programme, the York management were particularly careful to promote the respectability of the films given the rather titillating titles which were typical of Hollywood at that time – *Red Hot Romance* (1922)[14] and *Tarnished Reputations* (1920).[15] The programme contains a summary of the plot of the latter followed by the assertion that it was 'A drama of tarnished reputations and clean character'. This theme of clean entertainment was continued in a paragraph on the back of the front page about a coming attraction:

> 'The Song of Life', an all-star production to be shown at the York on Saturday next, is said to be an absolutely censor-proof picture. Based on mother love, the story presents a true profile of life on New York's East Side with all the romance, heart interest and adventure that O. Henry found in that great melting pot, but without even a suggestion of a sex complication to feed the hungry shears of the censor boards.

In such comments the York management distanced themselves from the activities of the censors at the same time that they informed their patrons that their current and forthcoming programmes were inoffensive.

Webb was also well aware that 'the regular patron – the captious critic always – wants something different to what he has been seeing for years. Thus it is that novelty and originality be served up at frequent intervals'.[16] The continuous search for novelty had also been the driving force in the development of exhibition strategies devised by American picture theatre managers. In an article in *The Mentor* in July 1921, Samuel Rothapfel, the 'father of the American picture palace', described how a programming strategy evolved until:

Finally, a formula for program-making was worked out that covered the field of music, general news topics, drama, comedy, education, dancing, and architectural effects. The American is appreciative of the beautiful, but he is impatient, and will not sit through a long tedious performance. He wants his entertainment well done, but quickly done. The type of performance that suits him and attracts him is marked by rapidity and diversion.[17]

Webb followed this 'formula' on 22 April 1922 by constructing a programming of eight items: an overture, three short films (two 'topicals' and a comedy), two songs and two feature films. At first glance the programme appears to be a haphazard collection of unrelated items. When it is compared with the arrangement of items on vaudeville programme outlines given by an Australian performer, Valentine Napier, who worked as a contortionist in Australia and other countries, and by American vaudeville historian Robert Snyder, however it becomes clear that the arrangement of the items on the programme is deliberate.[18]

The York programme began with an overture of excerpts from Gilbert and Sullivan's *Iolanthe*, followed by a Fox *Gazette*, a newsreel of topical interest with items of local and/or British interest. Napier suggests that the first item, which had the lowest status on the bill, should be 'something nice and bright to open' such as a dancing act, and should be followed by 'an act which only required a small stage area and could work in front of a cloth dropped in the first set of wings'. Snyder suggests starting with a dumb act, which 'will not be spoiled by the late arrivals seeking their seats', followed by 'anything more interesting than the first act'.[19] For the third item, the York showed a comedy film, *Dodge Your Debts* (1921). Napier stipulates a full stage act, acrobat, aerial act, skating, or musical, and Snyder suggests 'something to wake up the audience'.[20] The fourth item at the York consisted of Baby St Clair with a song. Napier recommends a comedian for fifteen to twenty minutes, and Snyder suggests 'an act to strike home, ideally a name performer who will rouse the audience to expect better things from the show'. To end the first half of the programme, the York presented a feature film. Napier suggests that a 'noisy act with some excitement was the thing' and Snyder recommends another big name, 'something the audience will talk about during the intermission'.

Snyder considers the first act after the intermission 'a difficult slot to fill', because it had to sustain audience interest without overshadowing the remaining acts. The sixth act had to begin a build-up that was 'infinitely' faster than that of the first half, one that would quickly put the audience in a 'delighted-expectant' attitude. Napier solves this problem with more of item one; the York screened a second newsreel. According to both Napier and Snyder, the seventh act should be stronger than the sixth, in order to set up the eighth act, which was 'the star the crowd was waiting for'. At the York, Miss Edith Moore sang 'Waiting', before the presentation of the major feature film, Pathé Pictures' *Tarnished Reputations*, starring Dolores Cassinelli. Both Snyder and Napier finish their programme outlines with a specialty act 'to keep the people in the theatre' and 'to send them home pleased'.

In all three programmes, a build-up of tensions was planned to retain the interest of the audience and to keep them in their seats until the most prominently featured artist or film was presented, illustrating Richard Koszarski's claim that 'silent-picture-palace managers . . . clearly saw this part of their business as closer to the work of vaudeville managers than operators of legitimate houses'. [21] Although this exhibition strategy was actively pursued by American and Australian picture theatre managers, it was not freely available to British picture theatre managers, because in Britain, buildings were licensed either as cinemas or theatres, but not for both kinds of performance, as was the case in both Australia and the US. American-style vaudeville programmes had been part of the landscape of Australian entertainment since the middle of the nineteenth century, so the application of that format to film exhibition was an accepted practice and was not regarded as a cultural imposition. [22]

A closer reading of the content of the items on the York programme results in a significant difference between it and the vaudeville programme outlines, however. A vaudeville programme usually consisted of a selection of individual acts which were not connected in any way: there was no plot or narrative, no producer and no master of ceremonies. At the opposite end of this scale of continuity was the drama theatre programme, consisting of one continuous narrative in which the actors were under the control of a producer. The York's programme falls somewhere in between, because although it contains a medley of apparently unrelated items, they have been carefully arranged with a common theme by the picture theatre manager. The overture, a selection of items from Gilbert and Sullivan's *Iolanthe*, tells the story of a thwarted romance between Strephon, an Arcadian shepherd, and Phyllis, a ward of Chancery. The first film was a romantic comedy and the second a romantic melodrama. It is not known which song St Clair sang but the title of Miss Edith Moore's offering is suggestive of lovers waiting to be reunited. The existence of a theme of romance running through the programme suggests a programming strategy more reminiscent of a variety show than of vaudeville. Variety shows occupied the middle ground in popular musical entertainments between vaudeville and musical shows. The latter had a plot, a script and a producer whereas a variety show consisted of a number of items with a theme running through them constructed by a producer and connected by a master of ceremonies (often a comedian).

To satisfy his 'captious critic', Webb's programme allowed the two American films to be part of a respectable show that included local performers, and the presence of a child performer added another sentimental note to the programme. In using a romantic theme to achieve a balance between respectability and vulgarity, and between local content and foreign content, Webb might have been accused of promoting too much sentimentality. This was a favourite topic in the Commonwealth Film Censor's reports:

> Sentimentality, or 'sob-stuff' is the greatest moral and artistic shortcoming of the modern film, and it is the reason why many people of intellect dismiss films in general as trash. It might very well be maintained that this sentimentality does, in the long run, more harm than the positively indecent scenes can do. Its influence is of a more insidious kind. It establishes for the unthinking an entirely false scale of values. [23]

Like other showmen, however, Webb knew that sentiment sold seats.

## The Picture Theatre Manager and the Performer

In addition to the theme of romance running through the programme, further continuity was provided by the sound of the York Theatre Orchestra, led by Signor Lombardi, who, incidentally, also gave Babs St Clair violin lessons. The musicians and their music were an integral part of the programme, as much a feature as the films themselves. The opening item, featuring the orchestra in a selection from a popular operetta first performed in London in 1882, set the tone of the evening as one of patriotic good taste. The music continued throughout the programme as accompaniment to the songs and all the film items, and shared equal billing on the front of the programme in the claim that the York was 'The apex in excellence in pictures and music'. When *Orphans of the Storm* (1921) was shown at the York on 14 October 1922, the entire musical accompaniment to the film, selected by the conductor, was listed on the programme by title and composer.[24] Patrons of picture theatres could be as attracted by the quality and quantity of the music offered to them as they were by the quality of the films.

All the music on the programme was provided by local performers. The featured singers, Baby St Clair and Miss Edith Moore, were both well known to Adelaide audiences. The distances between city centres in Australia meant that Webb had to rely on local talent, unlike his American counterparts who were often part of a circuit of 'small-vaudeville' acts, which would be pre-booked to each venue.[25] At the time of this performance, St Clair was a child of eight and possessed of a voice that could fill a theatre with ease. Because she was petite, she was always promoted as being two years younger than her actual age. She was a product of local dance schools and ambitious parents and had been performing professionally for about two years:

> I had to learn to get everywhere by myself, otherwise you were an amateur. You never approached a theatre manager – to whom you went every week – with your hand in your mother's. I had to get on the tram which passed our door all dressed up [and] wait to see the manager myself . . . You would do the rounds and even the old good acts like the comedians would do the rounds because people didn't have agents in those days.[26]

Her scrapbook shows that she was chosen by the York manager to feature in prologues prior to the screening of the Mary Pickford vehicles *Orphans of the Storm*, week of 14 October 1922, *Little Lord Fauntleroy* (1921), week of 27 October 1922,[27] and *Tess of the Storm Country* (1922), week of 5 May 1923, so it would appear that Webb approved of her professional approach to her work.

Although the picture theatre manager's relationship with musicians and performers was basically that of employer and employee, it was given an added professional depth by Webb's theatrical background, which he described in a 1924 article in *Everyones*:

> [I] joined the Lynch Family of Bellringers as touring manager, and travelled practically through every small town in Australasia. I was with this organisation for three years, after which I joined the late Alfred Dampier, whom I personally consider to be one of the finest all round actors Australia has ever seen. At that time one had to be a man of many parts – manager, touring manager, and actor was a part of everyday work.[28]

That was followed by more stock company work and a trip to America where he joined a touring company as treasurer and later became manager. After surviving the San

Francisco earthquake in 1906, Webb returned to Australia where he was employed at the Theatre Royal, Brisbane, in stock drama. This theatrical experience gave him the ability to select performers and produce stage presentations of a professional standard at the York, and meant that local performers such as Baby St Clair had the benefit of working with an experienced actor/producer/manager.

## The Relationship Between the Performers and the Audience

While the documentary evidence of this performance provides enough detail to construct a rounded portrait of the picture theatre manager's view of his patrons, there is much less evidence describing the relationship between the performers and the audience. Some connections between them can, however, be made if the cultural arena is extended to the local community in which both groups lived.

The photographs, newspaper cuttings, programmes and epidiascope (magic lantern) slides in the scrapbook of Babs St Clair show that she was a versatile performer who was able to obtain work in vaudeville, pantomimes and musicals as well as at the picture theatres. She was one of a considerable number of girls and young women who were to be found in front of an audience on the stages of picture theatres, legitimate theatres, town halls, boxing stadiums and dance halls almost every night of the week, except Sunday, in all the major cities. They were the students of local music teachers and dance schools situated in the neighbourhood.

There were at least three well-known dance schools in Adelaide in the early 1920s.

Babs St Clair, 1922

Glass slide for epidiascope used for pre-event promotion.

Louise Larsson, who taught St Clair, and Trixie Wilson taught all forms of stage danc-ing, while Nora Stewart taught both stage and ballroom dancing.[29] Stage dancing included 'styles such as tap dancing, national dancing, musical comedy (now jazz bal-let), acrobatic, classical (which was barefoot dancing) and operatic dancing (the term used for what is now known as classical ballet)'.[30] Larsson provided dancers from amongst her students for all the J. C. Williamson productions which came to town and Jennie Brenan did the same in Melbourne. Lesser-known schools existed in the suburbs and provided classes for one shilling.[31] The same witness continued:

> And the children who learnt dancing, of course, that was a night's entertainment
> because Mum and Dad would come with them to the classes and if Auntie May or Sally
> was there for tea, she would come down too . . . in my day there would be more parents
> kicking around than students.[32]

As well as watching the classes, the parents and other members of the community made costumes and scenery, acted as chaperones and dressers, and provided the music. The participatory nature of the activities surrounding the dance school meant that the com-munity became informed spectators of performance. As one well-known Australian vaudeville performer said in an interview, there was a 'kinder audience then who knew about it . . . Every second house had a piano which could be rented for five shillings down and two shillings a week' and there was a 'camaraderie around the suburbs'.[33] Other autobiographers, such as Hal Porter in *The Watcher on the Cast Iron Balcony* and Brian Dixon in *Sunday at Kooyung Road*, mention the weekly Saturday night gatherings around the piano.[34] From their participation in the activities of the dance school and through making their own entertainment at home, these ordinary people gained con-siderable knowledge about theatrical performance and took this knowledge with them when they went to the picture theatre. Thus they became participants in the event, as well as spectators of it. If we regard the York's 'balanced show' as a totality, the perva-

siveness of this community engagement with the performers provides a significant counterweight to the common critical argument that cinema's representational mode of performance brought about the demise of the more direct address to the audience provided by vaudeville and variety's presentational mode.

Another connection between the audience and the performers was the physical context in which the performance was seen on that night in 1922. The effusive report of the opening night of the York in November 1921, praised the 'spaciousness and elegant simplicity, the beautiful lines and the refined taste exhibited in the decorative effects'. A picture theatre management manual invests these 'decorative effects' with the capacity to

> make up the atmosphere of a palace, to stimulate the imagination of tired minds and re-create the strength of weary hearts. The architect has mastered the psychology of the theatre-goer. He understands the patron's love of adventure and the craving for the beautiful and luxurious, and with deft touches excites the spirit of romance by the very structure and decoration of the theatre.[35]

The York may well have had this effect on the audience and, therefore, reinforced the theme of romance, which was already present in the programme. But it had one attribute above all others which 'shaped the way mainstream films could be received – and reinterpreted – by non-mainstream audiences': it was Australian.[36]

This factor was emphasised in the newspaper report by highlighting the use of local materials:

> Then in the vestibule it was good to learn that the marble of the stairs was obtained from Agaston [forty miles from Adelaide]. In the opinion of the architect, C. S. Smith, it is superior to the imported article. Likewise the mosaic tiling compares favourably

with imported material.

And, like its companion house, the Wondergraph, the colour scheme and decorations of the York also had Australian themes:[37]

> Brown and buff are the predominant colors, tinged with blue, and picked out with touches of gold wattle groups. The walls are covered with beautiful landscape effects, representing different phases of Australasian scenery, and when the full scheme is completed the York will be second to none for the delightful character of its artistic embellishments.

The report ends on a resoundingly nationalistic note: 'The most interesting feature about the York Theatre is the fact that this magnificent building, certainly second to none in the Southern Hemisphere, is almost entirely the work of Australian genius and material'.[38] This Australian building was the venue for entertainment designed by an Australian picture theatre manager for an Australian audience. The conditions of reception were consequently thoroughly Australian.

## Conclusion

The programme presented on 22 April 1922 was an event overlaid with all the social and psychological complexities inherent in any situation where a cultural product is created and consumed. In this case, part of the product was imported and thus impregnated with foreign values and attitudes. The role of the picture theatre manager was pivotal in muffling this siren song by encasing the films in a programme that balanced imported films with local live performance, education with entertainment, comedy with melodrama and narrative with spectacle. The diversity of the items on the programme attracted the regular patron and allowed him a participatory role through his knowledge of the local entertainment industry in which the performers were embedded. The Australian conditions of reception enabled the audience to negotiate the American films. A balance had been struck between imported and local cultural input; between the spectacle of live performance, and the narratives embedded in the feature films; between the visceral (live action) and the cerebral (film); and between the moral virtue of respectability and the spicy desire for vulgarity. Considerable irony, however, lay in the fact that the format of the programme was itself an American cultural import, accepted without question.

### Notes

1 For an analysis of the contents of amusement columns in one paper in each state capital between 1920 and 1935 see Anne Bittner, 'A balanced show: a cultural history of the relationship between stage attractions and film in Australia from 1920 to 1935', unpublished PhD thesis, La Trobe University, 2000, Appendix A.

2 Janet Staiger, *Interpreting Film: Studies in the Historical Reception of American Cinema* (Princeton: Princeton University Press, 1992), p. 9.

3 Ibid., p. 7.

4 *Everyones*, 30 January 1924, p. 3.

5 Ina Bertrand (ed.), *Cinema in Australia: A Documentary History* (Sydney: New South Wales University Press, 1989), p. 69.

 6  Ross Thorne, *Cinemas of Australia via USA* (Sydney: University of Sydney Press, 1981),
    p. 381.
 7  *Everyones*, 30 January 1924, p. 3.
 8  Kristin Thompson, *Exporting Entertainment: America in the World Film Market*
    (London: BFI, 1985), p. 42.
 9  Bertrand, *Cinema in Australia*, p. 73.
10  *Bulletin*, 15 May 1924.
11  *Everyones*, 16 March 1927, p. 5.
12  Diane Collins, *Hollywood Down Under: Australians at the Movies, 1896 to the Present
    Day* (North Ryde, Sydney: Angus & Robertson, 1987), p. 38.
13  Ina Bertrand, *Film Censorship in Australia* (St Lucia: University of Queensland Press,
    1978), p. 57.
14  John Emerson and Anita Loos, *A Red Hot Romance*, Joseph M. Schenk, 1922.
15  Léonce Perret (author), *Tarnished Reputations*, Pathé Exchange Inc., 1920.
16  *Everyones*, 30 January 1924, p. 3.
17  S. L. Rothapfel, 'Making the program', *The Mentor*, July 1921, p. 33.
18  Valentine Napier, *Act as Known*, (Melbourne: Globe Press, 1986), pp. 21–2; Robert
    L. Snyder, *The Voice of the City: Vaudeville and Popular Culture in New York* (New York:
    Oxford University Press, 1989), pp. 66–7.
19  Ibid.
20  Hal Roach (author), *Dodge Your Debts*, Pathé, 1921
21  Richard Koszarski, *An Evening's Entertainment: the Age of the Silent Feature Picture
    1915–1928* (Berkeley: University of California Press, 1990), p. 53.
22  Cf. Richard Waterhouse, *Minstrel Show to Vaudeville: the Australian popular stage
    1788–1914* (Sydney: New South Wales University Press, 1990).
23  Commonwealth Film Censorship report for the year 1925, *Commonwealth
    parliamentary papers 1926–28*, Vol. 5, p. 7.
24  Babs St Clair, scrapbook, in the possession of the author.
25  See Robert C. Allen, *Vaudeville and Film: A Study in Media Interaction 1895–1915* (New
    York: Arno Press, 1980).
26  Anne Bittner, transcript of interview with Babs St Clair, 16 November 1990, p. 6.
27  For an analysis of that prologue and the accompanying programme, see Anne Bittner,
    'Little Lord Fauntelroy: an example of the relationship between vaudeville and film', in
    *Screening the Past: Aspects of Early Australian Film*, National Film and Sound Archive,
    Canberra, 1995, p. 107.
28  *Everyones*, 30 January 1924, p. 3.
29  Nora Stewart is mentioned as the teacher of the young Robert Helpmann, who later
    became Sir Robert Helpmann, artistic director of the Australian Ballet 1974–5, in both
    Mary Helpmann, *The Helpmann Family Story* (Adelaide: Rigby, 1967) and Elizabeth
    Salter, *Helpmann: the authorised biography* (Melbourne: Angus & Robertson, 1978).
30  Margaret Abbie Denton, *Joanna Priest: her Place in Adelaide's Dance History* (Adelaide:
    Joanna Priest, 1993), p. 22.
31  Anne Bittner, transcript of interview with Renee Mooney, The Renee Mooney
    Collection, Performing Arts Museum, Melbourne, p. 9.
32  Ibid., p. 4.

33 Charles Norman, interviewed by Frank Van Stratten, November 1980, Performing Arts Museum, Melbourne.

34 Hal Porter, *The Watcher on the Cast Iron Balcony* (London: Faber & Faber, 1963); Brian Lewis, *Sunday at Kooyung Road* (Melbourne: Hutchinson of Australia, 1976).

35 John F. Barry and Epes W. Sargent, *Building Theatre Patronage: Management and Merchandising* (New York: Chalmers, 1927), p. 12.

36 Miriam Hansen, *Babel and Babylon: Spectatorship in American Silent Film* (Cambridge, MA: Harvard University Press, 1991), p. 100.

37 For a photograph and description of the Wondergraph, see Thorne, *Cinemas of Australia via USA*, p. 378.

38 *Advertiser* (Adelaide), 5 November 1921.

# 4
# Cowboys, Jaffas and Pies: Researching Cinemagoing in the Illawarra

Nancy Huggett and Kate Bowles

'The Illawarra' is a term used to describe the region south of Sydney, Australia, centred on the city of Wollongong.[1] The two geographical features that have contained the growth of the region's suburban and small town communities are the large national park, which segregates the northern mining villages from Sydney's southerly suburban sprawl, and the dramatic sandstone and rainforest escarpment, which has confined the Illawarra's westerly development to a widening coastal strip clinging to the foot of steep, thickly forested cliffs. Road, rail, telegraphic, telephonic and networked communication between Sydney and Wollongong have all been channelled by this distinctive geography. Meanwhile, the primary drivers of development in the region have been mining and steel production in the city and northern suburbs, and dairy farming towards the south.

The Illawarra has been extensively researched by labour historians, social geographers and geoscientists, establishing a blunt logic to the idea of the region as a research object. Researching cultural memory in the Illawarra – including the history of cinemagoing – reveals the fragility of research agendas set by grouping together these diverse small towns and suburbs, however. In his study of the Illawarra during the 1930s Depression, Len Richardson remarks on the way in which the contemporary understanding of the region's shared experience and priorities may lead to a poor appreciation of the 'intense parochialism' of the separate communities within the region in earlier periods, as a result of which 'people from settlements a few kilometres apart considered each other outsiders'. Richardson argues that this parochialism is a resilient feature of local discourse, and that many locals 'still consider themselves to belong to Coledale or Bulli or Port Kembla and only secondarily to Wollongong'.[2] Our research has substantially supported this characterisation of the region as a series of parochial communities, within which personal stories of everyday life can be told. We believe, however, that the recurring pre-occupations of Illawarra cinemagoers may also describe some of the common character-istics of the picture theatre experience in non-metropolitan areas, both in Australia and elsewhere, and it is in this respect that local stories play a distinctive part in the study of the global cinema audience.

The initial aim of our research project, conceived in 1997, was simply to provide an oral history of cinemagoing in the region, in part to offer a corrective to the metropol-itan bias in Australian cinema historiography, and in part to 'thicken' the descriptions of cinemagoing provided by conventional analyses of production or distribution econ-omies. Australian cinema studies has produced some intense parochialism of its own, not least in the persistent tendency to account for the difficulties faced by the local production industry exclusively in terms of the distribution arrangements fostered by the Hollywood studios. This inspection of the past through the prism of nationalist resentment has so far not encouraged specific research into the audience experience of cinemagoing, but rather has generated an inferred and rather sketchy account of the imagined Australian audience as helpless (at best) or actively collaborating in their own subjection to the powerful American imperative. The first phase of this research (twenty-six oral history interviews conducted by Nancy Huggett with thirty-five local seniors between 1995 and 1999) aimed to provide the detail missing from the public record of regional cinema exhibition available in local archives, and in the Australian Theatre Historical Society's publication on Illawarra cinema buildings and their history, *Guaffered Velour*.[3] Findings from this first phase generated an extension of the project, which commenced in 2002, exploring the potential for using undergraduate students at the University of Wollongong to recruit and interview family members to add their accounts to a digitally archived and indexed database.[4]

In this chapter, we reflect on the successes and limitations of this research methodology, and make some cautious recommendations for the accommodation of oral history techniques to more commonly deployed strategies for researching cinema history in regional, national and comparative contexts. We begin, however, by offering a preliminary contextual sketch of early exhibition history in the Illawarra, compiled by combining oral history and other archival and published sources. In a sense, this is where we originally imagined the research project might conclude: in a demonstration of the value of oral history in amplifying and shading what can already be found on the public record. As our concluding remarks will argue, however, our reflections on the harvesting and selective exploitation of these accounts has led us to a modest renegotiation with the discipline of cinema studies; and to a partial resolution of the conflict of interest between ethnographic media audience research and the historiographic practices which are commonly used to convey information about audiences of the past.

## Cinema and the Illawarra

The first moving pictures to appear in the Illawarra came in the form of a one-night performance of Edison's cinematograph in Wollongong on 10 February 1897.[5] The exhibition of moving pictures in mixed vaudeville programmes and eventually in specialist programmes continued throughout the region courtesy of picture-showmen who operated from the late 1890s onwards. The showmen were jacks-of-all-trades, operating the equipment, providing commentary to the moving pictures, supplying additional entertainment, and cajoling local women into playing piano accompaniment, if a pianist was not already part of the picture show outfit. According to Cec Clark, who was a travelling showman in the region in the 1920s and 1930s, a showman would not have a particular territory, but would scout out locations in advance to determine which communities were without regular pictures, and would build up a circuit from his initial investigations.[6] The showmen hired their selection from film exchanges in Sydney, and were charged with travelling hundreds of miles around the region with the films and the exhibition equipment, all of which was highly vulnerable to fire, before returning the films in good condition to the exchanges. These hardy entrepreneurs exhibited at local town halls and public buildings, which might include the local

The King's Theatre, Thirroul.

School of the Arts, the Friendly Society hall, or the Agricultural hall, a practice which
saw another small revenue stream emerge from the licensing of premises for the showing of pictures. Given the growing popularity of the pictures, local entrepreneurs soon
moved to set up more regular picture shows in their suburbs, a practice that undercut
the position of the travelling showmen.

By 1911, Sydney had over one hundred temporary or permanent picture shows.[7] The
Illawarra's first designated picture venue was the Wollongong Garden Picture Palace
which opened in July 1911, followed three months later by the Crown Picture Palace.
Elsewhere in the district, the Woonona Princess and the Corrimal Princess opened in
January 1912 and in 1913 Thirroul also had a purpose-built venue in the first Kings
Theatre. In all, around fifteen new theatres were built in the first two decades of the
twentieth century. The first purpose-built theatres in the region were initially open-air
venues that showed pictures on fine evenings. However, the loss of revenue through
inclement weather soon made owners reconsider. For example, Olga Ferguson of
Scarborough remembers going to the Arena open-air theatre in Thirroul in 1920 when
a southerly blew up, overturning seats and upsetting the audience. Similarly, Cec Clark
recalls an outdoor screening where he and his partner had trouble keeping the film
steady as the wind flapped the screen fiercely. As a result, most of the picture theatres
quickly acquired partial or complete roofing.

At first, the theatres themselves were simple, barn-like structures, but as cinemagoing
became increasingly popular, so the picture venues gradually became more solid and
elaborate. By the 1920s some larger suburbs even had more than one 'luxury' theatre
competing for patronage.[8] The 1910s, therefore, witnessed the decline of the picture-
showmen, as some retired from the business and others became independent exhibitors. As the decade drew on, even the independents in the region faced tough
competition as theatre owners became involved in more than one theatre, and the

major players slowly began to move towards setting up a local chain. In 1923, Herbert Boland formed Wollongong Theatres Propriety Limited, a company that dominated cinema exhibition in the Illawarra until 1966. Boland had been the owner of the Crown theatre, the first recorded exhibitor at the Thirroul School of Arts, and a co-leaseholder at the Strand theatre in Corrimal from 1921. Under his influence the company extended its scope, building and acquiring picture theatres around the region, and forcing smaller independent operators to diversify or quit. In 1924, Wollongong Theatres leased the Theatre Royal in Bulli, and the following year built the New Kings theatre in Thirroul. In order to protect these investments, the company then bought out rival theatres in the same areas and turned them into dance halls.

During the reign of Wollongong Theatres, other entrepreneurs secured ownership of more than one theatre, but the dominance of one powerful chain in the region was hard to shift. The Yardley brothers of Coledale first became interested in cinema when the Coledale Empire fell into their hands through a defaulted loan in 1918,[9] and the two brothers were soon also running the Palace theatre at Scarborough, switching features, newsreels and serials between the two theatres via motorbike courier, according to Olga Ferguson. By 1926, however, the Yardleys had been persuaded to sell their assets to Wollongong Theatres, after protracted wrangles with the local council over sanitary conditions and leasing rights. Owning many venues enabled Wollongong Theatres to employ similar economies of scale, hiring films that they then showed in various locations. Theatres in close proximity to one another would even swap film programmes in the same evening. Ron and May Klower recall that the Bulli Royal and the Thirroul Kings, for example, would screen the main feature and the supporting programme in different halves of the evening to allow the programme to be split and exchanged by courier during the interval. Charlie Anderson, a local theatre manager, extends our understanding of this practice in his observation that control of more than one theatre meant that programme swaps could occur within the same evening without the film exchange knowing about the switch, thus providing double takings for the price of hiring one programme.

This account of local resourcefulness (which contravenes official records) demonstrates the contribution of oral history accounts of the period to reshaping our understanding of the role played by, for example, metropolitan distribution companies in the cinemagoing culture of the region. Such practices cannot simply be inferred from archival records, newspaper advertisements, playbills or even box-office takings. By including them in the history of regional cinemagoing, however, some aspects of the public record are subject to a qualified re-reading. Jack and Rene Hodgeson recall the enterprising larrikinism[10] of local 'character' 'Sherlock Jones' who 'pinched a roll of tickets' and handed them out at a screening at the Coledale Empire during the Depression. 'And we all got in and showed our ticket. Poor old Charlie [Charlie Dyer, the proprietor of the Coledale Empire] thought he had a big house but there was no money!' From the Hodgesons, we also learn about the struggling Dyer brothers, who managed small venues in the mining communities of the northern suburbs and were not well-placed to keep up with developments in motion picture technology or building standards in the 1920s, relying instead on a combination of entrepreneurial spirit and community loyalty to keep their audiences coming back. The Dyers combined the attraction of movies and the dance hall by screening silent films over the heads of dancers on the dance floor at the front of the theatre. Rene remembers that 'when you were dancing with a chap and you wanted a bit of a canoodle, you'd nick up the back [to the picture stalls] and then got back on the dance floor before the dance was finished'.

## Cinemagoing and Local Identity

In addition to increasing our understanding of the ways in which local exhibition practices worked, and were affectionately appreciated by local audiences, our conversations with local seniors illuminated for us many instances such as these in which audiences were distracted from the screen by the social dramas around them. These accounts of a lively local culture of cinemagoing provide an important corrective to the image of pre-war Australian audiences as passively absorbing Hollywood screen content. Recollections of cinemagoing demonstrate that the rituals and routines associated with going to the pictures – who sat where each week, and with whom, and what they wore – and the personal stories and relationships that depended on the experience, take narrative priority. This immediately challenges the impression gained from conventional historical descriptions of moviegoing, which have been biased towards the metropolitan experience, and have imagined the moviegoer as isolated and anonymous, fixated only on the screen – an icon of modernity enacted in the familiar photographic image of the mass cinema audience at the urban picture palace, all facing forwards with an expression of intent focus on the screen, certainly not chatting, canoodling or checking each other out.

Furthermore, these accounts have enabled us to appreciate a little-known feature of regional cinema history, in terms of the specific role played by cinema in the construction of community identity. The strength of community bonds in small towns and suburbs, mentioned by Richardson and borne out by many of those interviewed, had their origins in some of the distinctive labour-related hardships of the region, especially during wartime and the Depression. These bonds were consolidated first in specific community traditions in sport, surf lifesaving and churchgoing, and were then further enhanced by emerging public leisure practices such as cinemagoing, which once more enabled the community to keep an eye out for (and on) each other. Where proprietor and patron, projectionist and ice-cream seller all came from the same small village or suburb, we see the distance between exhibition and audience significantly diminished, resulting in a distinctive sense of community ownership of, and loyalty to, local cinema. Furthermore, with several other local businesses depending for their patronage on the cinema audience – from bus companies to bottle shops operating as confectioners during intervals in the programme – suburban and small-town movie-theatres functioned as indexical to the more general fate of the local economy.

The northern suburb of Thirroul provides an interesting case study in this hyphenation of cinema and prosperity. In the early years of the twentieth century, Thirroul was a settlement in the middle of the thriving coal-mining communities along the northern coastal strip, where the railway industry had built a busy marshalling yard. The first two decades of the century witnessed Thirroul's growth as a holiday destination popular with residents of Sydney, boasting a surf beach and several guesthouses. This trend saw Thirroul becoming, by 1922, the largest town in the region after Wollongong and Port Kembla. Shortly thereafter, however, the tourist trade began to decline, and it appeared by the mid-1920s that the town had passed its peak. The original Kings theatre had been built in the suburb in 1913, co-existing with open-air venues such as the Arena. In 1923, the Yardley brothers of Coledale constructed the luxury Arcadia cinema, and the local newspaper, the *South Coast Times*, used its opening to talk up the potential of the town, claiming that the theatre 'is the most striking proof of the confidence in the prospects of Thirroul: it is big enough for a city, adds greatly to the appearance generally of the town, and suggests indeed that entertainment is the chief raison d'etre of Thirroul'.[11]

The Arcadia faced competition when Wollongong Theatres opened the New Kings theatre just a few blocks up the street, but even this modest regional suburb was able to sustain two theatres for one year. Following the 1926 sale of the Arcadia to Wollongong Theatres, who converted it to a Palais de Danse, the Kings theatre became the main cinema venue in Thirroul and one of the flagship theatres of the Wollongong Theatres chain. When the talkies arrived at the Kings in 1929, the local newspapers once again saw the occasion as an indicator of the rising status of Thirroul. The *Illawarra Mercury* reported that

> A traffic scene worthy of a city was all created by reason of Union Theatres Ltd introducing to Thirroul 'the talkies' . . . Never previously has such a crowd assembled at Thirroul. The number of adults and children who gained admission totalling in the vicinity of 1500 and the luxurious Kings accommodated them comfortably . . . It was a distinction for Thirroul that this famous picture [*The Rainbow Man* (1929)] should be presented by the Kings prior to being shown at any other community venue in Australia.[12]

The local conceit that cinema made Thirroul nationally distinctive was echoed in the holiday brochures advertising the town in the first half of the century, where the local cinema often featured as part of the package of attractions available to Sydney-siders planning to spend long periods at the coast.[13]

The high profile of cinema in measuring the attractiveness and independent sustainability of a community can be explained in two ways. In the first place, cinema was squarely associated with progress in a way that other community traditions were not, and at the same time it drew on very traditional social practices in order to make technical novelty, as well as images of distant lands and their cities, seem safe and familiar. For example, elements of the programme at many cinemas specifically encouraged community participation: community singing, competitions for children, and the playing of the national anthem. Second, cinemagoing was popular right across the community, with the social geography internal to the picture theatre itself able to cope with any perceived class, age or denominational differences in the audience. Going to the pictures was an entertainment available to women and children who were excluded from other popular activities such as boxing or drinking at the local pub.[14] It was also an entertainment popular with local migrant populations, with screenings at migrant hostels, and specific weekend programmes for the ethnically and racially mixed audiences at the Whiteway theatre in Port Kembla, the suburb servicing the majority of the migrant and local workers at the Port Kembla steelworks to the south of Wollongong city. And although some regional Australian theatres were closed to Aboriginal audiences, oral history accounts suggest that urban Aboriginal communities to the south of the city of Wollongong were part of the audience at the Whiteway.

Cinema attendances throughout the region dropped during the Depression, but even relatively acute poverty was no absolute barrier to attendance. Picture-showman Cec

The Whiteway Theatre, Port Kembla

Clark recalls that during the Depression, there were 'hundreds and hundreds out of work, no job, no future, no money, no nothing [except] to be able to go along to the movies . . . and if they didn't have the money they came in for free of course'. Similarly, theatre owner Charlie Anderson remembers a siren which alerted people living in camps at some distance from town to the start of the programme or main feature.[15] Jack Hodgeson's awareness that the struggling Dyer brothers were 'battling for quids' during the Depression is balanced by his recollection of the resourcefulness of the local audience in finding ways into the Dyers' screenings for free, even without the assistance of the wily Sherlock Jones:

> See, we had no money. Nobody had any money in those days. There were two big doors at the front; they opened in, and perhaps you'd pay for one to go into the pictures – which would only be about thruppence or something – and just as the lights went out he would sneak up and pull the bolts on the double doors and we'd all scoot in.

## Shared Meanings and Cinemagoing

These highly localised accounts of moviegoing during the Depression do a great deal more than simply unearth specific practices associated with cinemagoing that cannot be gleaned from archival research. Their broader value lies in revealing the discursive landscapes of what Alistair Thomson calls 'particular publics', assembled by common interest or adversity, within which cinema was no more than a landmark – albeit a prominent one. Illawarra cinemagoers recall the 1930s within wider stories of larrikin behaviour that challenged the capitalist system which was failing regional and rural communities. Even when the 'victims' of such larrikinism were also local, this behaviour was admired and acknowledged as a necessity. The Hodgesons, for example, recall instances of sneaking into the movies for free in association with stories about other local people swiping

cargo from slow-moving goods trains passing through Coledale, poaching rabbits, steal-
ing chickens and scrumping apples. When entire communities such as the mining villages in the northern suburbs were suffering hardship, the 'us' of the community united
behind activities that bent the rules in order to provide for their members. Larrikinism,
or acting up, was also seen as a uniting discourse for the younger members of the community, with cinemagoing providing one venue in which to stage minor acts of rebellion
such as ticket-stealing, calling out, throwing lollies and even skimming unscrewed seat
arms down the aisles – generally testing the patience of adult patrons and theatre staff.
In these ways, the cinema reveals itself as a smaller and contained version of the community at large – a safe yet public place where individuals challenged authority in minor
ways, made reputations and starred in their own serial dramas.

Embedded within these contextualised accounts of larrikinism, we find another commonly discussed aspect of cinemagoing: eating, particularly at times when food in general
was scarce. Again, this situates cinemagoing within a narrative of community life which
serves a wider purpose. Audience members recalled both food on screen, and food that
played an important part in the cinema visit itself. Stan Chesher, for example, described
in detail the pies that his brother would buy at the paper shop opposite the pictures.
Darryl Walker also recalled these pies, claiming that 'you could just get drunk on the smell
of the pies, beautiful'. Olga Ferguson spoke of home-made ice-cream being the interval
speciality at the Scarborough shop, replaced in the winter months by hot saveloys. And
Pam Bain remembered dashing up from the Savoy theatre in Wollongong to Dales shop,
where she and her friends would see who could drink down a fresh fruit smoothie fastest,
before running back to the pictures. Many of these food narratives revealed particular
accompanying rituals: for example, the common practice of a man buying a box of choc-
olates for his date at the cinema, and the equally customary practice of the woman eating
just one or two and saving the rest of the box to take home to her mother.

The most common reminiscence concerned the particular brands of sweets and lollies available within the theatre itself, with the senses of smell and taste vividly recalled.
These connected to the most commonly recalled community ritual in the Australian cinemagoing context: rolling 'Jaffas' down the theatre aisles.[16] This practice has been extensively written into Australian filmgoing lore and continually emerges in oral history
accounts, although there are some significant variations in Jaffa-rolling behaviour!
Arthur Parkinson explained that Jaffas rolled by mistake when they were dropped, while
Darryl Walker remembered this as a deliberate tactic to defuse the suspense during a
tense part of the movie, and Pam Bain recalled Jaffas being thrown like missiles from the
dress circle to the stalls in the Dapto theatre in particular. In this way, we can see that
what might be called a 'general public' discourse (the Australian association of cinemagoing with Jaffa-rolling, of which those interviewed were clearly aware) intersects with a
'particular public' experience, which is in turn interpreted in various ways by different
individual audience members.[17] Similarly, while Illawarra audiences consumed the same
brands of sweets as other cinema audiences nationally, they recall these in narratives
which also take in particular and local experiences of food such as the Scarborough shop
ice-cream, the smoothies from Dales, and the unsurpassable pies outside the Bulli Royal.
It is the purposefully constructed significance of these local memories which plays an
important part in our appreciation of the role that cinemagoing played in marking out
the social contours of the region.

In particular, as argued at the start of this chapter, such details enable us to reopen the question of parochialism – to take issue with the idea of the national or even regional audience that is inferred from archival histories of motion picture distribution. When this audience is envisaged in terms of its response to exhibited screen content only, a more homogeneous impression is gained: the same movies constructing the same audiences wherever they played. Conversely, conversations with local people repeatedly explored the way in which one suburb or community viewed another, using their respective cinemas as the focal point of the comparison. For example, when comparing the cinemas of the northern suburbs, the Kings theatre in Thirroul was widely considered a 'better' venue than the smaller pictures shows at Scarborough or Coledale, described by projectionist Ron Klower as 'little dumps'. Similarly, interviewee Cecelia Jackson argued that Scarborough 'wasn't a theatre, it was a picture show'. In turn, the Kings paled by comparison with the picture palaces of Wollongong itself, most notably the Wollongong Crown, which many interviewees regarded as the grandest in the region – although the Whiteway in Port Kembla and the Regent in Wollongong were also occasionally associated with glamour. While individual comparisons did not always reach the same conclusions (others finding the Whiteway 'pretty grotty' and the Regent 'depressing'), the general observation can be made that specific picture theatres were part of a discourse which countered any tendency, either in research or municipal ambitions, to subsume the smaller communities of the Illawarra into a homogeneous region. Demarcations within and between theatres were used to mark rites of passage for local cinemagoers, who graduated to different seats, different session times and eventually different theatres as their community status changed. Children were sent to Saturday matinees at the local cinema because the staff could be relied upon to keep an eye on them; but, as the children grew older, they were occasionally allowed to travel to cinemas a little further away with their friends. Courting couples came to prefer certain cinemas to others, and marriage further changed the cinemagoing habits of many.

Mr Charles Anderson, Manager of the Whiteway Theatre, Port Kembla 1946–52

Meanwhile, the spatial politics within cinemas roughly preserved existing social, economic, class or religious identifications, while encouraging a kind of aspirational
mobility which was specific to the picture theatre. Courting couples and women in particular recall their elevation to the upper stalls, well away from the hazardous seating in
the 'spit and hangovers' or 'peanut alley', as the cheaper seats closer to the screen were
commonly known. Some also recall their seating choices as children being driven by
social factors: their parents' fears of 'bad influence', peer pressure from friends, or religious and school loyalties which may or may not have been encouraged by parents (children from Anglican and Catholic schools choosing to occupy different areas of the
Kings in Thirroul, for example).

The unwritten rules that governed where people sat in larger cinemas, or when and
how they progressed from the 'little dumps' to the more glamorous venues, applied to
children and adults alike. These spaces played an important role in the way in which the
community as a whole observed and regulated social classifications. In many of the
smaller cinemas, it was possible for audience members to see exactly who was at the pictures, and with whom. This was made easier by the tendency for local people to sit in
the same seats each week, and for regulars to assume a particular profile, both in the
eyes of the community at large, and in the recollections of theatre staff. Charlie
Anderson, for example, knew his regulars and noted their attendance at specific ses-
sions. The Hodgesons could look around the Arcadia in Thirroul and see who was there
and who was not. In their recollections, audience notables such as the loner 'Mrs Swan'
play a particular role in underscoring the distinctiveness of community-based cinemagoing:

> *JH*: But you'd look around as you went in and you could tell who was who, 'so and so's
> not here tonight!' There was a lady called Mrs Swan from Coledale. She lived in the
> bush along Coledale station and she went to the pictures in Thirroul every night.
> *RH*: Walked!
> *JH*: Walked from Coledale. And she sat in the same seat in Thirroul every night and to
> think she must have seen the same pictures every night! On her own.
> *RH*: She never missed a one
> *JH*: And she always took a bunch of flowers with her. I could never work out where she
> got the bunch of flowers from because she didn't have a garden! . . . She used to get
> into the pictures for nothing! She used to take this bunch of flowers.
> *RH*: She was such a regular they couldn't have taken money from her every night.

Commonly, these conversations recreate a local experience of cinemagoing that is not
so much concerned with the programmes and features that were on offer, as with the
social networking fostered by the regular and highly public nature of the event. Under
these circumstances, individuals such as Sherlock Jones and Mrs Swan were as much the
subject of scrutiny and speculation as the stars on the screen. Similarly, the genres of
American cinema became part of the ways in which Illawarra locals made sense of each
other. Alan Jeffrey told the tale of Bill 'Tex' Singer who used to dress in cowboy gear and
ride his horse to the Whiteway if a Western was screening, and Jack Hodgeson remembered that the owner of the Scarborough picture show, Bob Forster, had such a reputation as a womaniser that when the cry 'Who is the Lone Ranger?' went up at the end of

an episode of the popular serial, the Scarborough audience would cry 'Bob Forster!' Through these discourses of localisation and incorporation, Illawarra audiences kept things in perspective, enjoying American movies and their promotion, appreciating American stars, and subscribing with some enthusiasm to Hollywood gossip, but they did this in the context of their local experiences and community concerns. Indeed, if there is a generalised flaw in the media imperialism thesis which underwrites nationalist histories of American cinema as a species of local 'home-wrecker', it is this tendency to underestimate the persuasive power of the local and the everyday – or, at best, to afford it only the surreptitious pragmatism of the subaltern.[18] What is revealed through the narratives of Illawarra moviegoers is something more interesting: the way in which Hollywood content was accommodated and adjusted to local situations, rather than any particular evidence that American cultural values came to dominate local thinking.

## Memories of Cinema: Some Preliminary Conclusions

As this account of our research to date indicates, from a relatively small number of interviews we have learned a great deal about the social experience of cinemagoing in the Illawarra region in the first half of the twentieth century. In quite straightforward ways, this research has acquired a certain urgency: the children and courting couples of the 1930s are now in their seventies, eighties and nineties. In particular, the adults who owned and staffed the early picture theatres, who have been so generous in sharing these reminiscences with us, are custodians of a history of local exhibition which is at risk of being lost, just as many of the picture theatres themselves have been lost or obscured by other uses.[19]

The methodological challenges faced by this research are equally significant. In particular, we are concerned not simply to rush to exploit the recollections of our local community – to harvest cinema-specific historical information and disregard the rest. Neither are we proposing a workaround for the supposed problem of unreliable memory or biased narration. Rather, in following the critical approach of the Popular Memory Group, a methodological framework which has been adopted by a number of Australian oral historians, we are interested in research protocols which enable us to co-produce memories of cinemagoing *as memories*, situated within broader narratives of personal identity, and appreciated in theoretical terms both as narratives and reminiscences.[20] Rather than switching off the tape recorder when interviewees talk about their present life, or about events other than cinemagoing in the past, we are interested in seeing exactly how stories of cinemagoing function as part of a complex of strategies by which older narrators situate themselves, in relation not only to their younger selves, but also to us and our research goals.

One consequence of this, of course, is that the resulting archive may be of greater interest to gerontology than to cinema studies, whose organising principle has so often been to abstract cinema from its social context, or at best so to prioritise the study of cinemagoing over other habits, ideas and everyday pressures as to significantly distort its relationship to that broader context. Nevertheless, the project of making this intensely parochial research useful in a comparative cinema studies context, particularly in terms of the study of the reception of Hollywood cinema in its non-metropolitan markets is an ongoing preoccupation. Do common discourses of cinema and community life emerge in local populations of particular size? Have particular historical periods or economic circumstances produced similar cinemagoing tactics in non-metropolitan cinemagoing communities? Can the experience of informal social segregation in picture theatres, whether according to class, race or ethnicity, be extrapolated from one small regional community to another, one country to another?

In the meantime, what is already evident from oral histories of cinemagoing in the Illawarra is the resilience of local cultures – their tactical and self-confident accommodation of American cinema (the overwhelmingly dominant screen fare in Australia in the early twentieth century) to local economies of production and to the everyday routines of childhood, courting and ageing in small communities. To the extent that interviewees recall specific movies at all, they do so largely in order to tell stories about the community: what it meant to watch Hollywood movies, or the occasional British or even Australian movie, in the local picture theatre with neighbours, friends, family, and under the watchful eye of local theatre staff. In this context, rolling Jaffas down the theatre aisles was a emerging tradition which was understood to be both national and local, whether the Jaffas were rolled or thrown, and whatever was on the screen – whereas eating the local pies, travelling on local buses and dodging the ticket seller were appreciated at a more intimate level. However, this is not to suggest that any of these were regarded as resistant practices, but more simply that there was a great deal to be distracted by in the relatively novel experience of cinemagoing. Neither are we seeking to argue that oral history demonstrates in any conclusive way that individual movies or movie stars were peripheral *at the time*.

We do however learn a certain amount from this relatively (and perhaps deliberately) forgettable nature of screen content. It seems reasonable to argue that Hollywood's interests were well served wherever audiences themselves formed the habit of going to the pictures for reasons that were locally adapted even before the curtains opened, and thus locally satisfied, no matter what played on the screen. The modest role allocated to the movies themselves in these narratives of cinemagoing supports, rather than undermines, the notion that it was also pre-eminently in Hollywood's interests that the movies were designed for widespread smooth adaptability and, by implication, only minimal cultural impact.

## Notes

All images courtesy of Wollongong City Library's Illawarra Images collection

1 Occasionally – and particularly from the perspective of Sydney – 'Wollongong' itself is also used as the descriptor for the entire region. While the precise boundaries of the Illawarra shift in different interpretative contexts (see Peter Knox, Once Upon a Place: Writing the Illawarra, unpublished MA thesis, Faculty of Arts, University of Wollongong, 2001, p. 3), for the purposes of our research into the history of cinemagoing in this region, we have taken the small towns of Helensburgh to the north and Kiama to the south as the limits of the territory.

2 Len Richardson, *The Bitter Years: Wollongong During the Great Depression* (Sydney: Hale and Iremonger, 1984), p. xii.

3 Robert Parkinson, *Guaffered Velour: A History of Motion Picture Exhibition and Picture Theatres in the Illawarra District of NSW 1897–1994* (Campbelltown: Australian Theatre Historical Society, 1994).

4 See Nancy Huggett, 'A Cultural History of Cinema-going in the Illawarra 1900–50' (unpublished PhD thesis, Faculty of Arts, University of Wollongong, 2002).

5 Parkinson, *Guaffered Velour*, p. 1.

6 Full transcripts of the interviews conducted by Nancy Huggett, as well as audio recordings of thesis interviews, are found in the appendices of her unpublished PhD thesis (see note 4 above) and are also held in the library of the University of Wollongong. A list of the specific interviews from this collection referred to in this paper is given below.

7 Graham Shirley and Brian Adams, *Australian Cinema: The First Eighty Years* (Hong Kong: Angus and Robertson, 1983).

8 In 1925–6, for example, Thirroul cinemagoers could choose between the Arcadia and the New Kings theatre. Parkinson, *Guaffered Velour*, p. 55.

9 Ibid., p. 50.

10 Larrikinism is a popular Australian term whose meaning has drifted slightly over time from its original indication of rough or disorderly (male) youths larking about in public, to a more general and affectionate description of mischief, anti-authoritarianism and acting up, often assumed to embody authentically 'Australian' characteristics of irreverence and non-conformism.

11 *South Coast Times*, 15 June 1923, p. 18.

12 *Illawarra Mercury*, 27 September 1929, p. 14.

13 Local author Joseph Davis points out, however, that one of the reasons the neighbouring suburb of Austinmer succeeded as a rival tourist resort was precisely because the New Kings theatre was on the northern side of the town, within walking distance of the Austinmer guesthouses. It seems that Thirroul would have lost some lucrative guesthouse patronage precisely because of the accessibility of its theatre to the tourists in the neighbouring suburb. See Joseph Davis, *D. H. Lawrence in Thirroul* (Sydney: Imprint, 1989), p. 40.

14 Diane Collins, ' "More than just entertainment": 1914–1928', in Ina Bertrand (ed.), *Cinema in Australia: A Documentary History* (Sydney: New South Wales University Press, 1989), p. 69.

15 The second phase of our research has unearthed some rare accounts of families who did not attend the movies at all, and this appears to be due not so much to the absolute cost of theatre admission than to the problem of there being no cinema within even remote walking distance (although in other accounts we have heard of determined cinema patrons walking several miles to the cinema, in the absence of suitable bus transport).

16 Jaffas are small, hard, round, chocolate-coated orange-flavoured sweets, introduced to the Australian confectionery market in 1931. See Diane Collins, *Hollywood Down Under: Australians at the Movies 1896 to the Present Day* (Sydney: Angus and Robertson, 1987), pp. 51–2.

17 For a discussion of 'general public' and 'particular public' discourses see Alistair Thomson, *Anzac Memories: Living with the Legend* (Melbourne: Oxford University Press, 1994), p. 9.

18 Useful to our research, however, is Cindy Patton's formulation of 'subaltern memory' in 'Embodying Subaltern memory: Kinesthesia and the Problematics of Gender and Race', in Cathy Schwichtenberg (ed.), *The Madonna Connection: Representational Politics,*

*Subcultural Identities, and Cultural Theories* (Sydney: Allen and Unwin, 1993), pp. 81–106. Like the work of the Popular Memory Group, to which we later refer, this draws on Foucauldian ideas of popular memories of everyday practices as resistant to dominant historiographic trends.

19  The Whiteway is a shell; the Regent is sitting somewhat uneasily on prime real estate adjacent to the central Wollongong shopping mall; the Scarborough theatre is a small house; and the Thirroul Kings, which has been operating for many years as a roller skating rink, is subject to a development application to turn it into a 'high-tech' police station and retail precinct.

20  The Popular Memory Group (PMG) operated briefly at the Centre for Contemporary Cultural Studies at Birmingham University from 1979–85, and defined 'popular memory' using Foucault's conceptualisation of the term as an oppositional force in service of a radical political agenda. To the PMG, popular memory could be seen as a 'privatised sense of the past which is generated within a lived culture', distinct from and mobilised against dominant and public discourses (Popular Memory Group, 'Popular memory: theory, politics and method', in R. Johnson, G. McLennan, B. Schwarz and D. Sutton (eds), *Making Histories: Studies in History Writing and Politics* (London: Hutchinson, 1982), pp. 205–52.). See Lyn Spigel, 'From the Dark Ages to the Golden Age: Women's Memories and Television Re-runs', *Screen*, vol. 36, no. 1 (1995), pp. 16–33, for one reflection on the usefulness of their method to media audience research.

## Oral history interviews cited

Charlie Anderson, theatre manager
Pam Bain, audience member
Stan Chesher, audience member
Cec Clark, picture-showman
Olga Ferguson, audience member
Jack and Rene Hodgeson, audience members
Cecelia Jackson, audience member
Alan Jeffrey, audience member
Ron Klower, projectionist and May Klower, audience member
Arthur Parkinson, audience member
Darryl Walker, audience member

# 5
# Hollywood and the Multiple Constituencies of Colonial India

Priya Jaikumar

[I]t would be wrong to ignore the original and, I would say, the enabling rift between black and white, between imperial authority and natives, that persisted during the entire period of classical imperialism. The problem, then, is to keep in mind two ideas that are in many ways antithetical – the fact of the imperial divide, on the one hand, and the notion of shared experiences, on the other – without diminishing the force of either: a task that is particularly important when dealing with works of art or culture.

*Edward Said*[1]

After the news, we had twenty minutes of the worst type of American so called dance comedy, indecent and with no redeeming features . . . is it possible, when self-government is given to India, to prohibit films which have already been passed as fit for European and American audiences?

*Unidentified letter from India to the Bishop of London, 12 February 1935*[2]

The *Bombay Government Gazette*, which lists the proscription and endorsement of films by the Bombay Board of Film Censors, has an interesting ruling next to the US film *Crown of Thorns*. The film, distributed in India in 1937 by M. B. Bilimoria of Madan Theatres, is licensed 'For Christians Only'.[3] In the potentially incendiary context of nationalism in late colonial India, censors typically assessed films for their political, religious and salacious content. But while censors emphasised distinctions based on national, racial and ethnic affiliations, film screenings were in fact secular and public events that confounded segmentation. To the anonymous letter-writer quoted in the second epigraph, screenings of US films which were acceptable in Britain seemed 'embarrassing and unsuitable in a mixed audience of East and West' in India. The clumsy desire to restrict a film to 'Christians only' was in opposition to the ways in which audiences were sorting themselves into groups of cinematic allegiance in colonial India's multiracial and multidenominational society.

State anxiety about Indian (predominantly Hindu and Muslim) anti-British senti-ments played a significant part in defining official responses to Hollywood films in colo-nial India. Nevertheless, the early sound era in India was as much a time of cinematic possibilities as it was one of official anxiety over Indian nationalism. A compelling aspect of the two decades of cinema preceding India's independence was that, along with British India's censors and policy-makers, India's film-makers, Britain's film producers and Hollywood's distributors jostled to determine the viewing options of Indian audiences, with varying levels of interest and success. Any assessment of US films in India must occur within this purview of prevalent uncertainties and debates over the composition of film audiences, film form and film content in the colony. To this end, studying the reception of individual US films in colonial India is less enlightening than charting dominant discussions about cinematic practices, possibilities and challenges in the colony, in order to interrogate their assumptions about Hollywood cinema.

Key official respondents to US films in India included members of the British film industry interested in India's film market; representatives of the British parliament concerned with colonial affairs; British India's film censor boards; members of the Indian film industry; Indian film journalists, nationalists and opinion leaders; and US film representatives in India. Each of these constituencies had a specific investment in film content and image control, which defined their disposition towards Hollywood films in India. Here, Said's observation about 'shared experiences' over an 'imperial divide' between Britain and India holds particular relevance. Both coloniser and colonised faced Hollywood's onslaught in their domestic film markets, and Hollywood films were viewed by British as well as Indian viewers in India. Troubled by this shared space, the British Indian state justified film censorship and asserted a hierarchical notion of audiences, deeming Indians unfit for certain cinematic content. In response, Indians attacked racist representations of imported films while simultaneously drawing attention to the state's discrimination between audiences along race and class lines, thus opposing both their censors and Hollywood cinema.

In terms of trade, Britain assessed India's potential as an overseas outlet for British films, while the Indian film industry defined a national cinema *despite* Britain's interest in an empire film market and Hollywood's dominance of the market. In 1921, only sixty-four of a total of 812 films endorsed by the censors were of Indian origin, and over 90 per cent of the imported films were from the US.[4] By 1935, Hollywood and other film imports led by a narrower margin, constituting a little over half of the total feature films screened in India.[5] Even as Indian film exhibitors collaborated with American studios, by the 1930s Indian film-makers had successfully differentiated their domestic film product from Hollywood cinema and cultivated a strong audience base. Any account of Hollywood in colonial India must make room for these apparently discordant but mutually influential historical narratives.

## Collaboration and Competition

The story of film in India would continue to be, for many years, a story of American and Indian films.

*Barnow and Krishnaswamy*[6]

50 per cent Nationalist and 50 per cent His Majesty the American.

*Samik Bandyopadhyay, quoting* Filmland, *24 January 1931*[7]

The 1930s were an important decade in Indian film history, because several aspects of its film industry coalesced during this period and anticipated India's takeover of its domestic market. The decade saw the collapse of Madan Theatres, a major importer of US films, the success of India's Bombay Talkies, New Theatres and Prabhat studios, and

Indian cinema's cultivation of its domestic audiences. While some Indian exhibitors continued to collaborate with Hollywood to facilitate film imports, several producers adapted aspects of Hollywood films in creating a distinctive idiom for an indigenous cinema. The following paragraphs will analyse the collaboration between Hollywood and its Indian film importers, and discuss the simultaneous processes through which Indian film producers differentiated their domestic film product from Hollywood's fare to become a competitive product in their home market.

As Indian film producers dealt directly with exhibitors during the silent era, India's distribution network was primarily established by importers of Hollywood films.[8] Bombay was the port of entry for most film imports, and the subcontinent was divided into six major geographical regions for their distribution: the North West (managed by booking offices in Lahore and Karachi), North (Delhi), North East (Calcutta), East (Rangoon), Centre and West (Bombay) and South (Madras, Bangalore, Colombo).[9] M-G-M, Paramount, Universal, United Artists, Warner Bros., 20th Century-Fox, Columbia Pictures and RKO had their own distribution offices in India, with some of them (such as Universal and M-G-M) also distributing films from other US as well as British companies.[10] US studios also entered into contracts with Indian exhibitors, demanding block and blind bookings in return for exclusive screening rights. India's Madan Theatre chain distributed and exhibited films for Columbia, DeMille Pictures, Paramount, RKO, United Artists and Warner, becoming the largest importer of Hollywood films during the 1920s and for much of the 1930s.

In addition to blind booking, it was reported that studios such as Universal expected monetary compensation from Indian exhibitors who accepted a film from any other producer.[11] Interviews given by members of the Indian film industry to the Indian Cinematograph Committee, a body constituted by the government in 1927 to assess the condition of cinema and censorship in colonial India, are a testimony to the friction created by such monopolistic import practices. While Ardeshir Bilimoria (Director, Madan Theatres, Bombay) acknowledged the growing demand for Indian films with 'the Indian audience and uneducated people', he was firm in his opinion that his theatres were best filled when he screened western (that is, primarily Hollywood) films to attract Europeans and educated Indians. In his view, Indian films had a solely regional appeal in India in contrast to American films, which had a national appeal. Additionally, he considered theatres to have dedicated audiences. Bilimoria felt that he was better served showing western films even in those Madan-owned theatres which were located in 'the Indian locality' of Bombay, such as the Empress and the Edwards, because viewers identified Madan theatres with Hollywood films. Consequently, when Madan Theatres produced a film in its studio in Bengal and released it in Bombay, Bilimoria was of the view that it either failed because of its parochial content, or succeeded when screened at a theatre *not* identified with Madan, such as the exhibition sites of the Crown or Imperial companies.[12]

Bilimoria's views ratified the notion of a segregated audience in India, but others saw them as somewhat self-serving. In discussing the difficulties with distributing Indian films in Bengal, the West and the North West, where Madan had a near-monopoly in the late 1920s and early 1930s, Mr Desai (film producer and member of the Bombay Cinema and Theatres Trade Association) pointed out: 'They [Madan] do not take other pictures, nor do they take any films made in India. They import American and other continental films from abroad and exhibit them. They make large contracts according to their requirements'.[13] In fact, according to most accounts, Indians of all classes viewed Indian films, educated Indians, Anglo-Indians and Europeans attended imported films, and the filmgoing attendance of the 'illiterate classes' was increasing more rapidly than the educated classes in the late 1920s.[14] A theatre's location and the gradation in ticket prices maintained a separation of audience by class, race and nationality, but self-conscious attempts on the part of Indian film-makers in the 1930s to evolve a 'national' visual and linguistic idiom for cinema were breaking down the segregation of domestic Indian viewership. To elaborate on this, it is useful to create a conceptual distinction between 'audience segregation' and 'audience differentiation'.

Importers recognised variations in the filmgoing habits of Europeans and elite Indians on the one hand and mass Indian audiences on the other. Indian film-makers, however, attempted to differentiate a cross-section of Indian audiences that might watch *both* Indian and Hollywood films from those who patronised imported films exclusively. While assumptions of segregated audiences informed import practices,[15] film-makers competing against these imports tended to incorporate elements of Hollywood cinema in their film-making and marketing strategies, redefining them along national lines to differentiate (and create) a cross-section of Indian audience for Indian films. Even as the exhibition practices of importers catering primarily to Europeans and elite Indians entrenched a segregation of audiences, the production and marketing strategies of Indian film-makers increasingly dismantled this segregation. Non-elite and non-urban film audiences were not treated as primary audiences for imported films, which were rarely original prints and were given their first run in cities as a matter of course. They were usually on their tenth or eleventh run by the time they were exhibited in rural areas.[16] This did not mean that Hollywood films were unpopular with mass Indian audiences; rather, the screening of imported films reinforced a hierarchy of audiences by class and education. Producing film in India meant a self-conscious attempt to bridge those gaps and seek a national audience.

Indian film producers attempted to reach a broader Indian audience by articulating the differences between Indian films and imported films. Comparing leading English-language newspapers (which would imply a readership of primarily urban, educated Indians) and film journals from the early 1930s against their editions from the early 1940s suggests a shift in the framing discourse of Indian cinema and its altering position in relation to Hollywood films. In the early 1930s, news of Hollywood and Indian film releases shared the same page in newspapers, with similar film titles, visual images and appeals. This altered in the 1940s. As an example, film news was usually carried on page 15 of *The Hindustan Times* (Delhi) in 1930–1. Advertisements for Fay Wray and Gary Cooper in *The Legion of the Condemned* playing at the Elphistone, Mr Jal and Miss Sulochana in *Sword to Sword* ('A Tale of Rajput Valour', 'with Coloured Bath Scenes') playing at Cinema Majestic, and Harold Lloyd's *Haunted House* at the Gaiety Picture Palace are printed together.[17] The Indian film *The Web*, starring the 'Indian Douglas-Master Vithal' playing at Imperial Picture, is advertised alongside *The Drake Case* ('100 percent Universal All-Talking Picture') at the Capitol and Harold Lloyd's *Speedy* at the Elphinstone.[18]

By 1941, *The Hindustan Times* had separate pages in the same edition for Hollywood and Indian films. News of Indian film releases, such as *Naya Sansar*, *Himmat*, *Shadi* and

*Asra*, take up page 3, which also includes some brief synopses of English-language films. Hollywood films, such as *Sing You Sinners* with Bing Crosby or *Stella Dallas* with Barbara Stanwyck, appeared on page 9.[19] *The Times of India* (Bombay) is similar to *The Hindustan Times* (Delhi) in its coverage pattern. In 1930–1, every Saturday edition of the newspaper had one full page of new releases from Hollywood and India, titled 'The Screen in Bombay'. Illustrations from US and Indian films were followed by brief film reports. We see an advertisement for Surya Film Company's *Kingdom of Love*, with the caption 'India's Hollywood makes another fine film' alongside Hollywood's releases.[20] On another Saturday, Joan Crawford's *Blushing Bride* is announced next to 'Noorjehan's *Lust for Gold*', an 'Arabian romance'.[21] By 1941, Indian and Hollywood films had their own pages released on different days of the week. Hollywood news was typically published on Fridays under the title 'On Bombay Screens' and Indian film news on Saturdays under the header 'On Indian Screens'.[22] Semiotically, these titles associated Indian films with national audiences while linking Hollywood to Bombay, giving Hollywood's films a more restricted and urban connotation.

The immediate conclusion we may draw from this is that the increase in Indian film production (from twenty-eight films annually in 1931 to 170 films in 1940) necessitated more detailed coverage.[23] Additionally, while there continued to be an overlapping audience for Hollywood and Indian films among English-speaking Indians, the autonomous address to audiences of Indian cinema by the 1940s acknowledged a growing elite Indian interest in indigenous cinema and an expansion of discourses surrounding Indian film culture.[24] Placing this phenomenon of expanded and autonomous Indian film reports in English-language Indian newspapers within a larger cultural context may permit a broader interpretation: paradoxically, Hollywood was serving as a template by which Indian films were progressively differentiated from their western counterparts in the sound era. An exhaustive discussion of this argument is beyond the scope of this chapter, but some representative examples will highlight Hollywood's role in Indian cinema's acquisition of its own domestic audiences.

Hollywood's celebrated international reach was countered by the Indian creation of stars (encouraged by sound and studios),[25] as well as an 'indianisation' of Hollywood's content. Citing Indian films from the early 1930s such as *Dynamite, Mr. X, Fashionable Wife, Educated Wife, 300 Days and After* (advertised as 'India's first picture in the American Style') as examples, Aruna Vasudev argues that early Indian film-makers were imitative of themes and genres in US films – ranging from stunt films, comedies, crime and action thrillers to the serials of Pearl White, Eddie Polo and Douglas Fairbanks, Sr – because they wished to avoid controversy with the censors, who were overly sensitive about films depicting nationally relevant topics in India.[26] The prevalence of mythological and historical genre films in early Indian cinema complicates this observation, because they successfully evaded censorship despite being repositories of cultural nationalism and allusive anti-colonialism. Nevertheless, Vasudev is right in noting that the predominance of US films in the silent era supplied Indian film-makers with a range of popular genres. To create an indigenous identity, however, popular Hollywood themes and stars were reinvented within the evolving marketplace and aesthetics of Indian cinema.

In a study on Indian female stars from the 1930s to the 1950s, Neepa Majumdar argues that notions of stardom in India 'were consolidated with the coming of sound and the change in genre emphasis to more "socials" [i.e., film with themes that addressed social issues] in the 1930s'.[27] She notes that references to American and Indian stars in film journals of the 1920s and the early 1930s carried a clear sense of what stardom meant in the US but were more ambiguous in the Indian context, where different cultural assumptions about private and public information, individuality or fame applied. In her view, Hollywood stars were of interest to Indian journals in the 1930s in part because 'Hollywood was the pre-eminent model of modernity which is the subject of negotiation' in Indian star discourse and its social genre films.[28] Modernisation was a fraught process for a colonised nation, as it carried connotations of a compromise with westernisation and imperialism. Classical American cinema, as Miriam Hansen suggests, was a sort of 'global vernacular' that mediated rival national and cultural discourses on modernity.[29] In the case of India, to a significant extent Hollywood came to symbolise a fascinating but potentially degenerate medium of western modernisation, against which modern India's cinema found its definition. One paradigm through which Indian film culture incorporated Hollywood into its self-definition was as a form of oppositional modernity.

In 1931, the Indian film company Imperial advertised its film *Hell's Paradise* with the image of a woman in a sari bowing to a woman in a dress, to publicise the 'Story of a Prince craving something new and novel, never realizing the intrinsic value of a home and a devoted wife . . .'[30] In multiple ways, the sound era consolidated a national identity for Indian films, and women's bodies were a central locus for this work. During the

Kanan Devi endorsing Bathgate Castor Oil, *The Hindustan Times*, 23 June 1941

silent period, Anglo-Indian and European actresses (such as Ermaline, Ruby Meyers, Patience Cooper and Nadia), who were willing to be on camera despite its social stigma in India, were renamed and re-presented as 'Indian'. In the opinion of a star-struck writer for the popular Indian magazine *Filmfare*, Sulochana aka Ruby Meyers' twelve-year period of glory in Indian cinema (1925–37) was 'a period of the Indian movie-goer's enchantment with a heroine cast in the mould of stars appearing in Hollywood and French serials'.[31] By the mid- to late 1930s, the growing industry had attracted actresses such as Gohar, Jaddanbai, Pheroze Dastoor, Nurjehan, Sardar Akhtar, Kananbala, Suraiyya and Manorama, whose facial features and singing voices mutually reinforced a traditional Indian-ness. Garnering public attention involved exploiting this identity within and outside film texts. Newspaper readers of the 1940s saw products advertised by icons of (Hindu-ised) Indian womanhood in a sari, replacing images of white women with a *bindi*.[32] In the 1940s, we read Sardar Akhtar's recipes for Indian cooking,[33] see Kanan Devi endorsing Bathgate's castor oil,[34] and Khursheed advertising Colgate talcum powder.[35] Instead of product endorsements by European or westernised women, domestic products for a modern India were given the face of female Indian stars, and their images became simultaneously the agent and object of commodification and intimate national address.

By this period, discussions of Hollywood's female stars were incomplete without an equivalent discussion of national stars who acquired status through their association with and differentiation from Hollywood's discourse. Regional film journals are a case in point, as they demonstrated the increasingly qualified creation of a local taste that distinguished itself from Hollywood as well as the hegemonic national Indian cinema. When *Talk-A-Tone*, a Madras-based film journal, published its seventh Annual Madras Film Ballot results for the most popular stars of the 1940s, these were:

Foreign Male Artists: Clark Gable, Charles Laughton, Errol Flynn
Foreign Female Artists: Greta Garbo, Bette Davis, Norma Shearer
North Indian Male Artists: Motilal, Ashok Kumar, Saigal
North Indian Female Artists: Leela Chitnis, Sardar Akhtar, Kanan Devi
Tamil Male Artists: P. U. Chinnappa, M. K. Thyagaraja Baghavathar, Serukalathur Sama
Tamil Female Artists: M. S. Subbulakshmi, K. B. Sundarambal, T. R. Rajakumari.[36]

By the 1940s, the Tamil and Telugu film industries had spawned a large regional fan base, in no small part because the visual aesthetics, narrative themes and musical traditions which informed south Indian films varied from their northern counterparts. Classical musicians in the Tamil and Carnatic tradition, such as Thyagaraja Baghavathar and M. S. Subbulakshmi, listed among the artists above, had a long-term influence on southern film music, giving it a distinctively different sound than the Bombay film industry's songs, which had their roots in Hindustani music. For the Indian audience, Hollywood was part of a generic 'foreign' cinema while Indian films were identifiable in all their national and local variations. Desire was more differentiated at the national level.

Additionally, Hollywood offered an aesthetic that was a point of both reference and alterity for Indian film directors. Critical responses to V. Shantaram's masterful film *Admi* (aka *Manoos* aka *Life is for the Living*, 1939) exemplified this duality towards

Gohar on the songbook
cover of *Prabhu ka Pyara*
(Chandulal Shah, 1936)

Hollywood films. Shantaram's film was arguably a remake of M-G-M's *Waterloo Bridge*, but in India it was seen as a better and more socially responsible rendition of the story. In M-G-M's film, a military officer goes to war leaving behind his girlfriend who is a ballet dancer, only to find that conditions have forced her to take up prostitution in his absence. Her traumatised conscience prevents her from marrying him and after confessing her truth to his mother, she commits suicide. In Shantaram's film, Moti, a policeman, falls in love with the singer and prostitute Kesar. She leaves this life for him, though he remains fearful of the social stigma attached to her profession. When he finally introduces her to his mother and gathers the courage to propose to her, she cannot bring herself to marry him. As she runs away, she is confronted by her extortionist pimp whom she accidentally kills. She is imprisoned, but leaves the suicidal Moti with a life-affirming message to not give up life for love.

The plot is an insufficient account of the film, but it provides adequate context to make comprehensible *filmindia* editor Baburao Patel's assessment of *Waterloo Bridge* as 'a romance pure and simple' that 'makes light of hunger, poverty and unemployment' with 'no social significance' in comparison to *Admi*, 'perhaps the most vivid document of human emotions. Its bedrock is the regeneration of lost souls.'[37] In fact, Shantaram's film distinguished itself from M-G-M's film in several ways. In addition to its strong female character, *Admi* successfully combined the critically admired style of social realism with aspects of German Expressionism and Indian musical sequences. The film reinterpreted elements of European art cinema and Hollywood melodrama to create a distinctively Indian form. In effect, for leading Indian film-makers experimenting with film form, Hollywood was not the sole international model of film-making nor the primary critical standard for 'good' cinema. In 1941, the magazine section of *The Hindustan Times* was not averse to publishing at length a conversation between the British actor Leslie Howard and film critic C. A. Lejeune, criticising the escapism of 'the average Hollywood picture which bears no relation to life'.[38] Hollywood's spectacle-oriented genres faced the criticism of those in India who saw cinema as an artistic medium with a social responsibility.

Here was an unexpected alliance, with entirely divergent motivations, between those in Britain who were concerned about the effect of Hollywood's sensationalist fare on colonial subjects (discussed in the next section) and those in India worried about Hollywood's potential to debase Indian cinema. Both viewpoints perceived Hollywood films as commercially slick but morally empty. Samik Bandyopadhyay notes that:

> Both *Filmland* and *filmindia* in the thirties were fighting a lost battle against what they considered the 'Bombay brand picture with all action but no psychology'. Even as Prabhansu Gupta (*Filmland*, 31 January 1931) upheld Murnau Stroheim and Lubitsch as models, 'as sworn allies of emotional pictures and . . . not panoramic and advocates of motion as the Yankee directors are', and Niranjan Pal held up the 'technique' of German cinema, and 'art and life' of Russian cinema against the 'well made, sophisticated film plays to tickle our fancies – sugary, peppery, undress spectacles and so called sex-dramas' churned out by Hollywood; *Filmland* itself recognized the popularity of . . . '50 per cent Nationalist and 50 per cent His Majesty the American' (*Filmland*, 24 January 1931).[39]

As Bandopadhyay implies, after the 1940s dominant Hindi-language cinema was a distinctively national form that had assimilated elements of Hollywood blockbusters, so that alternative cinemas in India self-consciously mobilised an antithetical reference to European and Soviet art cinema. The influence of European cinema's modernist and realist traditions was most evident in the films produced in the late 1940s and 1950s by the IPTA (Indian People's Theatre Association), a progressive group of playwrights, artists and film-makers informally affiliated with the Communist Party of India. Their avant garde films combined Indian folk forms, neo-realist and expressionist aesthetics, and socially relevant themes to create alternatives to the commercial products generated by the Indian and US film industries.[40] Thus, though members of the nascent Indian film industry continued to be receptive to advice and assistance from those affiliated with Hollywood,[41] films from the US were also evaluated with a measure of skepticism and censure.

In the long term, collaborating with Hollywood did not always pay off as a business proposition for Indian distributors and exhibitors. Importers such as Madan were left vulnerable to US trade decisions. One of the Indian licensees of RCA Photophone, Madan invested heavily in the conversion to sound. The combination of these costs with the breakdown of a deal with Columbia is believed to have led to Madan's own collapse.[42] In cultural and aesthetic terms, however, Indian cinema proved its viability within its domestic and regional market. The controversial and colourful Baburao

Patel's journal, *filmindia*, always a good source for sensationalist news items that nevertheless conveyed the temper of the times, printed a report that Bette Davis 'learned Dancing from an Indian Girl'. [43] Upon reading the article we learn that Davis' teacher was an English woman who was born and raised in India. Yet the article's assertive title assimilates Hollywood to India to give the latter a place of equivalence and legitimacy. Like another regular feature in *filmindia* that humorously interweaves accounts of Indian and Hollywood stars, comparing Clark Gable to Ghulam Mahomed and Slim Summerville to Master Vithal, the article on Davis is an affirmation of the Indian film audience's cosmopolitanism and fluency with international as well as national film news and gossip. [44] By the early 1940s, Hollywood no longer dominated the subcontinent. It existed as a parallel cinema.

## Opposition

To the vast mass of black, brown and yellow people, the inner life of the European and especially that side of it which flourishes in centers of crime and infamy, was unknown: until the American film showed them a travesty of it.

*'Pernicious Influence of Pictures on Oriental Peoples', A treatise*[45]

The fact is, the Americans realized almost instantaneously that the cinema was a heaven-sent method for advertising themselves, their country, their methods, their wares, their ideas, and even their language, and they have seized upon it as a method of persuading the whole world, civilized and uncivilized, into the belief that America is really the only country which counts.

*Lord Nelson, in the House of Lords*[46]

In the development of the [British film] industry particular attention is being paid to overseas markets, especially those within the Empire where the product of British studios has good reason to be particularly welcome. In all the great Dominions (Canada, Australia, New Zealand and South Africa) the demand for British-made films has increased tremendously in the last few years. Conditions in India (with its huge non-European population) naturally differ from those in other British territories and there is important local production . . .

*Memorandum, Federation of British Industries*[47]

In the process of assessing the possibility of an empire film market, British film producers evaluated India's receptivity to British films. They were cognisant of the colony's predominantly non-white, non-English-speaking population, which was developing competitive local film production against the large volume of Hollywood imports. To make headway in the absence of protectionist imperial film policies in India (such as a quota for British films), Britain faced the dual challenge of competing with local as well as Hollywood cinema. Placed in a context where the production sector of the British film industry was seeking new markets, Britain's concern over the image of Europeans in India takes on a new aspect.

Though information on cinema in colonial India is sporadic, the Indian Government Gazettes, British parliamentary proceedings, and the British Indian Home Department's political files inform us of the censors' process and rationale for proscribing films in India. Film censorship in colonial India was not centralised in one board but housed in the provinces of Bombay, Madras, Calcutta, Punjab and Rangoon. The Bombay Board was the most important, as it was the main port of entry for foreign films, with the Madras and Punjab boards mainly re-examining films previously seen by other boards and Rangoon chiefly handling Chinese films.[48] The commissioner of police for the province was the *ex officio* chairman of the board, which meant that the heads of the boards were British. A certificate issued for a film by any one board was valid throughout the country, though any province could re-examine the film and suspend it. District magistrates and commissioners of police were also empowered to revoke a film's certification.[49] Banning films was relatively easy because a certified film could be 'uncertified' by the central government at any point. The central government did not feel answerable for censorship decisions, however. Repeated requests in the British parliament for an enumeration of films prohibited for exhibition in India met with infrequent answers, and the question was considered inappropriate because executive action on censorship was taken by the provincial censor boards.[50] Hence, despite the fact that film censorship was on the central and state list, it was considered outside the central government's responsibility.

Indian films were primarily censored for their potential to foster nationalist or anti-state sentiments, and Hollywood films for sexual, moral and racial content in addition to implicit messages of political disaffection. Few British films were censored in India, partially because not many were imported into the country. In her thorough study of the Indian reception of imported films depicting imperial themes, Prem Chowdhry notes that the colonial Indian state adopted policies to ban or shelve thirty-seven Hollywood films about India in the years 1939–40 for fear that they would agitate Indian sentiments or portray the white race in a negative light.[51] Hollywood representations of the subcontinent certainly invited close scrutiny. For instance, the original version of Warner Bros.' *The Charge of the Light Brigade* was refused a certificate on 20 April 1937 because 'it was likely to offend a friendly foreign nation, and to stir up racial feelings'. It was passed after 'drastic excisions' (of 3,340 feet) were made to the film, including 'reference to tribal warfare on the Northern Frontier and the attack and subsequent massacre at Chikoti'.[52] This bowdlerization of all scenes depicting a political or social struggle seems to have been maintained consistently over time and also applied to Hollywood films that did not specifically depict India. Cecil B. DeMille's *The Volga Boatman* (1928) was censored because the film 'portrays class hatred and violence which accompanied the Bolshevik Revolution' in addition to its 'scenes of degrading lust and brutality'.[53] Columbia Pictures' *The Scarlet Lady* (1930), distributed in India by Near East Film Distributors, was 'prohibited on the grounds that it is likely to promote disaffection against and resistance to Government and to cause breach of law and order'. Fox's *The Red Dance* (1930), distributed by Fox in India, was prohibited 'on the grounds that it contains many revolutionary and mob scenes and is full of sentiments of class hatred and class domination'.[54] Columbia's *The Side Show* (1930), from Near East Film Distributors, was passed with this endorsement: 'Omit the words "Gandhi the Great" wherever they occur in the film and substitute for them the words "Rama the Great".'[55] Paramount's *Showdown* (1930), distributed by Madan, was passed with the requirement to cut a scene in which the 'hero is shown looking at a girl dancing in a semi-nude condition'.[56]

Indian public opinion was vocal in its contempt for overzealous censorship. When

M-G-M's *The Scarlet Letter* (1928) was refused a certificate because the character Pastor Dimsdale's role 'is calculated to bring the ministry of the Christian religion into contempt, or, at any rate, to tarnish its repute', an editorial in the *Indian Social Reformer* deplored the censors' inability to trust India with a Nathaniel Hawthorne story that was 'written in a profoundly religious spirit'. Another writer in the journal observed that excisions from a silent Hollywood Western *The Santa Fe Trial* included the intertitles: 'My people, soon there will be no place for the Red Man. His treacherous, white brothers, step by step, day by day, are invading his domains . . . how long will the Indian endure if he is driven from the plains'. The commentator notes:

> The word 'Indian' seems to have been on the brain of the Censors. The film version of a chapter from American history, made in America, and digested by the Americans, White and Red together, is deemed too hard for the stomachs of the Brown ones in India . . .[57]

There existed, certainly among the literate Indian classes, an acute awareness of the censors' presumption of colonial susceptibility and ignorance, and censorship's support of a political status quo.

At the same time, as Prem Chowdhry discusses, Indians strongly opposed orientalist and racist fictions in Hollywood and European cinema. In the 1930s, the Indian Legislative Assembly faced frequent questions about the possibility of government action against 'anti-Indian films' made by other countries, and the topic was discussed at length in film journals and popular Indian presses.[58] Indian nationalists seized upon Hollywood films that depicted India in a negative light as evidence of their ruling state's lack of interest in taking diplomatic action on behalf of the subject country. With an awkward turn of phrase, a journalist observed: 'The questions would naturally arise as to why of all the countries India is selected for being victimized. Because India is a subject country and she has not the means of adopting any corrective measures against her slanderers'.[59] The Indian revolutionary leader Subhash Chandra Bose recommended that films 'slandering India' be met with 'diplomatic action' and called for a 'boycott of goods coming from countries producing such films, beginning with a boycott of films'.[60] In effect, although the overprotective censors hoped to pre-empt such objections, Hollywood films were a platform for Indian nationalists to launch their criticisms against the state. Indians used Hollywood films strategically in their anti-colonial movement, to underline the ways in which the imperial government was not representative or protective of Indian interests.

In Britain, criticism of Hollywood films screened in the colonies served a different end. British film producers and concerned citizens frequently quoted the putatively negative effects of foreign films upon the colonial populace. The following memorandum, which solicits intergovernmental co-operation between the imperial nations of Great Britain, France, Japan and the Netherlands, offers an evocative example of such anxieties:

> The simple native has a positive genius for picking up false impressions and is very deficient in the sense of proportion . . . The pictures of amorous passages, many of which, according to his ideas, are very indecent, give him a deplorable impression of the morality of the white man and, worse still, of the white woman. The prolonged and often erotic exhibitions of osculation frequently shown on the screen, cannot but arouse in the minds of unsophisticated natives feelings that can better be imagined than described.[61]

As I argue at length elsewhere, imperial panic over unpoliced images viewed by excitable colonial inhabitants allowed British film producers to demand some form of state support for the promotion of British films in India.[62] It offered justification to the request for a 'more general distribution in India than hitherto, so as to present the British rather than the foreign (or American) angle of things to the vast audiences which annually attend film pictures in India'.[63] Such efforts were unsuccessful in drawing state support and the Indian film industry resisted all attempts to pass protective laws in favour of British cinema, arguing that most Indians perceived no difference between a US and a British film. In their view, state intervention into the film industry was permissible only if it was in support of Indian cinema.[64]

Despite the British film producers' overall failure in acquiring British state assistance, British opposition to Hollywood films in India succeeded in rehearsing arguments about India's cultural and historical proximity to England. As a report on 'British Films and the Empire' claimed: 'The civilisation and outlook they [Hollywood films] reflect are too alien for the people of India to imitate . . . England and India understand each other much better than do India and America'.[65] Rejecting this interpretation of empire as empathy, Indians conceded that Britain's familiarity with India was not shared by North America. Hollywood's gross ignorance and 'inevitable blunders' about the subcontinent were often commented on in Indian film journals.[66] The Indian *Film World Weekly* wrote about RKO's *India Speaks* (1935):

> That same Hollywood which made the brilliant and popular 'Cavalcade' has made yet another 'Indian' film which can be described in but one word – stupid . . . [In it] Mohamedans were given Hindu names and Mohamedans were shown to wear sacred thread . . . [by] the same Hollywood which pays thousands of dollars on little details such as the size of palm trees . . .[67]

*India Speaks* was felt closely to resemble Katherine Mayo's *Mother India* (1927), a best-selling book in the US that caused a great storm in India. There were several debates and objections over the book and the film, which claimed to offer an authentic portrayal of India as a strange and barbaric land of polygamy, nudity and human sacrifices. In response, *Father India*, 'an Imperial super-special with Miss Sulochana, Mr Jal, Miss Jillu and Mr Jamshedji' was advertised in Indian newspapers as

> A Trenchant Crushing Reply to *Mother India* picturising the effects of Modern civilisation on the lives of our young generation and the victory of our age-old culture and civilisation which has taught and developed self-control, self-sacrifice, and subordination of surging passions.[68]

The practices of US film distributors in India also attracted criticism. By the 1930s several Hollywood studios had established distribution centres in India. In the article 'A Crore of Rupees Dissipated In Foreign Entertainment', *filmindia*'s editor Baburao Patel argued that US distributors were responsible for an enormous drain on the Indian economy.[69] According to Patel, US nationals working in the Indian film distribution offices took close to Rupees (Rs) 12 lakhs in salary, leaving Rs 3 lakhs to be distributed over 500 Indian employees.[70] In addition, foreign distributors took hefty bribes from

Indian exhibitors and insisted that they spend over Rs 13 lakhs a year on film publicity. These facts and figures are hard to substantiate, but they convey a sense of the perceived disparity between Indians and US nationals working in India, as well as the prevalence of aggressive US trade practices. According to *filmindia* again, the US used diplomatic pressure to restrain the exhibition of Indian films in the region. Iraq, then a US ally, was 'suspected of being influenced by rival American interests' as a number of Indian films languished in Baghdad without getting censor certificates. Reports from a variety of Indian newspapers from the 1940s onwards indicated that Iraqi exhibitors applying to their censor board to screen Indian films were threatened with the cancellation of their licenses, and no Indian film had been allowed exhibition in Iraq since the Indian stunt-action film *Hurricane Hansa*'s four-week run in 1937.[71]

In brief, a key aspect of Hollywood's presence in colonial India may be assessed in relation to the British and Indian film industries' opposition to Hollywood's film content and trade practices. They used their criticism of Hollywood strategically, to draw attention to the British and Indian film product. Legitimated by concerns about the kinds of films viewed by colonial subjects, Britain's opposition to Hollywood cinema was equally about trade. The British Intelligence Bureau suspected the US of exploring 'fields for the post-War development of US trade' in India.[72] Hollywood's predominance until the 1940s suggested to Britain that cinema was such a field. On its part, the Indian film industry opposed Hollywood's discriminatory images and practices but, as discussed previously, it also collaborated with US film companies and reinterpreted aspects of Hollywood's cinema to define a uniquely Indian film form, overtaking its domestic market via cultural specificity rather than state policy.

The context of British imperialism was central to the manner in which Hollywood films were deployed and received by those affiliated with the film industry in India. As mentioned earlier, the possibility of mixed audiences of Europeans, Christians, Hindus and Muslims provoked an overly cautious attitude towards film censorship. Potentially mixed exhibition sites in a colonial situation also provoked class- and race-based anxieties in audiences who did not wish to fraternise with the mass of Indian audiences. In particular, Indian exhibitors of foreign films participated in decisions – ranging from security precautions and the pricing of seats to hygiene regulations – that rigidified a segregated viewership. The extent to which exhibitors were willing to appease their white and anglicised Indian audiences provoked the ire of Indian public opinion, particularly closer to the securing of independence. One such controversy arose over the playing of the British anthem 'God Save the King' at the close of Hollywood film screenings.

The anthem was played at the initiative of local theatre proprietors, and not by any government ordinance. On 25 October 1944, a letter from the Secretariat of the Viceroy of India was sent to the Governor of Bombay expressing concern over the news that Indians had been walking out during the playing of this anthem, as 'this practice tends to neutralise the object of playing the National Anthem if not reduce it to a farce or worse'. This initiated an investigation, in which it was found that the anthem was not played in all the Bombay theatres, but only at the Regal, Eros, Excelsior, Empire and Metro cinemas which screened Hollywood films. As the office of the Governor of Bombay reported, these theatres showed 'imported pictures in which the dialogue is in English' and were frequented mostly by the 'Defence Services, European civilians, Parsis and other more well-to-do Indians', who purchased higher-priced tickets. The

Governor of Bombay advised the Viceroy that it was premature to initiate action to stop the anthem, as the war had brought a large number of men from the defence services to theatres. The people who walked out were only in 'the lowest class of seats', 'ordinarily filled by Indian boys and servants'. Therefore, 'the arrangement has some educative value as walking out comes to be regarded as a sign of low social status'.[73]

By 1946 and 1947, harsh criticism of the practice of playing the British anthem appeared in Bombay's *Free Press Journal* and in Baburao Patel's *filmindia*. During those two years, India's independence was visibly close and an interim government was in place to oversee the transfer of power. The Union Jack and 'God save the King' were declared 'alien' and 'badges of slavery' by the *Free Press Journal*, and the respect expected from Indians was considered 'humiliating and unnecessary'. The protests were noted by the Home Department of the government, which acknowledged that playing the British anthem after Hollywood films was creating an awkward situation in India. No state action was taken to prevent the playing of the anthem, and with Indian independence finally achieved in 1947, this became a moot issue.

Another form of audience segregation that occurred with the screening of Hollywood films in the absence of any overt enforcement but as a consequence of colonialism's implicit hierarchies was visible in India's cantonment theatres. Exhibition sites in cantonment areas typically screened European and Hollywood films and were patronised by British soldiers, as Indian soldiers of the British Army preferred to travel to civilian areas to watch Indian films. As a consequence of this division, cantonment theatres became easily identifiable targets for anti-colonial aggression. During the Civil Disobedience Movement in 1942, three cases of bomb explosions were recorded in Ahmednagar's cantonment theatres, in the province of Bombay. A bombing at the Sarosh Talkies resulted in injuries to eighteen British soldiers and three members of the staff, one of whom died. At the West End cinema, a similar bomb was safely removed while the Capitol cinema bombing killed one and wounded twelve British soldiers.[74] In more ways than one, Hollywood's presence in colonial India highlighted the sociopolitical rifts and antagonisms, engendering and, in Said's words, 'enabling' a colonial society.

## Conclusion

This chapter has accommodated film regulators, producers, distributors and journalists within the category of India's film 'audiences'. Admittedly, there is an archival convenience in including individuals who left a record of their responses where general viewers did not. However, these accounts are important because they allow us to consider state officials and industry professionals as active audiences of domestic as well as imported films. They also permit an interpretation of industrial and aesthetic practices as adaptive to and determining of historical constraints, by extending the reception context to industry members and state representatives.

These 'audience constituencies' have been further categorised according to implicit overlaps in their relationship to US films in particular, and their perceptions of cinema's role in India's cultural and political life in general. In foregrounding discourse, heterogeneous groups have been systematised based on their perception of cinema. This is not to obliterate hierarchies between audiences, but a heuristic device that permits contradictory affiliations to emerge. For instance, at the official end of responses, the British Indian state and India's provincial censor boards investigated and tackled questions about the content of imported as well as domestic films viewed in India. These institutions tended to evaluate the effect of US films on Indian audiences as potentially detrimental to Indo-British relations. With interesting overlap, Indian nationalists gave definition to their nationalism through their agitation against specific US films. In part, these constituencies anticipated each other, as the state machinery wished to avoid the very thing that the nationalists aimed to provoke: a group of people unified in their articulation of an oppositional stance against an imported film. In this, the nationalists were similar to state representatives in treating US films as primarily political, with a direct impact on colonial relationships. Hollywood became the pretext for a confrontation over colonial inequities.

Between the British state and the Indian nationalists fell a wide variety of audience constituencies. Among them were British and Indian viewers who attended screenings of Hollywood films in India, and Indian journalists who catered to these audiences by printing news, reviews and fashion comments about Hollywood films and stars. Such constituencies perceived US films along the registers of trade and culture rather than politics. They responded to them as a cinematic achievement worthy of imitation, as a rationalised business practice, as a pleasurable distraction or an index of modernity. Interestingly, some of the British state's correspondence with British film producers reflected a similar notion of US films in India. By the late 1930s, members of the British state were hesitant to intervene on behalf of British films, particularly given the strength of anti-colonial nationalist movements in the subcontinent. They suggested that British film producers turn to commercial rather than regulatory means to promote their industry in the colony. Arguing against legislative intervention, British state representatives offered Hollywood films as an example of a product that combined a successful narrative formula with efficient distribution to corner film markets through competitive trade rather than state policy.[75]

In responding to Hollywood films in India, each key constituency variously evaluated the import as an object of trade, culture or politics. In this chapter, these have primarily been treated as mutually contested categories. This makes it possible to note overlaps between Indian nationalists and the British state officials who criticised Hollywood's political content, in opposition to Indian film exhibitors who collaborated with the US film trade. However, rigid schemas are not sustainable in a context where Britain's political opposition to Hollywood facilitated arguments made by British film producers hoping to promote their own films in India. In addition to imperial discussions of Hollywood's suitability for colonial subjects and Indian protests against Hollywood's racism, Britain and India shared an investment in competing against US film trade in the colony. Where British film producers argued unsuccessfully for state intervention, Indian film-makers competed against Hollywood on cultural and aesthetic terms with greater success.

## Notes

1  Edward Said, 'Always on Top', *London Review of Books* (20 March 2003), p. 5.

2  IOR, L/P&J/1995, File 372. Collections of the India Office Records (IOR) are housed at the Indian and Oriental Studies annexe of the British Library, London.

3  *Bombay Government Gazette*, 15 April 1937, p. 792. The *Gazette* published a monthly register of films examined by the Bombay Board of Film Censors during the preceding month.

Several of these are available at the National Film Archives of India (NFAI), Pune, India.

4  *Indian Cinematograph Committee 1927–1928: Evidence Volume I* (Calcutta: Government of India, Central Publication Branch, 1928), p. 83. Available at the NFAI, Pune.

5  See Prem Chowdhry, *Colonial India and the Making of Empire Cinema: Image, Ideology and Identity* (Manchester: Manchester University Press, 2000), p. 15, and Ashish Rajadhyaksha and Paul Willemen, *Encyclopaedia of Indian Cinema* (Chicago: Fitzroy Dearborn, rev. edn, 1999), p. 30. According to Rajadhyaksha and Willemen, in 1935 annual Indian film production was up to 233 films, with a majority (154 films) in the Hindi language. A comparative ratio of Hollywood, British and Indian films endorsed for screening across the winter and summer months of 1930 and 1935 tell a similar story: in January 1930, of the number of features released in India, eight were Indian, three British and thirty-four American. In June 1930, twenty-six were Indian, two British and fifty-four American. By January 1935, ten features were Indian, one British and ten American, and in June 1935, twelve were Indian, one British and nine American. *Bombay Government Gazette*, 6 February 1930, pp. 241–66; 14 February 1935, pp. 318–23; 17 July 1930, pp. 1831–6; 8 July 1937, pp. 1572–78.

6  Erik Barnouw and S. Krishnaswamy, *Indian Film* (New York: Oxford University Press, 2nd edn, 1981), p. 58.

7  Samik Bandyopadhyay (ed.), *Indian Cinema: Contemporary Perceptions from the Thirties*, selected by Dhruba Gupta and Biren Das Sharma (Jamshedpur: Celluloid Chapter, 1993).

8  Barnouw and Krishnaswamy, *Indian Film*, p. 145.

9  *filmindia*, vol. 6, no. 2 (February 1940), p. 57; *filmindia*, vol. 4, no. 8 (December 1938), pp. 12–13.

10  As examples, based on listings in the *Bombay Government Gazette*, 6 February 1930, p. 241; 5 June 1930, p. 1411; and 11 September 1930, p. 2311, M-G-M India distributed newsreels for Hearst Movietone and United Artists distributed Alexander Korda's films in India.

11  Bilimoria's testimony in *Indian Cinematograph Committee 1927–1928: Evidence Volume I*, p. 330.

12  Ibid., pp. 326–7.

13  Ibid., p. 12. Desai later adds that Madan took Indian films from Kohinoor and Sharda Film Company, but not from the Imperial and Hindustan Company, p. 13.

14  This was expressed frequently throughout the interviews. See the very first response in ibid., p. 1.

15  Importers such as Madan were also producers, so I do not distinguish between importers and producers as much as the *practice* of film importation and production.

16  *Indian Cinematograph Committee 1927–1928: Evidence Volume I*, pp. 334–5.

17  *The Hindustan Times*, 3 April 1930, p. 15.

18  *The Hindustan Times*, 27 April 1930, p. 15.

19  *The Hindustan Times*, 27 June 1941, pp. 3, 9. Also, as is evident from the titles, the practice of giving Indian films an English title became less frequent, though it persisted in some degree into the 1940s. English titles were mostly abandoned in the post-independence era with the exception of regional (non-Bombay) and art films, marking the need to make them comprehensible to national audiences in the case of the former and international audiences in the latter.

20  *The Times of India*, Saturday edition, 11 April 1931, p. 16.

21  *The Times of India*, Saturday edition, 18 April 1931, p. 16.

22  As an example, see *The Times of India*, 'On Indian Screens', 14 July 1941, p. 8 and 'On Bombay Screens', 20 July 1945, p. 8.

23  Rajadhyaksha and Willemen, *Encyclopaedia of Indian Cinema*, p. 30.

24  Coverage included features and news items on industry deals, film awards, star performances and future releases.

25  In this context, a study of extra-cinematic performances would yield interesting insights. For example, in February 1930 Sangam theatre near Jamma Masjid in Delhi, which typically screened Indian films, publicised a performance where 'European Artists will give Indian Songs and Dances' (*The Hindustan Times*, 23 February 1930, p. 8). In 1941, audiences at the Jubilee theatre in Delhi, which screened Indian films as well, were entertained by the singing of Indian star Nurjehan and routines by the comedian Shanti Lal (*The Hindustan Times*, 27 June 1941, p. 3). Contrary to Bilimoria's assessment, then, this indicates that some Indian exhibitors mixed attractions and appealed to a sense of novelty by exploiting cultural difference in 1930, when the future of the Indian market was still an unknown quantity. The same promotional strategy was implausible by the 1940s, because the extra-cinematic appeal of Indian stars singing to audiences fortified the Indian filmic text and rendered the novelty of non-Indians in Indian dress somewhat less attractive.

26  Aruna Vasudev, *Liberty and Licence in the Indian Cinema* (New Delhi: Vikas Publishing House, 1978), pp. 49–52.

27  Neepa Majumdar, 'Female Stardom and Cinema in India, 1930s to 1950s', PhD dissertation, Indiana University, June 2001, p. 14

28  Neepa Majumdar, 'Female Stardom', p. 41.

29  Miriam Bratu Hansen, 'Fallen Women, Rising Stars, New Horizons', *Film Quarterly*, vol. 54, no. 1 (autumn 2000), pp. 10–22.

30  *The Hindustan Times*, 4 January 1931, p. 15.

31  Hameeduddin Mahmood, 'Sulochana: Movie-queen of Yesteryear', *Filmfare*, 15–28 October 1976, p. 17.

32  A *bindi* is the mark on the forehead worn by Hindu women. Advertisements using non-Indian women wearing a *bindi* may be found in most Indian newspapers from the 1930s and 1940s, but as an example see *The Times of India*, 14 April 1941.

33  *filmindia*, vol. 6, no. 3, (March 1940) p. 62.

34  *The Hindustan Times*, 23 June 1941, p. 7.

35  *The Times of India*, 26 April 1941, p. 11.

36  *Talk-A-Tone*, vol. 5, no. 5 (1941), p. 9.

37  *filmindia*, vol. 6, no. 10 (October 1940), pp. 39–40.

38  'The Cinema of the Future', *The Hindustan Times Magazine Section*, 23 June 1941, p. 3.

39  Bandyopadhyay, *Indian Cinema*, pp. 12–13.

40  For more details, consult Nandi Bhatia, 'Staging Resistance: The Indian People's Theatre Association', in Lisa Lowe and David Lloyd (eds), *The Politics of Culture in the Shadow of Capital* (Durham: Duke University Press, 1997), pp. 432–60; Rajadhyaksha and Willemen, *Encylopaedia of Indian Cinema*, p. 109.

41  This was particularly true during the conversion to sound. For example, in 1931, Wilford Deming, a sound technician from Hollywood, was hired to work on India's first

all-sound feature *Alam Ara*, though Rajadhyaksha and Willemen note that the film's
director Ardeshir Irani went on to do most of the film's recording himself (*Encylopaedia
of Indian Cinema*, p. 109). In 1932, R. C. Willman of RCA Photophone was placed in
charge of the technical division of Bengal's East India Company as it became India's first
sound studio to produce 'Indian talking pictures with Hollywood sound quality'.
*Filmland*, vol. 3, no. 125 (3 September 1932). We also find journals publishing opinion
pieces from Hollywood representatives such as A. A. Walters, the Warner representative
in India, Burma and Ceylon, who writes about the importance of playing gramophone
music during film intervals to coincide with the tone of the film. Such an article was
directed at Indian viewing conditions, given that 'the principle of the interval' was part
of every Indian film screening and rarely used with Hollywood films in India. See A. A.
Walters, 'Better Showmanship Means Better Business', *filmindia*, vol. 6, no. 7 (July 1940),
pp. 47–50 and *filmindia*, vol. 7, no. 1, (January 1941), p. 39.

42  See the accounts in Rajadhyaksha and Willemen, *Encylopaedia of Indian Cinema*, p. 139
and Bandyopadhyay, *Indian Cinema*, p. 13. Bandopadhyay quotes the former General
Manager of Columbia films (India), S. V. Money as saying: 'They closed down suddenly
with just a month's notice. Even a person in my position was left without a job and out
of the trade circuit'.

43  *filmindia*, vol. 6, no. 10 (October 1940), p. 45. The English woman Roshanara was born
and raised in India, and taught at the Mariarden School of Dancing in New
Hampshire.

44  'Pointers of Progress', *filmindia*, vol. 1, no. 3 (June 1935), pp. 9, 40.

45  'Pernicious Influence of Pictures on Oriental Peoples', A treatise for the International
Parliamentary Commercial Conference (5 August 1932), IOR, L/P&J/1995, File 372.

46  Lord Nelson giving notice to His Majesty's Government to inquire into the causes of
the British film industry's depression, *Parliamentary Debates* (House of Lords), Fifth
Series, Volume 61 (14 May 1925), p. 274.

47  Film Industries Department, Federation of British Industries, 'Memorandum: Films for
Exhibition in India', 18 April 1934, IOR, L/E/8/137, Ref. 340/Z/2.P.13: 1.

48  'Film Censorship in India', IOR, L/P&J/1995, File 372, handwritten page number 451.

49  Prior to 1922, a film banned in one province could run in another, but subsequent to a
case over D. W. Griffith's *Orphans of a Storm* (1921) (banned in Bengal but screened in
Punjab), it was decided that if a province banned a film it had to send a copy of its
order to the other provinces. For further details on colonial Indian film censorship, also
consult S. Theodore Bhaskaran, *The Message Bearers: The Nationalist Politics and the
Entertainment Media in South Asia, 1885–1945* (Madras: Cre-A, 1981) and Stephen P.
Hughes, 'Policing Silent Film Exhibition in Colonial South India', in Ravi S. Vasudevan
(ed.), *Making Meaning in Indian Cinema* (New Delhi: Oxford University Press, 2000),
pp. 39–64.

50  See repeated questions from 1929 to 1937 about the origin and titles of films prohibited
in India from one Mr Day (also referred to as Colonel Day) in IOR, L/PJ/6/1995 and
*Home (Political)* file no. 21/XVI/1928 (National Archives, New Delhi).

51  Chowdhry, *Colonial India and the Making of Empire Cinema*, p. 44.

52  *Bombay Government Gazette,* 10 June 1937, p. 1303.

53  *Home (Political)* 1928, file no.38 (Maharashtra State Archives, henceforth MSA).

54  *Bombay Government Gazette,* 24 April 1930, serial no. 8843, p. 797.

55 *Bombay Government Gazette,* 15 May 1930, serial no. 9035, p. 1213.

56 *Bombay Government Gazette,* 6 March 1930, serial no. 8707, p. 463.

57 *Home (Political)* 1928, file no. 1 (MSA). See *Indian Social Reformer* editorial (21 January 1928) and *Indian Social Reformer* letter to the editor (4 February 1928).

58 Some of the films that drew particular attention were Hollywood's *Lives of a Bengal Lancer* (1935), *Charge of the Light Brigade* (1938) and *Gunga Din* (1939) and Alexander Korda's British film *The Drum* (1938). In conjunction with Chowdhry's analysis, see *Home (Political)* 1935 file no. 71; *Home (Political)* 1938 file no. 173l; and *Home (Political)* 1938, file no. 237/38 I (MSA).

59 In *Home (Political)* 1935, file no. 71 (MSA), see Satya Bhusan Sen, 'Organise Film against Vilification of India', *People,* 20 October 1935.

60 In *Home (Political)* 1935, file no. 71 (MSA), see *Bombay Chronicle,* 30 April 1935.

61 'Pernicious Influence of Pictures on Oriental Peoples'. Also consult Poonam Arora, ' "Imperilling the Prestige of the White Woman": Colonial Anxiety and Film Censorship in British India', *Visual Anthropology Review,* vol. 11, no. 2 (autumn 1995), pp. 36–50.

62 Political and moral grounds for censoring Hollywood films were more defensible than the economic vetoing of such films through imperial quotas or state subsidies supporting British films in India, as India's active anti-colonialism would not have permitted such a move. For an extended discussion of this, see Priya Jaikumar, 'More than Morality: The Indian Cinematograph Committee Interviews, 1927–28', *The Moving Image,* vol. 3, no.1 (spring 2003), pp. 82–109 and its companion article 'An Act of Transition: Empire and the Making of a National British Film Industry, 1927', *Screen,* vol. 43, no. 2 (summer 2002), pp. 119–38.

63 The Film Group of the Federation of British Industries (FBI), 'Memorandum: Films for Exhibition in India', 18 April 1934, IOR, L/E/8/137, Ref. 340/Z/2.P.13, p. 1.

64 Consult the report of the *Indian Cinematograph Committee 1927–1928: Evidence Volume I* for an account of these arguments.

65 Winifred Holmes, 'British Films and the Empire', *Sight and Sound,* vol. 5, no. 19 (autumn 1936), pp. 72–4.

66 *filmindia,* vol. 6, no. 1 (January 1940), p. 47.

67 Editorial titled 'An Insult to India', in *Film World Weekly,* vol. 1, no. 33 (15 September 1933), pp. 5–6.

68 *The Hindustan Times,* 5 April 1930, p. 15.

69 *filmindia,* vol. 4, no. 8 (December 1938), pp. 12–13. The exchange rate in this period was complex as both Britain and India were on the pre-decimal system, and there was significant controversy over whether the Indian rupee should remain linked to gold and sterling rates after Britain went off the gold standard in September 1931. The 1927 exchange rate held for most of the 1930s, calculated in the following way: 1 Indian Rupee = 1 shilling 6 pence in British terms. (In British currency before decimalisation in 1971, £1= 20 shillings and 1 shilling = 12 pence). Regarding the term 'crore', 1 crore = Rs 10 million.

70 Rs 100,000 = 1 lakh.

71 *filmindia,* vol. 6, no. 12 (December 1940), pp. 38–41 collating reports from *The Sunday Times* (Madras), *The Hindustan Times* (Calcutta), *Cochin Argus* (Kerala), *Indian Express* (Madras) and *Sunday Standard* (Bombay).

72  *Home Political (Internal)*, file no. 99/1944 (National Archives, New Delhi).

73  *Home (Special)*, 355(26)G-I/1938–40 (MSA).

74  *Home (Special)*, 1110 (4)-b(7)-A-I/1942 (MSA).

75  IOR, L/E/8/137.

# 6

# 'Home of American Movies': The Marunouchi Subaruza and the Making of Hollywood's Audiences in Occupied Tokyo, 1946–9[1]

Hiroshi Kitamura

The end of World War II ushered in a dramatic change in the cinematic landscape of Japan. During the period of American occupation (1945–52), General Douglas MacArthur's Supreme Command for the Allied Powers (SCAP) and the American film industry orchestrated a large-scale cultural campaign to promote democracy and pro-American values throughout Japan through motion picture exhibition. Working via the Central Motion Picture Exchange (CMPE), a distribution subsidiary of the major US studios founded under SCAP's direction, the occupiers disseminated over 500 Hollywood features nationwide. These films reached large metropolitan centres as well as the local cities (*chiho toshi*) and smaller towns where Hollywood culture had hitherto received minimal exposure. Just over a year into this campaign, a CMPE representative boasted that Hollywood's business was already 'far ahead of pre-war figures'.[2] Four years later, a top Hollywood representative in the US happily reported that Japan had become one of the industry's 'best market[s]'.[3]

The purpose of this chapter is to explore the impact of this remarkable (and understudied) campaign through a case study of film exhibition in early post-war Tokyo.[4] The social history of Japanese movie theatres has received little attention in English-language scholarship. Moreover, few studies – in Japanese or English – have investigated the exhibition of Hollywood cinema in Japan.[5] This scholarly void reflects two broader shortcomings in the growing literature on Hollywood's overseas trade. The first issue concerns geography. Since Thomas Guback's pioneering study of such trade, film scholars have produced insightful studies on the development of the industry's business in key European markets.[6] In contrast, far less attention has been paid to the American film industry's expansion in non-European societies, including Japan – one of the largest overseas consumers of Hollywood movies in the past few decades.[7]

Second, scholars have yet fully to address the social and cultural ramifications of the international film trade. Since standard studies of Hollywood's globalisation concentrate primarily on the top-level negotiations over tariffs, quotas, censorship and the distribution of film prints, we are left largely in ignorance concerning the impact of this worldwide phenomenon on the 'ground level'. Where did foreign consumers see American movies? How were they sold and presented in the markets overseas? Who went to see them (and who did not)? How did the penetration of Hollywood cinema help reshape and transform foreign societies? The answers to these questions require a closer scrutiny of the *reception* of Hollywood cinema abroad – a concept Robert C. Allen defines as the issues 'surrounding the confrontation between the semiotic and social'.[8]

The focus of this study is a prominent site of 'confrontation' between Hollywood cinema and Japanese consumers in the nation's capital: the Marunouchi Subaruza. During the three-year period after its opening on 31 December 1946, this movie theatre flourished as a nationally acclaimed outlet for Hollywood's new releases. Movie fans idolised the theatre, which was emblazoned with the epitaph 'Home of American Movies' on the front wall. The trade championed the mid-sized venue as a an 'ideal' exhibition site.[9] Praising it as the 'promise of a new Japan', the CMPE recognised Subaruza with an award as one of the Ten Best exhibitors in 1947.[10] The recollection of the glamour and aura that characterised the theatre's early career (which some would later think of as its 'golden years') endured throughout Japan's recent past. Forty years later, one film critic recalled the occupation era and emphatically declared that: 'One cannot discount Subaruza from any social history of postwar Japan . . . [The theatre was] beyond first-rate'.[11]

Subaruza's first three years reveal the unique strategies a novice exhibitor employed to survive and thrive in a competitive business field. Subaruza was no ordinary exhibitor, however. As a 'chosen' movie theatre enjoying a privileged relationship with the CMPE, Subaruza strove to distinguish itself as a culturally respectable exhibitor of American films. The theatre not only screened Hollywood's high-end feature films under a coveted roadshow system, but amplified the prestige value of the films through various off-screen strategies. It published lavish movie programmes touting American cinema in general as producing culturally sophisticated and mature products. It cultivated an air of refinement in the theatre by adopting reserved seating, orderly screening and a 'good manners' policy. Subaruza also organised gala premières and special events for the Japanese elites. Through these extensive efforts to elevate the cultural status of American cinema, Subaruza constructed its patronage primarily from what might be considered Japan's 'educated mainstream'. This broad social category included office workers, students and public officers; men, women and couples; Tokyoites and out-of-towners; as well as families and middle-aged consumers.

The business of this prominent movie theatre also offers a means of understanding the broader dynamics of cross-cultural transmission in the context of the Allied occupation. The years under SCAP's rule are often remembered as an 'American interlude' or a 'forced Americanisation' – a moment in which US policy-makers stepped in to remould the war-shattered nation independent of Japanese will. In *Embracing Defeat: Japan in the Wake of World War II*, however, John Dower challenges this perception by demonstrating the diverse ways in which the Japanese population actively shaped their own historical experiences in the face of a devastating defeat. In Dower's account, occupied Japan was not simply the experience of SCAP's top-down coercion and control. Instead, it functioned as an interactive space in which the Japanese 'embraced' the victor's values and meanings in reconstructing their new identities under America's neo-colonial presence.[12]

The case of Subaruza suggests that Hollywood's trans-Pacific penetration was not simply a 'forced Americanisation'. Although the US film programme during the occupation stemmed in part from the top-level policy-making of SCAP, Hollywood and the

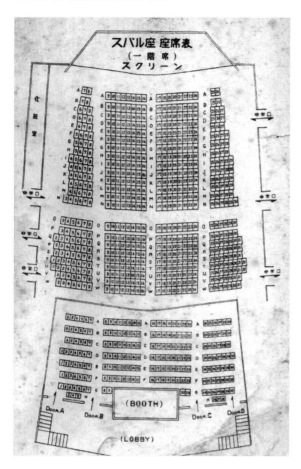

スバル座 座席表
(一 階 席)
スクリーン

The seating plan for the
Marunouchi Subaruza

US government, the culture of American cinema did not reach the Japanese filmgoer unmediated. Before meeting the everyday consumer, Hollywood cinema encountered various local intermediaries, including local studio employees, film critics, publicists, fan representatives and exhibitors who consumed, reinvented and promoted the meanings of American cinema at the 'ground level'. The early career of Subaruza shows how some of Hollywood's exhibitors in occupied Japan mediated American cinema and the Japanese consumer through an active 'embrace' of the victor's narrative products. Subaruza did not 'just show' the movies, but actively constructed a unique entertainment culture that surrounded them. In so doing, this novice theatre became a centripetal force that facilitated Hollywood's trans-Pacific trade in the early aftermath of World War II.

## The Birth of a Roadshow Theatre

The American film trade in occupied Japan formed part of a larger cultural campaign generated by SCAP. During the six-year period after World War II, the occupation government launched a large-scale campaign to transform the formerly militaristic state into a peace-minded 'democratic' nation.[13] In addition to the political, business and constitutional reforms conducted on the top level, the occupiers also orchestrated cultural programmes to disseminate pro-democratic and pro-American values to the mass population. Finding cinema a useful tool in encouraging the Japanese public to embrace the 'American way', occupation authorities monitored the production of Japanese feature films through a complex censorship apparatus, while facilitating Hollywood's trans-Pacific market penetration through the CMPE.[14] As a hybrid institution that represented the interests of SCAP and US film studios aligned under the Motion Picture Export Association (MPEA), the CMPE pursued the dual objective of aiding SCAP's efforts to transform Japan from a warring militaristic state into a peace-minded, 'democratic' nation while also facilitating the more general penetration of Hollywood films across Japan. Starting with a one-room office in the heart of Tokyo, the CMPE soon established regional branches in Nagoya, Osaka, Fukuoka and Sapporo, and launched a nationwide distribution campaign of American feature films.[15]

Subaruza came into existence during the CMPE's first year of operation. The origin of the theatre can be traced to 9 February 1946, when a group of nine Japanese men gathered in Tokyo to inaugurate an exhibition company, the Subaru Enterprises Co. Ltd. Most of the founders were formerly bankers and corporate employees of the Mitsubishi conglomerate. Although none of them had run a movie theatre before, they expressed a strong determination to break new ground in the movie business. In part to show their commitment to the business, the company's founders named it after a famous constellation of stars – the Pleiades (which, in Japanese, is translated as 'Subaru'). To the founders, this symbolised co-existence, teamwork and collaboration. Armed with a modest capital of 180,000 yen and a novice's zeal, Subaru Enterprises set out to make a name for itself in Japan's post-war market.[16]

The immediate climate of the theatre business was a vibrant and disorderly one. Following the destruction of over 500 movie theatres and the damaging of many others, the war-shattered nation witnessed a dramatic 'theatre craze' that extended the size and scope of the theatre business beyond prewar levels.[17] This mainly consisted of the recovery of Toho and Shochiku's nationwide chains, as well as what *Eiga Geino Nenkan*, the yearbook of the motion picture and entertainments industries, described as the 'unending growth' of new circuits and independent venues across the nation.[18] Exhibitors established new outlets in a variety of neighborhoods and spaces, including vacant lots, department stores, office buildings, warehouses and other available places. *Kinema Junpo*, a leading trade magazine, reported that movie theatres sprouted as fast as 'bamboo shoots right after a shower'.[19] In Tokyo, a special control order was issued immediately, in order to prevent the proliferation of 'quickie' constructions.[20]

Subaru Enterprises sought to distinguish its theatres from its rivals through two strategies. The first strategy was to become a regular exhibitor of Hollywood's high-end films, then distributed by the CMPE. The idea of doing business with the MPEA-CMPE appealed to Subaruza, which perceived US feature films as a better alternative to what was otherwise available in the early post-war market. In the company's prospectus, Subaru Enterprises expressed a strong excitement at the opportunity to showcase Hollywood's ready-made 'superior films', while denouncing others for screening 'low-brow films', which presumably meant low-cost Japanese feature films produced under shortage-prone conditions.[21]

The second strategy was to enhance its mode of presentation. Although the theatre business was growing dramatically in Japan, the culture of film exhibition appeared nothing short of 'degenerate' in the eyes of Subaru Enterprises. Theatres were 'unsanitary' spaces into which the 'masses' (*taishu*) swarmed *en masse*. Exhibitors did little to reform the filthy and chaotic atmospheres. Audiences experienced 'agony' instead of 'entertainment', 'degeneration' instead of 'education'. What was worse, this tendency turned away the 'truly . . . cultured people' (*bunkajin*) from moviegoing. In response to this disorderly climate, Subaru Enterprises declared that it would improve the quality of film presentation. Looking upon the Astor theatre in New York as a model for the exhibition business, the company promised to present its theatres as 'cultural institutions', not 'vulgar' venues.[22]

The desire to pursue these two strategies led Subaru Enterprises to approach the CMPE and the occupation forces. Although the actual negotiation process is unclear, a contemporary report suggests that Toyama Fukio, the exhibitor's inaugural president, was the driving force. Known as an energetic businessman, Toyama capitalised on his personal acquaintance with the CMPE's first managing director, Michael Bergher, to secure favourable screening arrangements with Hollywood.[23] Bergher responded to Toyama with enthusiasm. In a memo dated 17 April 1946, the CMPE representative not only 'welcomed' the company's idea of building an 'upscale' theatre that would showcase Hollywood films, but also requested that Japanese authorities allow Subaru Enterprises to build its theatres in spite of the control order. Favourable backing also came from SCAP's Civil Information and Education Section (CIE), which oversaw the reconstruction of the media in Japan. In a memo to Subaru Enterprises, Major H. L. Roberts gave 'full support' for the construction and maintenance of the theatre.[24]

The occupiers' support enabled Subaru Enterprises to inaugurate its exhibition business with three theatres in the heart of Tokyo. The first venue, Marunouchi Meigaza, opened on 10 September 1946. Located in the basement of the Mainichi Shinbun Sha building, this modest subterranean space exhibited pre-war US exports as well as new releases. The second theatre, Marunouchi Orionza, debuted three months later as a first-run exhibitor of American feature films. The third venue was Subaruza, a two-storey wooden structure that seated 804 people. On New Year's Eve 1946, it opened with the release of *Always in My Heart*.[25]

At the time of its birth, Subaruza was one of the forty-one movie houses that showcased Hollywood feature films in the nation's capital.[26] What distinguished it from others was the roadshow format.[27] Employed by New York's Astor theatre to showcase such prestige productions as *Gone with the Wind*, the roadshow system granted exclusive screening of a given film before it reached first-, second-, or lesser-run houses in the region.[28] It also made it possible for particular films to have longer runs. At the time, Japanese exhibitors switched feature presentations frequently, typically on a weekly or bi-weekly basis. The roadshow system allowed theatres to alter the length of exhibition in light of the film's popularity. On 25 March 1947, with the opening release of *Rhapsody in Blue*, Subaruza made history by becoming the first long-term roadshow theatre in Japan.[29] The six films released before the Gershwin story were each shown for only two weeks. Under the new presentation format, the turnaround time commonly extended to three, four or six weeks. Successful features remained for over two months. The longest lasted on-screen for seventeen weeks.[30]

The roadshow system rewarded Subaruza with a privileged line-up of Hollywood

The Subaruza movie
programme, 25 March 1947,
for *Rhapsody in Blue* (Irving
Rapper, 1945)

feature films. Because of this unique distribution format, the CMPE supplied Subaruza
with a number of prestige films that promised high turnout for multiple weeks. The distributor also used Subaruza to boost the reputation of the selected films before they
reached first-run (and lesser-run) theatres across the nation.[31] As a result, the line-up
was largely devoid of the B-Westerns and *Tarzan* movies that circulated in less favoured
venues. Instead, Subaruza received what one manager labelled 'artistically high' films
that transcended 'mere entertainment'.[32] The list included literary epics (*Jane Eyre*),
Broadway adaptations (*The Philadelphia Story* and *Arsenic and Old Lace*), acclaimed
melodramas (*Random Harvest* and *Waterloo Bridge*), biographical films (*Rhapsody in
Blue*), Technicolor productions (*Gulliver's Travels* and *The Yearling*) and prestigious
'male melodramas' (*The Lost Weekend* and *The Best Years of Our Lives*). A third of the
theatre's releases were Oscar-winners.[33]

One possible drawback of the roadshow theatre was its admission price. At Subaruza,
tickets cost over twice as much as at other theatres. The admission fee for *Rhapsody in
Blue*, for example, was 25 yen, at a time when tickets for first-run houses were 10 yen.
Moviegoers, nonetheless, flocked to the theatre every day.[34] Before implementing the

roadshow system, Subaruza struggled to make ends meet. A manager complained in February 1947 that weekday attendance, especially in the mornings, was 'absolutely hopeless'.[35] After *Rhapsody in Blue*, tickets were often sold out days ahead.[36] 'Long lines [of ticket buyers]' observed *Nihon Bunka Tsushin*, 'formed in front of the theatre' on a regular basis.[37] Responding to popular demand, Subaruza soon added new seats in the back rows and middle aisles.[38] The theatre's popularity made it an attractive site for scalpers, who would charge unreasonably high prices to desperate ticket-seekers.[39]

## Hollywood Cinema in Print

Subaruza's attempt to distinguish itself in the business went further than simply screening Hollywood's high-end films. Eager to amplify the quality of the on-screen narratives, the theatre also published its own movie programmes for sale. The idea of producing such publications was actually not a novel one. Since the pre-war years, elite exhibitors had commonly issued their own movie programmes to advertise new releases, stars, and the theatres themselves. Subaruza's, however, were generally more lavish in design and substantial in content than those produced by rival moviehouses.[40] At a time when a typical theatre programme was a two- or three-page broadsheet, Subaruza's publications – popularly dubbed 'Subaru souvenirs' (*Subaru miyage*) – were neatly stapled booklets that could run to up to forty pages.

The programmes promoted the showcased feature presentation, containing articles and essays written by film critics, industry professionals and other prominent individuals. These texts conveyed at least three kinds of information: they provided synopses and content descriptions of the films themselves; they also introduced the film's stars, cast and production staff; and they outlined the customs, beliefs and lifestyles of foreign societies (especially the US). The booklets added colour and glamour with a myriad of still photos, sketches and illustrations of the films and their cast of characters. Major stars commonly made their appearances in full-page stills and portraits. While the themes they highlighted varied from film to film, the programmes as a whole supported the films' claim to the status of artworks. They also celebrated Hollywood's on-screen world as a representation of 'high culture' and 'sophisticated' lifestyles – usually, of course, those found in the United States.

The programme of *Rhapsody in Blue* serves as a case in point. Beginning with the exhibitor's greetings, this twenty-three-page booklet provided a two-page introduction to the movie, as well as brief biographies of its cast and production crew. The central figure, however, was the film's subject: George Gershwin. The programme profiled Gershwin in six full-length essays that scrutinised the famed composer from multiple angles. The writings discussed his professional career from the early jazz age, Tin Pan Alley, to Hollywood; the 'making' of the songs in the movie; the musicians whom Gershwin knew and interacted with in real life (e.g. Oscar Levant, Paul Whiteman, Al Jolson, Hazel Scott, Anne Brown and Tom Patricola); the differences between Gershwin's music and classical music; and the subsequent work of the short-lived composer. The programme, as one of its essays boasted, celebrated the 'luscious music' of Gershwin, whom it hailed as the 'greatest American composer'.[41]

The *Old Acquaintance* programme characterised this Vincent Sherman melodrama as a film for 'adult' women that crystallised the difference between 'film art' and a simple 'moving image' (*katsudo shashin*). The central figure of this programme was the

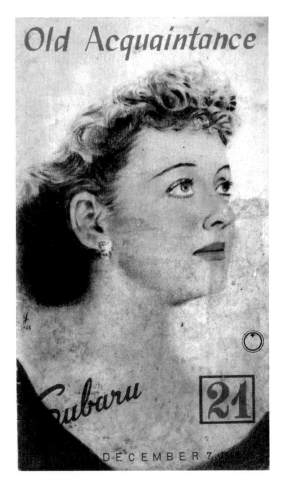

The Subaruza movie
programme, 7 December 1948,
for *Old Acquaintance* (Vincent
Sherman, 1943)

film's star, Bette Davis. Her solemn face decorated the programme's front cover, while a
plethora of illustrations and still photos of her appeared on page after page. The writings on Davis identified her as a 'renowned actress' and 'top star' of Warner Bros. who
encapsulated the 'highest intelligence of Hollywood'. One essay reminded its readers
that the highlight of a Bette Davis movie was always the actress herself. '[When one
watches] a movie with Bette Davis', the film critic Nanbu Keinosuke wrote, 'it is good
[enough] if you can feast on her performance'.[42]

The most impressive element of *The Long Voyage Home*, according to its programme,
was not the on-screen stars, but the film-makers. Following the synopsis of the movie
and the introduction of the major cast of eight characters (including John Wayne, Barry
Fitzgerald, Ian Hunter and Thomas Mitchell), the programme included a two-page
essay that lauded this 1940 movie as a 'high level art film'. Tamura Yukihiko, the author
and a founding member of Subaru Enterprises, specifically praised the efforts of
'America's top film director', John Ford, who 'absorbed the original story well and
turned it into a representative art film'. Equal acclaim was given to the 'splendid camera[work]' of cinematographer Gregg Toland. His mixture of 'bright high key' and 'dark
low key' shots, Tamura wrote, produced one of the most 'outstanding cinemato-

graph[ies]' that he could remember.[43] The remaining pages extended the discussion of Ford and Toland in a total of four full-length essays, two for each figure. Other articles were devoted to the playwright Eugene O'Neill and the screenwriter Dudley Nichols.

The programme for *The Best Years of Our Lives* also used most of its pages to promote the actors and the film-making crew. Following a two-page introduction to the movie, the programme devoted page-long essays to each of the main performers (Myrna Loy, Fredric March, Dana Andrews, Teresa Wright, Harold Russell, Virginia Mayo, Cathy O'Donnell and Hoagy Carmichael), outlining their upbringing, careers and past performances. In the many pages that followed, the programme also examined the personal and professional careers of the film-makers, praising the producer, Samuel Goldwyn, for his 'sublime . . . truly polished [and] especially beautiful' movies. William Wyler, the director of the Oscar-sweeping film, received applause as a 'first-rate' film-maker who strove to 'incorporate . . . an even higher, even deeper [degree of] artistic value to cinema [than general entertainment movies]'. Once again, cinematographer Gregg Toland was lauded, this time as a 'cameraman with an artist's heart'.[44]

The programme also reminded its readers that the Wyler movie embodied 'serious lessons' for Japanese audiences. In a three-page essay titled 'American Society and Life', the cultural critic Nakano Goro expressed his admiration for the movie, not solely for its entertainment and artistic values, but also because it represented what he saw as the essence of America: a 'democracy in action'. This story about the three war veterans and their struggles to adapt to civilian life after World War II, wrote Nakano, represented the everyday lives of three different social classes (the rich, lower middle and poor classes) in an average American town – which he compared to 'Middletown' (in reality, Muncie, Indiana), the US small-town community studied by sociologists Robert and Helen Lynd.[45] Praising the film's depiction of the 'problem [of] war veterans' as well as the 'passion', 'humanity' and 'love' of the 'average American', the critic concluded that this 'great picture based on a great idea' could ultimately stimulate, facilitate and encourage Japan's own 'democratisation'.[46]

## Dignifying Space

In addition to programme publication, Subaruza strove to improve the social atmosphere of the movie theatre itself. While they were confident that the films they showed would continue to be superior, the exhibitors worried that the experience of moviegoing could ruin the actual pleasure of watching them. As many contemporaries lamented, the physical state of movie theatres in the wake of a devastating war was hardly good. In addition to vandalism, theft and other disruptive behaviours that characterised many theatres, exhibitors in general struggled with the problem of over-congestion. At this time, theatres commonly employed policies of 'packing-in' (*tsumekomi*) or 'pouring-in' (*nagashikomi*), cramming audiences into the venue until it was literally jam-packed. By prioritising profit over comfort, packing-in theatres fostered dangerously over-crowded atmospheres in which injuries, brawls and disorderly behaviour were familiar occurrences. This situation encouraged some theatres to employ various off-screen strategies to dignify theatrical space.[47]

One strategy adopted by Subaruza was reserved seating. Instead of allowing movie-goers to crowd in, the managers of Subaruza decided to limit the number of patrons to actual seating capacity. Three days before opening day, Subaruza took a block advertisement in *Asahi Shinbun*, a leading newspaper in Japan. Mentioning nothing of the show-cased film, the ad announced the theatre's adoption of a partial reserved seating system that would guarantee ticket-holders a seat. The first floor adopted an 'open restriction' method in which patrons chose seats on a first-come, first-serve basis. On each second-floor ticket, patrons found their row and seat numbers. After *Rhapsody in Blue*, Subaruza changed its policy to full reserved seating.[48]

Reserved seating helped restore spatial order in an otherwise chaos-prone atmosphere. At Subaruza, audiences no longer had to jockey for position or stand on their toes to watch the screen. As one company ad boasted, viewers could simply 'sit and relax in their seats'.[49] The new arrangement also functioned to restrain disruptive individuals who took advantage of congested spaces to bother others. Reserved seating also fostered an atmosphere of formality. In order to prevent chaos and confusion, the theatre employed usherettes, who escorted patrons to their designated seats.[50] Managers routinely inspected their uniform, hairstyle, make-up and bowing manners, and also corrected their use of language so that these young women would provide respectable services in the theatre. Usherettes guided the flow of people in the building to avoid confusion with the new seating practice.[51]

Subaruza's mode of business altered audience behaviour in another important way, by forcing moviegoers to follow the theatre's screening schedule. In most other theatres, patrons could wander in and out at will. Under Subaruza's policy, ticket-holders could attend just one screening, at the specific time and date inscribed on the ticket. This arrangement encouraged punctuality. Since tickets went on sale in advance, patrons had to plan ahead to secure their chance of watching a feature presentation. In one of its programmes, Subaruza's manager admitted that the theatre's seating system created confusion at first. Once audiences had sampled the less congested spaces, however, they appeared to enjoy it. The manager took pride in the fact that many of his patrons 'scheduled a few hours [of movie-viewing] in their monthly plans'.[52]

Subaruza's respect for its scheduled screening became apparent in the auditorium as well, where screen curtains were used as punctuation after each show, as well as between shorts (newsreels, trailers, etc.) and feature presentations.[53] The theatre's vice-manager also saw to it that each screening would run on schedule. In particular, he ensured that projectionists did not try to shorten their work hours by skipping reels or starting a reel before the previous one had ended. With the five to six projectionists thoroughly supervised, managers largely prevented these unprofessional practices (known as *oikomi*, or the 'run-on' of films) and maintained a clear temporal structure for their programmes.[54]

Subaruza also endeavoured to curtail disrespectful behaviour by establishing the theatre space as a respectable environment. In each of its programmes, Subaruza included a policy statement, which pleaded with audiences to cooperate by behaving like 'ladies and gentlemen'. The theatre made it clear that enforcement was strictly 'voluntary'. Employees, the statement continued, would not use microphone announcements to convey its policy or verbally humiliate those who disrupted the showings. 'We plead for your co-operation', Subaruza's management wrote, so that everyone might enjoy the 'highbrow and bright atmosphere' of the theatre.[55]

The creation of a 'highbrow and bright atmosphere' required efforts to curtail specific behaviour that disturbed patrons. The theatre thus urged (male) audiences to place their hats on their laps so as not to block the view of others. The policy also prohibited smoking everywhere but in the hallways.[56] Smoking was a serious problem because it clouded the screens, polluted the air and increased the possibility of a disastrous fire. Facing the dogged refusal of smokers to comply, the theatre adopted an additional tactic. Whenever fumes fogged the hall, employees walked up to the smoker, flashlight in hand, and silently handed out a small card inscribed with a 'no smoking' sign.[57] According to the CMPE, this strategy eventually succeeded in preventing smoking 'without any exceptions . . . [probably because] audiences felt their personalities were respected'.[58]

## The Elites Go to the Movies

Subaruza's effort to enhance its presentation encompassed a specific form of audience mobilisation: the incorporation of Japan's top elites. The exhibitor reached out to the most visible and prominent figures in Japan in part to co-opt them as patrons, but more importantly to elevate the prestige of the theatre itself. The presence of eminent public figures also drew extensive media attention. After watching Subaruza's showcased features, prominent members of society often voiced their own opinions about the movies through lectures, writings and radio broadcasts. The courting of the elite was a deliberate strategy to solidify Subaruza's prestige and to attract a wider range of patrons.

During the first months of its operation, Subaruza drew in the Japanese elite with two gala premières. The first took place on 17 March 1947, with the special screening of *Rhapsody in Blue*. For this event, Subaruza invited politicians, deans and professors of universities, company executives, SCAP officers, movie stars, novelists, writers, critics and composers, together with other distinguished individuals. A handful of imperial family members – including Prince Takamatsu, Prince Mikasa and Princess Higashikuni – were also present. What made this event even more unusual, one film critic recalled, was that spouses were also invited. Subaruza's lavish première appeared 'Americanised' to him in part because of the introduction of this Hollywood-style custom.[59] The Gershwin screening received wide publicity in newspapers, magazines and newsreels, and even appeared on the news abroad.[60] *Kinema Junpo* reported that the screening, which drew an 'unusual line-up of people', was a 'great success'.[61]

The second gala première took place on 21 July 1947, at the screening of *Random Harvest*, the theatre's third roadshow release. Just as with *Rhapsody in Blue* some four months earlier, the second première drew artists, business leaders, film stars, SCAP officers, imperial family members and a group of top-rank politicians: Prime Minister Katayama Tetsu and his Cabinet colleagues. This event received wide publicity in newspapers, magazines and newsreels. A radio crew recorded the excitement and broadcast it four days later. The recording, wrote *MPEA News*, 'effectively captured the atmosphere of the première show', and was 'very well-received'. The show overall displayed 'even more flamboyance' than the Gershwin première.[62]

Subaruza's involvement with the elite intensified after the birth of the American Movie Culture Association (AMCA), an organisation for American movie fans. Founded in Tokyo on 8 July 1947, AMCA soon blossomed into a nationwide organisation that developed regional branches in over sixty cities and towns nationwide. Unlike the movie clubs founded in high schools and universities, or a popular fan organisation such as Tomo no Kai (run by the movie magazine *Eiga no Tomo*), AMCA consisted primarily of professors, poets, novelists, critics, politicians, bureaucrats, musicians, artists and other distinguished members of society.[63] AMCA's core members included Haruyama Yukio (poet and cultural critic), Okano Hideki (head of the American Research Institute in Japan), Hayashi Fumiko (novelist), Kikuta Kazuo (playwright), Eito Toshio (councilor of Mainichi Shinbun), Hosoiri Totaro (professor of English literature), Nakano Goro (journalist and critic), Iijima Tadashi (film critic), Shima Teru (public relations representative of Japan Broadcasting Company), Honda Kensho (professor), Tatsuno Takashi (literary scholar) and Fujita Tsuguji (painter). In its regional branches, mayors, public officials, journalists, film critics and others played an active role in running the organisation.[64]

The elites of AMCA treated Hollywood cinema as a 'serious' cultural phenomenon that transcended 'mindless entertainment'. 'In order for Japan to grow into a worldly nation', stated AMCA, it was necessary to 'learn the finest things that America is spreading across the world through American movies'. The 'finest things', continued AMCA, encompassed 'artistic essence' as well as numerous cultural themes and ideas about America: lifestyle, thought, science, education, politics, religion, language, custom and even the 'inner workings of human nature'. The goal of the organisation was not simply to develop a 'correct' understanding of these cultural tropes and ideas among the Japanese elite, but to also disseminate that knowledge to the 'masses' across the nation.[65] AMCA thus promised to become a true 'educational institution' that would aid 'Japan's reconstruction into a democratic and cultural nation'.[66]

Subaruza decided to work with AMCA, believing that the latter could add another layer of respectability to the theatre. It encouraged ties with AMCA by supporting its foundation and by commissioning its members to write essays for the theatre's programmes.[67] Contributors usually delivered analyses and commentary using their own professional expertise. Shikiba Ryuzaburo, MD, discussed the movies from a medical point of view, in such essays as 'Movies on Amnesia' and '*The Lost Weekend* as an "Alcoholism Movie".'[68] Shima Teru, an amateur expert on American culture and society, offered his views on *The Yearling* in a programme that introduced the physical, social and cultural conditions of Florida, the film's geographical setting.[69] Relying in part on his first-hand experiences in the US as a journalist, Nakano Goro explored the meanings of democracy and community life in his essay for *The Best Years of Our Lives* programme. In *The Lost Weekend* programme, six AMCA members participated in a roundtable discussing the Ray Milland movie from various angles.[70]

Subaruza also organised special screenings for AMCA. Starting in December 1947, it offered itself for a series of AMCA screenings that featured lectures by experts in various fields – a group of people whom the AMCA newsletter boastfully described as the 'first-rate cultural elite'.[71] A typical event was held for *Arsenic and Old Lace*. This Frank Capra comedy involved a mentally disturbed uncle who believed he was a Theodore Roosevelt, as well as two aunts who shared a secret habit of poisoning their guests. The presence of such eccentricity prompted Shikiba to deliver a talk on psychoanalysis and cinema.[72] For the screening of *The Philadelphia Story*, a film that portrayed a wealthy American family through a daughter's marriage, Subaruza hosted a lecture by Shima, who frequently wrote about American cinema and society in movie magazines and programmes.[73]

The most visible act of collaboration took place on 26 March 1948, when Subaruza and AMCA co-hosted a première of *Gulliver's Travels*, a 1939 animation of Jonathan Swift's famous novel. As was the case with the theatre's other premières, this one welcomed prominent individuals from a variety of fields, including members of the cabinet and imperial family.[74] The highlight of the event was the attendance of a boy: the crown prince Akihito. Following World War II, the crown prince had become something of a popular celebrity, whose public appearances were greeted by crowds of onlookers.[75] His presence, therefore, transformed the première into a public spectacle. A Subaru Enterprises executive, who looked after visitors at the main entrance, later recounted the unforgettable moment of the price's arrival:

> The sound of the chimes rang through the theatre. It is now quiet in Subaruza. Silence has fallen outdoors as well. The speech of AMCA trustee [and professor] Hori Makoto seems to have begun. On the main street facing the theatre, uniformed and plain-clothed security guards await the arrival of the crown prince. An unusually tense feeling – one that I had never experienced in ordinary film previews – hung in the atmosphere. The sound of applause rippled from indoors. Education Minister Morito's speech is underway. Everything seems to be running according to schedule.
>
> The clock struck 2.20pm. The crown prince will arrive at any moment . . . From the direction of Yurakucho Station, two black automobiles appeared in sight . . . By this time a crowd had gathered to greet the crown prince. Guards and other personnel are doing their best to restore order.
>
> As I witnessed the prince step off the vehicle . . . I couldn't stop my tears from flowing out of my eyes. I stood there glancing at His Highness ascend the stairs, amidst the flare of strobe lights and spotlights. Newsreel cameramen and newspaper photographers were moving to and fro.[76]

This 'première of premières' further amplified Subaruza's respected status in the movie-going culture of defeated Japan. The flamboyance, the formal atmosphere, the media attention, and above all the presence of Akihito and the Japanese elite created a spectacle in itself, separating Subaruza from its contenders in Tokyo and the rest of the nation.

## The Educated Mainstream as Patrons

Subaruza's patrons were not limited to the elites who regularly attended the gala premières and AMCA-related activities. As a commercial enterprise in a competitive field of business, Subaruza encouraged elite patronage with the aim of boosting the theatre's prestige, garnering public attention, and eventually netting a wider range of moviegoers. The theatre's patrons, commonly identified by the trade as the *interi so* or *chishiki so* (both roughly translated as 'intellectual class'), included a diverse range of groups and individuals.[77] In terms of occupation, they included office workers, students and public officials. Both men and women patronised the theatre, often treating movie-going as a heterosocial event. Patrons also included families and middle-aged people. Overall, Subaruza used its films and unique mode of presentation to construct patronage around a broad 'educated mainstream'.

In order to identify Subaruza's audiences, it is necessary to consider geography. The district where Subaruza was located (Marunouchi) was the financial centre of Tokyo, adjacent to Ginza, a lively commercial district that flourished as a 'modern' urban centre during the pre-war years. As one of the central workplaces for the burgeoning new middle class, especially after the Great Kanto Earthquake of 1923, the neighbourhood attracted a wide range of commuters and visitors, many of them students and office workers.[78] The Marunouchi-Ginza area was a convenient access point for two major transportation systems: the train and the bus. Despite the damages wrought by air raids during the final months of the war, the nearby Yurakucho railroad station was averaging some 600,000 passengers daily by 1950, while a constellation of bus stops connected visitors to over twenty different routes.[79]

Although many multistorey buildings survived the air raids, the war left deep scars on the physical and social character of the Marunouchi area. Particularly in the early years of the occupation, its social composition was mixed and diverse: displaced veterans, orphans and black marketeers loitered on the streets while students and company workers passed by. A particularly visible group were the occupation forces, whose headquarters was in the Ginza-Yurakucho zone. The foreign occupiers, however, seldom visited Subaruza's regular screenings. Since SCAP had converted some of the existing theatres into their own entertainment centres (such as the nearby Takarazuka Gekijo, which was renamed the Ernie Pyle theatre), Japanese moviegoers rarely encountered GIs in the movie theatre.[80]

Who, then, did Subaruza attract? One place to start is with people working in nearby office buildings. The strong presence of office workers was not unique to Subaruza: reports indicate that a large portion of moviegoers in the Marunouchi area generally was drawn from the working population of the area.[81] This characteristic differed from other places in the metropolis, such as the more 'mass-oriented' (*taishu-teki na*) Asakusa district, where audience surveyors commonly detected a larger proportion of factory workers, engineers, small shopkeepers and farmers.[82] To Subaruza, office workers were welcome targets not just because of their proximity to the theatre, but also because they were more likely to afford the theatre's higher admission prices. In part to woo them to its shows, Subaruza offered group discounts and strategically marketed the films towards them.[83] A publicist of Subaru Enterprises noted that the theatre consciously reached out to the desk-working *sarari man,* or the 'salary man', by advertising its films in major newspapers such as the *Asahi, Yomiuri* and *Mainichi.* These publications, he continued, were effective because they 'penetrated deeply into households'.[84]

While drawing the working population in the vicinity, Subaruza also attracted other social groups, including students and public officials from outside the area.[85] What lured them to Subaruza's screenings? One can argue that the prime source of attraction was the films themselves. As a roadshow theatre in Tokyo, Subaruza was able to monopolise the novelty value of its films in the capital city.[86] Thanks to its unique presentation format, which guaranteed the possibility of longer screen runs, Subaruza was also able to allocate far more funds for advertising than average movie-houses. This enabled the theatre to generate extensive publicity campaigns across Tokyo, using posters, billboards, still photos, magazines ads, radio and electric newsboards – in addition to block ads in the daily papers.[87]

Moreover, Subaruza's drawing-power appears to have extended beyond Tokyo proper. Reports suggest that many out-of-towners visited Subaruza to enjoy its refined presentation of select Hollywood films. As a result of its wide popularity, the theatre soon earned a reputation as a 'specialty of Tokyo' (*Tokyo meibutsu*).[88] The theatre's drawing power was observed by *Nihon Bunka Tsushin,* which reported that exhibitors in 'satellite cities' such as Chiba, Urawa, Omiya, Hachioji, Yokosuka, Zushi and Kamakura, as well as those in the capital city itself, were losing part of their clientele because local moviegoers were pulled towards the Yurakucho-Marunouchi area. A ticket centre in Kamakura noted that its local fans preferred to watch American movies at Subaruza, even if it required an extra 70 yen to cover round-trip train fares.[89]

In addition, Subaruza became an attractive site for female audiences. One explanation for female attendance was the selection of the films. A number of its releases were 'women's pictures' highlighting heterosexual romance or strong female characters. The list included *The Constant Nymph*, *Always in My Heart*, *The Philadelphia Story*, *Waterloo Bridge*, *All This and Heaven Too*, *Anna and the King of Siam*, *Love Letters*, *Mrs Parkington* and *Old Acquaintance*.[90] The theatre also lured the woman consumer with the programmes. In addition to the still photos of Hollywood stars, these publications were peppered with consumer advertisements that specifically targeted women, promoting western clothes (*yofuku*) for women, cosmetics, handbags, shampoos, lipsticks and women's magazines. One local department store contributed a 'message ad' that encouraged women to wear perfume and white handkerchiefs to the theatre to help create a respectful atmosphere.[91]

The proportion of men and women must have varied in line with the film as well as the date and time of screening, but overall Subaruza attracted a high proportion of women.[92] Between September and November 1947, during the screenings of *Random Harvest* and *Jane Eyre*, the theatre commissioned a film club (*kenkyukai*) of Chuo University to assess the profile of the theatre's audiences. In this survey, just over half of the respondents (215 out of 416) were female. The study also discovered that women moviegoers were relatively younger. Whereas male respondents ranged widely in age, from less than twenty to forty, the majority of female audiences were under twenty-five.[93]

Many of these women treated moviegoing as a heterosocial event, visiting Subaruza with their male friends.[94] Although this practice was not new in the post-war decades, the occupation years fostered a cultural space that encouraged dating in public. Heterosexual romance became an increasingly visible phenomenon in the urban landscape, sometimes involving American GI's and Japanese women, but more often Japanese men and women.[95] As the Yurakucho-Ginza district revived from the ashes of war, it became a popular site for young couples to rendezvous.[96]

Subaruza capitalised on this growing trend with a unique selling strategy: they installed twelve love seats on the back rows of the theatre and labelled them 'romance seats'. These paired seats immediately generated a flurry of publicity.[97] Despite an initial plan to isolate each romance seat with curtains, the seats were actually placed in the open, in the back rows of the first and second floors.[98] While removed from the direct view of the rest of the audience, the couples in the rear were urged to act respectably as members of a shared common space. This popular seating arrangement encouraged young couples to go out to the movies, and to behave in a way modelled on the wholesome romance of a classical Hollywood film.

Finally, Subaruza appears also to have appealed to families and middle-aged moviegoers. The exhibitor stated, perhaps somewhat boastfully, that an 'overwhelming number' of its patrons were middle-aged family audiences and office workers.[99] The effort to encourage family attendance was perhaps strongest when the showcased film was a 'children's movie' such as *Gulliver's Travels*, or *The Yearling*, which was promoted as a film that 'men and women, young and old' could all enjoy.[100] Clearly, spatial comfort seems to have attracted a diverse range of audience groups, while helping to establish the theatre's reputation as a place where both 'children and the elderly can enjoy' the movies.[101] A familiar sight at Subaruza, stated the CMPE, was familial attendance, consisting of 'friendly parents and their children, brothers, sisters, [and] children with elderly mothers'.[102]

## Conclusion

Subaruza's career as a 'chosen' theatre ended on a sour note. Three years after its debut, the theatre abruptly lost its ties with the CMPE. At least two reasons account for this break-up. The first was over-ambition. Emboldened by the success of Subaruza (as well as its other theatres), Subaru Enterprises decided to extend its operations across a variety of projects. In addition to the three theatres in Marunouchi, the company acquired two other movie houses – one in Kyoto and the other in Osaka – and invested in a seaside bathing resort, a tennis club and an amusement park. This excessive investment, coupled with inexperience in the movie business, drove the company into debt. By late 1949, it temporarily lost its ownership of Subaruza and was forced to dismiss a quarter of its employees.[103]

The second reason was competition. The growth of the theatre enterprise during the occupation years prompted the appearance of new, attractive movie-houses that soon threatened Subaruza's status in the business. By the autumn of 1949, a manager of Subaru Enterprises admitted that their business had become 'even more challenging' because of competition from theatres with good facilities.[104] Subaruza was also unable to monopolise its roadshow status for long. Some of the larger and well-equipped theatres in Tokyo, such as the Yurakuza, Marunouchi Piccadilly, Shinjuku Hikariza and the 1,730-seat Hibiya Eiga Gekijo, were soon able to boast roadshow releases of European or American films. As a result, Subaruza's novelty value diminished as time passed. The CMPE turned to other, more attractive outlets in pursuit of profits and prosperity.[105]

The end came abruptly in 9 December 1949, when the CMPE announced its decision to discontinue ties with Subaru Enterprises.[106] Starting on New Year's Day 1950, the theatre adopted a new strategy for survival as an exhibitor of European films.[107] It managed to stay in business for three more years, until a mysterious fire broke out in the auditorium during a screening of *War of the Worlds*. The theatre burned to the ground (leaving some to wonder if the Martians were responsible). Die-hard fans of Subaruza would have to wait another thirteen years until the theatre celebrated a modest reopening in a subterranean space of the Yurakucho building.[108]

In conclusion, Subaruza's first three years offer an insight into the business strategies that a new exhibitor employed to survive in a competitive theatre business. As a 'chosen' theatre with favourable working relations with the CMPE, Subaruza flourished as an exhibitor of Hollywood's prestige films. What served to distinguish it even more were the various off-screen tactics it employed to elevate the quality of film presentation. In addition to presenting its films under a roadshow format, Subaruza published flamboyant programmes, adopted a deliberate strategy aimed at dignifying theatre space and organised special events to attract the Japanese elites. Through such efforts to amplify the prestige value of the on-screen narratives, the theatre strove to construct a patronage from a wide body of moviegoers in the 'educated mainstream': office workers, students and public officials; Tokyo-ites and out-of-towners; men, women and couples; and, last but not least, families and middle-aged patrons.

Subaruza's rigorous endeavours challenge the notion that the American film programme in occupied Japan was a 'forced Americanisation'. While initiated by SCAP, Hollywood and the US government, this massive cinematic campaign was not a process just imposed 'from above'. In the process of reaching the Japanese filmgoer, various local agents actively consumed, appropriated and reinvented Hollywood entertainment in ways that facilitated its penetration across the war-shattered nation. The case of Subaruza offers insight into the active agency of Japanese film exhibitors and the unique way in which Hollywood cinema was presented and promoted to the Japanese consumer. The early history of this new theatre exemplifies one way in which Hollywood entertainment was at times constructed 'from below'.

## Notes

1  An earlier version of this paper was presented at the 'Cinema and Everyday Life' workshop at the Society for Cinema Studies Annual Conference, Washington, DC, 26 May 2001. I wish to thank Robert C. Allen, Richard Maltby and Melvyn Stokes for welcoming me to join the session. I am also grateful to Greg Bond, Fujiki Hideaki, David Herzberg, Ishii Yosuke, Makino Mamoru, Mike Rawson, Togawa Naoki, Julia Thomas, Chris Wells and Yamada Noboru for their input and research assistance. Special thanks to Asaoka Hiroshi and Ishikawa Hatsutaro, two former employees at Subaru Enterprises. Japanese primary sources used in this chapter, unless otherwise noted, were gathered at the University of Maryland-College Park (Gordon Prange Collection), National Diet Library, and major university libraries in Tokyo. In this chapter, Japanese names, except for those whose works are authored in English, are presented with family name first. All translations from Japanese are my own.

2  *The Hollywood Reporter*, 10 July 1947, p. 15.

3  *Variety*, 21 November 1951, p. 3.

4  For an in-depth examination of Hollywood's trans-Pacific trade during the occupation, see Hiroshi Kitamura, 'Globalising Entertainment: Hollywood and the Cultural Reconstruction of Defeated Japan, 1945–1952', (PhD dissertation, University of Wisconsin-Madison, 2004). See also the following Japanese-language study: Tanikawa Takeshi, *Amerika Eiga to Senryo Seisaku* (Kyoto: Kyoto University Press, 2002).

5  There are some useful studies of film exhibition in Japan (in Japanese), however. See Fujioka Atsuhiro, 'Kyoto Nishijin Chiku Eigakan no Hensen', *CineMagaziNet!*, 4 (8 September 2000), http://www.cmn.hs.h.kyoto-u.ac.jp/CMN4/FUJIOKA/nishijin.html; Fujioka, 'Nyusu Eigakan "Tanjoki" no Kogyo to Sono Kino', *Eizogaku*, 68, 2002, pp. 28–46; Hase Masato, 'Kenetsu no Tanjo: Taisho Ki no Keisatsu to Katsudo Shashin', *Eizogaku*, 53, 1994, pp. 124–38; Kato Mikiro, 'Eigakan to Kankyaku no Rekishi: EigaToshi Kyoto No Sengo', *Eizogaku*, 55, 1995, pp. 44–58. An English version of Kato's article, 'A History of Movie Theatres and Audiences in Postwar Kyoto, the Capital of Japanese Cinema', is available on-line at *CineMagaziNet!*, 1 (autumn 1996), http://www.cmn.hs.h.kyoto-u.ac.jp/NO1/SUBJECT1/KYOTO.HTM.

6 Thomas Guback, *The International Film Industry: Western Europe and America since 1945* (Bloomington and London: Indiana University Press, 1969). Some notable works on the Euro-American film trade include Heide Fehrenbach, *Cinema in Democratizing Germany: Reconstructing National Identity after Hitler* (Chapel Hill: University of North Carolina Press, 1995), pp. 51–91; Andrew Higson and Richard Maltby (eds), *'Film Europe' and 'Film America': Cinema, Commerce and Cultural Exchange, 1920–1939* (Exeter: University of Exeter Press, 1999); Ian Jarvie, *Hollywood's Overseas Campaign: The North Atlantic Film Trade, 1920–1950* (New York and Cambridge: Cambridge University Press, 1992); Paul Swann, *The Hollywood Feature Film in Postwar Britain* (London and Sydney: Croom Helm, 1987); John Trumpbour, *Selling Hollywood to the World: US and European Struggles for Mastery of the Global Film Industry, 1920–1950* (Cambridge: Cambridge University Press, 2002); Jens Ulff-Møller, *Hollywood's Film Wars with France: Film-Trade Diplomacy and the Emergence of the French Film Quota Policy* (Rochester, NY: University of Rochester Press, 2001); Ruth Vasey, *The World According to Hollywood* (Madison: University of Wisconsin Press, 1997). Key overviews include Toby Miller, Nitin Govil, John McMurria and Richard Maxwell, *Global Hollywood* (London: BFI, 2001); Kerry Segrave, *American Films Abroad: Hollywood's Domination of the World's Movie Screens* (Jefferson, NC: McFarland & Company, Inc., 1997); Kristin Thompson, *Exporting Entertainment: America in the World Film Market 1907–1934* (London: BFI, 1985).

7 On Japan's growing significance to Hollywood's international trade in the post-World War II decades, see, for example, Toby Miller, 'Hollywood and the World', in John Hill and Pamela Church Gibson (eds), *American Cinema and Hollywood: Critical Approaches* (Oxford: Oxford University Press, 2000), p. 147; Segrave, *American Films Abroad*, pp. 214–15, 254–5, 289–90.

8 Robert C. Allen, 'From Exhibition to Reception: Reflections on the Audience in Film History', Annette Kuhn and Jackie Stacey (eds), *Screen Histories: A Screen Reader* (Oxford: Oxford University Press, 1998), p. 15.

9 *Nihon Bunka Tsushin*, 24 April 1947, p. 3.

10 *MPEA News*, 15, December 1947, p. 4; *MPEA News*, 13, October 1947, p. 1. The publication dates of *MPEA News* are approximate.

11 Kodama Kazuo, 'Natsukashi no Subaruza', *Subaruza no Ayumi: 40 Nen Shi* (Tokyo: Subaru Enterprises, 1986), p. 22.

12 John Dower, *Embracing Defeat: Japan in the Wake of World War II* (New York: W. W. Norton and the New Press, 1999), esp. pp. 24–5. Also see Sodei Rinjiro, *Senryo Shita Mono Sareta Mono: Nichibei Kankei no Genten wo Kangaeru* (Tokyo: Simul Shuppan, 1986) and Kitamura, 'Globalising Entertainment'.

13 Standard works on this subject include: Dower, *Embracing Defeat*; Michael Schaller, *The American Occupation of Japan: The Origins of the Cold War in Asia* (New York: Oxford University Press, 1985); Takemae Eiji, *GHQ* (Tokyo: Iwanami Shoten, 1982).

14 Kyoko Hirano, *Mr Smith Goes to Tokyo: Japanese Cinema under the American Occupation, 1945–1952* (Washington, DC: Smithsonian Institute Press, 1992).

15 On the operation of the CMPE, see Kitamura, 'Globalising Entertainment'; Tanikawa, *Amerika Eiga to Senryo Seisaku*, pp. 265–386.

16 Subaru Enterprises, *Subaru Kogyo 50 Nen Shi* (Tokyo: Subaru Kogyo, 1997), p. 13.

17  *Kinema Junpo*, 1 (1 March 1946), p. 4.

18  Jiji Tsushinsha, (ed.), *Eiga Geino Nenkan 1947 Nen Ban*, (Tokyo: Jiji Tsushinsha, 1947) p. 57.

19  *Kinema Junpo*, 5, (10 August 1946), p. 41.

20  Civil Information and Education Section, 'Weekly Report', 15 June 1946, Box 5304, Folder 3, Supreme Commander for the Allied Powers Papers, Record Group 331, National Archives II, College Park (hereafter NAII).

21  Subaru Enterprises, *Subaru Kogyo 50 Nen Shi*, p. 139.

22  Ibid., pp. 139–40.

23  Ibid., p. 13; *Rengo Tsushin Eiga Geino Kaisetsu*, 11 January 1948, p. 1.

24  Subaru Enterprises, *Subaru Kogyo 50 Nen Shi*, pp. 16–17.

25  Ibid., pp. 12–15.

26  *Sentoraru Nyusu*, 4 (January 1947), p. 1.

27  Originally, roadshowing signified a mode of distribution practiced in the United States since the 1910s. Under this method, the producer or importer would book a theatre on a percentage-of-gross basis, and run the exhibition of a given film. See Tino Balio (ed.), *The American Film Industry* (Madison: rev. edn, University of Wisconsin Press, 1986), p. 111. For a useful overview of the roadshow system in Japan, see a special forum titled 'Rodosho no Kenkyu', *Kinema Junpo,* 126 (15 August 1955), pp. 39–47.

28  Tino Balio, *Grand Design: Hollywood as a Modern Business Enterprise, 1930–1939* (Berkeley: University of California Press, 1993), p. 210.

29  According to *Kinema Junpo*, Hibiya Eiga Gekijo in Tokyo ran an *ad hoc* roadshow screening of *Tales of Manhattan* in August 1946. See *Kinema Junpo*, 8 (10 November 1946), p. 41.

30  Subaru Enterprises, *Subaruza no Ayumi*, pp. 83–4.

31  Ishikawa Toshishige, 'Rodosho no Igi to Sono Genjitsu', *Kinema Junpo,* 126 (15 August 1955), p. 39.

32  Murai Seiichi, 'Subaruza no Omoide', ibid., p. 40.

33  *Subaru Theatre News*, 8 (*Gaslight*, 3 June 1947); 'Subaru Kogyo no Seisaku wo Nozoku', *Eiga Engeki Shinbun*, March 1947, p. 6.

34  *Kinema Junpo*, 12 (1 April 1947), p. 37.

35  *Nihon Bunka Tsushin*, 10 February 1947, pp. 2–3. Also see *Kogyo Taimusu*, 14 February 1947, p. 6, in Box 8662, Folder 26, NAII.

36  *Kinema Junpo*, 12 (1 April 1947), p. 37.

37  *Nihon Bunka Tsushin*, 27 March 1947, p. 3.

38  *Zenkoku Eigakan Shinbun*, 15 October 1947, p. 2.

39  *Nihon Bunka Tsushin*, 4 August 1947, p. 1; *Rengo Tsushin*, 27 November 1948, p. 3.

40  On a history of movie programmes in Japan see Makino Mamoru, ' "Bunka Toshiteno Eiga no Dokyumenteshon": Bunken, Posuta, Puromaido Nado', in Kawasai Shimin Myujiamu (ed.), *Eiga Seitan 100nen Hakurankai* (Tokyo: Kinema Junpo Sha, 1995), esp. pp. 138–41.

41  *Subaru Theatre News*, 7 (*Rhapsody in Blue*, 25 March 1947), pp. 1–11, 14–16.

42  *Subaru Theatre News*, 21 (*Old Acquaintance,* 7 December 1948), pp. 6–11.

43  *Subaru Theatre News*, 27 (*The Long Voyage Home*, 20 May 1949), p. 13.

44  *Subaru Theatre News*, 17 (*The Best Years of Our Lives*, 1 June 1948), pp. 23, 29, 31.

45  Robert and Helen Lynd, *Middletown: A Study in American Culture* (New York: Harcourt Brace, 1929).

46  *Subaru Theatre News*, 17 (*The Best Years of Our Lives*, 1 June 1948), pp. 35–7.

47  *Nihon Bunka Tsushin*, 24 April 1947, p. 3.

48  *Asahi Shinbun*, 28 December 1946, p. 3; *Kinema Junpo*, 11 (1 March 1947), p. 36.

49  *Yomiuri Shinbun*, 30 December 1946, p. 2.

50  *Kinema Junpo Gyokai Tokuho*, 11 June 1949, p. 2.

51  Interview with Asaoka, 3 September 2000.

52  *Subaru Theatre News*, 8 (*Gaslight*, 3 June 1947). Also see *Zenkoku Eigakan Shinbun*, 15 August 1947, p. 2.

53  Interview with Ishikawa, 19 November 1999.

54  Interview with Asaoka, 3 September 2000; *MPEA News*, 28 (February 1949), p. 1.

55  See, for example, *Subaru Theatre News*, 8 (*Gaslight*, 3 June 1947), p. 32.

56  Ibid.

57  *Sentoraru Nyusu*, 5, February 1947, p. 4.

58  Ibid.

59  Interview with Togawa Naoki, 29 November 1999, Tokyo, Japan.

60  *Nihon Bunka Tsushin*, 14 March 1947, p. 2; *Sentoraru Nyusu*, 6 (April 1947), p. 1.

61  *Kinema Junpo*, 12 (1 April 1947), p. 37.

62  *MPEA News*, 10 (August 1947), p. 1.

63  Hiroshi Kitamura, 'Embracing Hollywood: Tomo no Kai and the Rebirth of American Movie Fandom in Defeated Japan 1947–1951', paper presented at 'American Cinema and Everyday Life' Conference, 26–8 June 2003, University College London.

64  *Amerika Eiga Bunka*, 1 (1 October 1947), pp. 1–2.

65  Ibid., p. 1.

66  *MPEA News*, 50 (November 1950), p. 1; *Amerika Eiga Bunka*, 1, p. 2.

67  Subaru Enterprises, for example, posted a block ad in the inaugural issue of *America Eiga Bunka*, AMCA's newsletter, to congratulate the founding of this fan organisation. See ibid., p. 1.

68  *Subaru Theatre News*, 9 (*Random Harvest*, 29 July 1949), p. 21; *Subaru Theatre News*, 12 (*The Lost Weekend*, 1 January 1948), p. 36.

69  *Subaru Theatre News*, 28 (*The Yearling*, 14 June 1949), pp. 24–6.

70  *Subaru Theatre News*, 12 (*The Lost Weekend*, 1 January 1948), pp. 29–35.

71  *Amerika Eiga Bunka*, 3 (1 December 1947), p. 2.

72  Interview with Asaoka, 2 October 2000. Shikiba had already contributed essays to *Subaru Theatre News*.

73  *MPEA News*, 17 (February 1948), p. 4.

74  Ibid., 18 (April 1948), p. 3.

75  See, for example, Hayashi Tadahiko, *Kasutori Jidai: Renzu ga Mita Showa 20 Nendai Tokyo* (Tokyo: Asahi Shinbun Sha, 1987), pp. 162–3.

76  *Zenkoku Eigakan Shinbun*, 1 April 1948, p. 3.

77  See, for example, *Nihon Bunka Tsushin*, 28 April, 1947, p. 4; *Nihon Bunka Tsushin*, 27 March 1947, p. 3; *Nihon Bunka Tsushin*, 21 April 1947, p. 1; *Zenkoku Eigakan Shinbun*, 1 February 1949, p. 2.

78  On Ginza's pre-World War II prosperity, see, for example, Yoshimi Shunya, *Tokyo no Doramaturugi: Tokyo Sakariba no Rekishi* (Tokyo: Kobundo, 1987) pp. 219–61.

79 The data is derived from 1950. See *Kinema Junpo*, new edn 4 (1 December 1950), p. 28.

80 On the Ernie Pyle theatre, see Saito Ren, *Maboroshi no Gekijo, Ani Pairu* (Tokyo: Shincho Shuppan, 1986).

81 *Nihon Bunka Tsushin*, 10 February 1947, pp. 2–3. According to *Kinema Junpo Gyokai Tokuho*, about 80 per cent of evening audiences were commuters to the area. 11 November 1947, p. 2. Also see *Kinema Junpo*, 64 (15 August 1949), p. 40.

82 See audience survey on *Kinema Junpo*, 67 (1 October 1949), pp. 24–5.

83 *Nihon Bunka Tsushin*, 27 March 1947, p. 3.

84 *MPEA News*, 16 (January 1948), p. 1.

85 *Eiga Bunka Tsushin*, 26 August 1947, p. 3; *Nihon Bunka Tsushin*, 27 March 1947, p. 3.

86 Subaruza did not retain this privilege for long, however. In November 1947, the Shinjuka Hikariza, a rival theatre in the Shinjuku area, became the second roadshow theatre that specialised in Hollywood feature films. See *MPEA News*, 14 (November 1947), p. 1.

87 *Kinema Junpo Gyokai Tokuho*, 21 September 1948, pp. 2–3.

88 *Eiga no Tomo*, May 1949, p. 24.

89 *Eiga Engeki Shinbun*, March 1947, p. 6; *Nihon Bunka Tsushin*, 26 August 1947, p. 3; *Nihon Bunka Tsushin*, 26 December 1947 p. 1.

90 On the 'woman's picture', see Balio, *Grand Design*, pp. 235–55.

91 *Subaru Theatre News*, 20 (*Mrs Parkington*, 16 November 1948), pp. 14 , 16; *Subaru Theatre News*, 2 (*The Yearling*, 14 June 1949), p. 29; *Subaru Theatre News*, 27 (*The Long Voyage Home*, 20 May 1949), p. 33; *Subaru Theatre News*, 25 (*Waterloo Bridge*, 22 March 1949), p. 29.

92 *Junkan Amerika Eiga*, 31 (1 August 1949), pp. 1–2; *Junkan Amerika Eiga*, 30 (1 July 1949), p. 4.

93 *MPEA News*, 17 (February 1948), p. 1.

94 According to Hori Hikari's findings, women went to the movies either alone or with (female) friends, whereas male audiences tended to prefer moviegoing solo. Hori, 'Eiga wo Mirukoto to Katarukoto: Mizoguchi Kenji, *Yoru no Onnatachi* wo Meguru Hihyo, Jenda, Kankyaku', *Eizogaku* 68 (2002), p. 56.

95 On the occupiers' fraternisation with Japanese women, see Dower, *Embracing Defeat*, pp. 123–38. On the changing customs of dating, see, for example, Tsurumi Shunsuke *Sengo Nihon no Taishu Bunkashi 1945–1980* (Tokyo: Iwanami Shoten, 1991), p. 23.

96 Hirosawa Ei, *Kurokami to Kesho no Showashi* (Tokyo: Iwanami Shoten, 1993), pp. 200–19.

97 'Romance seats' were first implemented at Osaka Subaruza, another theatre owned by Subaru Enterprises. These seats first appeared at Marunouchi Subaruza on 18 November 1947. See *Zenkoku Eigakan Shinbun*, 1 November 1947, p. 2; *Subaru Theatre News*, 11 (*All This and Heaven Too*, 1 November 1947), p. 32. On popular response to romance seats, see, for example, *America Eiga Monogatari*, July 1949; *Kindai Eiga*, 4 (8 August 1948), p. 11.

98 Subaru Enterprises, *Subaru Kogyo 50 Nen Shi*, p. 16.

99 *Nihon Bunka Tsushin*, 10 February 1947, p. 3; *Kinema Junpo Gyokai Tokuho*, 11 June 1949, p. 2.

100 *Subaru Theatre News* (*The Yearling*, 14 June 1949), p. 27.

101 *Nihon Bunka Tsushin*, 26 December 1947, p. 1.

102  *MPEA News*, 15 (December 1947), p. 4.

103  *Zenkoku Eigakan Shinbun*, 1 October 1949, p. 3.

104  *Kinema Junpo*, 65 (1 September 1949), p. 40.

105  *Zenkoku Eigakan Shinbun*, 11 July 1949, p. 2; *Kinema Junpo*, 52 (15 February 1949),
     p. 4. For more on Hibiya Eiga Gekijo, see *Kinema Junpo*, new edn, 4 (1 December
     1950), pp. 28–9.

106  Jiji Tsushin Sha (ed.), *Eiga Nenkan 1951* (Tokyo: Jiji Tsushin Sha, 1951), p. 56.

107  *Zenkoku Eigakan Shinbun*, 1 November 1949, pp. 2, 3; Jiji Tsushinsha, *Eiga Nenkan
     1951*, p. 56.

108  Subaru Enterprises, *Subaruza no Ayumi*, p. 14.

# 7
# The Making of Our America: Hollywood in a Turkish Context

Nezih Erdogan

This chapter examines the ways in which American cinema was represented in Turkey in the 1940s and the evidence for the existence of a growing connection between American cinema and the popular Turkish imagination during this period. It is based on an analysis of the popular film magazines of the time, as well as the memoirs and observations of writers interested in cinema. Issues of audience demand, of course, pose questions about the cultural identities involved in the experiences of identification and fantasy enjoyed by the film viewer. After describing the historical context in which American cinematic hegemony was established, the chapter will consider some of the ways in which Hollywood itself functioned as a kind of fantasy screen for the Turkish viewer. It will also touch upon European cinema since – as becomes particularly clear in the memoirs of film historian Giovanni Scognamillo – the tension between America and Europe, and thus between Hollywood and European cinema, is crucial to the mental machinery at work in the viewers' cinematic experience in its broadest sense.

These changes paralleled a number of political and sociocultural changes in Turkish society. In the two centuries leading up to World War II, the ongoing attempts at westernising Turkey were modelled on European patterns and precedents. By the mid-1940s, however, Europe was in ruins. At least for the time being, it could no longer act as the object of fascinated desire it had previously been. The United States inherited this mantle. Now, to the consternation of many pro-Europeans, Americanisation added its own cultural contradictions to such westernisation.[1] As well as championing the values attached to freedom, it was more 'western' than any European country in terms of its wealth, technological prowess, and the scale of its cities (the year the war ended, a Chicago taxi driver proudly insisted on showing Falih Rifki, a Turkish journalist, the 'biggest' things in the world).[2] In the post-1945 era, Turks found their thinking having to change to accommodate the rise of US power and influence. Their new perceptions revolved around a political axis that opposed America to the Soviet Union and a cultural axis that opposed America to Europe.

Although Turkey had not herself entered World War II, she still suffered from the pressures, restrictions, shortages and other damages it caused. This encouraged domestic social and political conflicts to rise to the surface. The western-oriented government found itself simultaneously under pressure from a nationalist movement with racist tendencies, an anti-western religious fundamentalist movement, and a left-wing movement based on an anti-imperialist discourse. These movements were treated by the

Turkish government in a manner that was simultaneously very delicate, in order not to upset western allies, and very harsh. The leftist movement, in particular, was closely monitored and mercilessly repressed. Conservative Turkish governments were determined to ensure that Turkey herself opposed communism and remained part of the free world. In his book, *My Silent War*, Soviet agent Kim Philby recalls how in the mid-1940s Turkey was considered the first point of resistance against the Soviet Union in terms of a global war.[3] The paranoia of the post-war years forced the West to try to defend Turkey against the threat from its old enemy, Russia, but during Philby's stay in Turkey (from 1946 to 1949), the United States took over this responsibility from the British.[4] David J. Alvarez notes that Americans saw Turkey as an indispensable ally, because

> policy-makers had decided that the independence of Turkey was vital to the security of the United States. They had concluded that the Soviet Union threatened that independence. Now they had committed America to assisting Turkey with arms and money, preferably through Great Britain but unilaterally if necessary.[5]

This beginning of a new alliance between two countries which did not really share any history together was symbolised by the visit of the American battleship *Missouri* in 1946, bringing home the body of the late Munir Ertegun, the Turkish Ambassador to the United States.[6] The appearance of the *Missouri* might stand as a metaphor for the entrance of 'America' into Turkish life, and the most crucial steps in the development of Turkey's political and economic relations with the US were taken immediately after its arrival.[7]

## Early Patterns of Movie Distribution in Turkey

The Turkish intelligentsia had sought to sponsor westernisation for many decades, in the process encouraging a eurocentric discourse. The introduction of cinema in Turkey immediately after the first screenings in Europe constituted a new space for this discourse. From the beginning, going to the movies was itself regarded as a western ritual. Sigmund Weinberg, a Polish Jew, arranged the first regular public screenings in Pera (now Beyoglu), a district of Istanbul where non-Muslim minorities had already adopted a much-envied western lifestyle.[8] A great majority of early theatre managers belonged to minority groups, or to use the specific term, *levantens*. The European films they exhibited were intended to appeal to upper-class Turkish intellectuals as well as to the non-Muslim minorities of Pera, who spoke a variety of languages including Greek, Armenian, Hebrew, French, Italian and Spanish. Thanks to their special schooling, religious upbringing and their contacts in Europe, these managers had developed decidedly European tastes. The films they showed presented 'glamorous' scenes from various parts of Europe. One of the first screenings, for example, announced that it would make available 'For the first time in Istanbul (Constantinople), the magnificent and awesome show which brings in the whole of Paris'.[9] The audience was able to have access to these films almost immediately after they were produced. By offering virtual travel to Turkish audiences, early cinema represented a kind of visual colonialism. It implied a sort of double articulation: the Turkish audience could not only 'travel' around Europe while sitting in a movie-theatre, but could also travel around the movie-theatres of the whole of Europe in a fantasy of westernisation. It was now possible to see the world from where the European viewer stood ('I am watching a film which the European viewer has also seen').

The first film companies to sell films in Istanbul were Lumière, Pathé, Gaumont and Ciné Theatrale d'Orient. After the pioneering activities of the Lumière brothers, Pathé authorised Sigmund Weinberg to distribute and exhibit their films in 1908, and the rest then followed. Consequently, early cinema in Turkey was predominantly French. Most of the first film magazines were bilingual – *Opera-Ciné, Le Courrier du cinéma, Artistic-Ciné, Ciné-Turc, Le Film* and *Ekran* – and, next to Turkish or Ottoman, French was the necessary language of cinephilia. The movie-theatres, many of them part of a chain, followed the same pattern until the 1930s: Ciné-Palace, Orientaux, Central, Parlant, Gaumont, Artistic and Pathé. American films were also shown from a comparatively early stage. According to film historian Giovanni Scognamillo, the film magazine *Musavver Türk Sinemasi* made reference during the 1920s to companies such as Kemal Film, Opera Film and Fanamet Films Ltd, which were already importing films from Universal, United Artists, Paramount, First National and M-G-M.[10] Theatre owners or managers had to provide a French title for American films, which were usually dubbed into French and subtitled in Turkish, or else subtitled in both French and Turkish. This continued until the 1950s, when Turkey began to enjoy closer cultural and economic/political relations with the US, including assistance from the Marshall Plan.[11]

The mid-1940s saw American cinema establishing its hegemony in Turkey. After war broke out in 1939, American films had gradually come to dominate the market, not only because of the crisis in the European film industries and difficulties in distribution, but also as a result of the rising popularity of the films themselves amongst Turkish audiences. Scognamillo comments that even though Turkish audiences were able to see some German UFA productions, French Vichy films, and also became acquainted with Hungarian cinema and liked it, Hollywood soon began to rule in the film market. The Turkish audience, he argues, wanted 'action, wealth, spectacularity and glamour . . . excitement and emotion. They want dreams and they pay to have their dreams.'[12] Some theatre owners resisted this apparently growing American dominance by claiming that Italian movies (such as the melodramas of Amedeo Nazzari and Yvonne Sanson, together with the comedies of Toto), as well as British films (especially Arthur Rank productions) were also big box-office success. 'But it is American cinema after all', Scognamillo (himself a *levanten*) recalls:

> [that] comes up with innovations – or they polish the old ones and present them as
> new – it dazzles, it fills the people with awe . . . Marvellous are these American films,
> these Hollywood productions and they really add something to our view of the world,
> to our taste.[13]

By the 1940s the minority groups of Pera were no longer in a position to decide which films to import. Even with three expanding Turkish film companies, Ipek Film, Kemal Film and Lale Film, the increasing demand from Turkish audiences could only be met by American companies.[14] Under the studio system, they were able to produce far more films than their European competitors and it was American-produced films that met the requirements of popular taste. A synchronicity now emerged between the domination of Hollywood and the domination of popular taste. As Andrew Higson observes,

Hollywood is not only the most internationally powerful cinema – it has also, of course, for many years been an integral and naturalised part of the national culture, or the popular imagination, of most countries in which cinema is an established entertainment form.[15]

Hollywood itself presents a complicated Other to national cinemas – an Other that is both within and an alternative to national culture itself. Hollywood, of course, was not naturalised for European national cultures in the same way that it was naturalised for Turkish culture. Unlike European viewers of Hollywood, who were already westernised, Turkish viewers desired to achieve this condition. Hollywood's appeal to the Turkish viewer must in consequence be analysed in relation to specifically Turkish sociocultural and psychological dynamics, especially the roles played by identification and desire in forming Turkish identities.

## Identifcation and Desire in Turkish Popular Film Magazines

Twenty film magazines were published between 1943 and 1947. Although many of them were short-lived, the figure indicates an increasing demand for information about Hollywood. Several of these magazines added the word 'Hollywood' to their titles.[16] The editor of one new magazine, *Sinema Alemi*, explained its *raison d'être*:

> Masses line up in front of the movie theatres just as they do in front of bakeries. Children play 'cowboys' in the streets. The best children games borrow their themes from the silver screen. Once, Paris was the pioneer of fashion. Now fashion is by and large influenced by the silver screen, particularly by Hollywood. Why all this? This is why we are publishing this magazine – to answer this question.[17]

Almost all the magazines devoted most of their pages to Hollywood. Through publicity materials, gossip columns, glamour photos, reviews, interviews and letters, they participated energetically in the construction of an image of 'Hollywood' and along with it an image of the 'American way of life'. Typical titles of articles included 'Hollywood creates vogue', 'Stars learning languages', 'Waists get thinner' and 'Tips from stars'. Writers focused their attention on love, sex, marriage, success and consumption, taking their material from Hollywood film companies' publicity departments, American film magazines and Turkish journalists who were then living in the United States.[18] Such magazines gave little room to European cinemas. When a reader asked, for instance, for some information about what was going on in German cinema, the editor of *Holivut Dunyasi* (*The World of Hollywood*) answered that they were not able to receive any films even from Switzerland, which had not taken part in the war, let alone Germany. 'You would not want us to make up stories, would you?' he commented, perhaps facetiously. Obviously, European cinema was not able to exercise the same power of publicity as that generated by the efficient marketing machinery of Hollywood.[19]

Popular film magazines both encouraged and reflected a growing Turkish admiration for Hollywood stars. These magazines offered a reading of Hollywood that positioned the star at the centre and America (more properly, the 'American way of life') in the background. Richard Dyer sees stardom 'as a version of the American dream, organised around themes of consumption, success and ordinariness. Throughout, however, there is an undertow that, as it were, "sours" the dream. In addition, love, marriage and sex are constants of the image.'[20] Films themselves hold an off-centre position: references to films constitute a discourse that revolves around the star.

In February 1945, *Holivut Dunyasi* published a questionnaire, allegedly produced by an American studio, suggesting that 'if you can answer these questions, the doors of the studios can open for you'. It offers a fascinating and sometimes amusing view of how Turkish readers were invited to construct stardom. In reprinting (or, more probably, inventing) the questionnaire, the magazine's editors revealed a good deal about their own perceptions of stardom and personal beauty. The survey was split into three sections. The first, 'Beauty of Body', asked six questions:1. Do you have a beautiful face?; 2. Can you walk swiftly?; 3. Does your hair cover your temples?; 4. (to women) Do you have beautiful hands?; 5. Do you have a nice profile?; and 6. Is there an elegance in the way you sit in an armchair? The second, 'Personality', wanted to know five things: 1. (to women) Do men like you?; 2. (to men) Do women like you?; 3. Are you well educated?; 4. Are you knowledgeable?; and 5. What makes you distinct when you are among other people? In the third and final section, on 'Artistry', respondents were asked seven questions: 1. Are you clever?; 2. Can you understand immediately what you are told?; 3. Do you have a strong memory?; 4. Do you have an accent?; 5. Can you express your feelings easily and communicate them to others?; 6. Have you ever experienced a disastrous event?; and 7. Do you have a beautiful voice? To show how fascinating and at the same time illusory fantasies of personal stardom were, 15,000 people completed the survey – but only 300 were deemed to have 'passed'.[21]

Nine months later, Esther Williams ('Star of the Day') was 'quoted' as summarising the ten 'rules' of stardom. While some of these were obvious, even jejune, they also help underline the ways in which American stardom was constructed in order to fit prevailing Turkish ideas on beauty and desirability. A star, according to Williams, ought: 1. to be metropolitan; 2. to be the best; 3. to speak many languages; 4. to dance well; 5. to have a trained voice; 6. to have a distinguished look; 7. to have taste; 8. to be taller than 175 cm; 9. to be chic; and 10. to have luck.[22]

Two years earlier, Hikmet Feridun Es had profiled six Hollywood stars. The qualities he discerned amongst them also shed light on what personal qualities Turkish writers perceived as essential for stars to have:

Joan Crawford: luck, talent, persistence
Deanna Durbin: photogenic-ness, luck, charm
Jean Blondell: agility, dance, good body
Bette Grable: agility, dance, good body
Clark Gable: sincerity, culture, labour
Spencer Tracy: unlimited love, unlimited knowledge.[23]

All these suggestions for appearance, habits, attractions, skills, knowledge and physical accomplishments not only indicate how Hollywood stars were represented, but also give evidence of the emergence of a new discursive re-configuration of the Turkish body and social behaviour. This re-configuration provided a new set of values and standards (for example, to be sophisticatedly metropolitan) and, by drawing attention to the qualities of individual stars, also pointed to new possibilities for Turkish bodies which had never danced, spoken, acted or looked this 'American' way before.

The relationship of film and star is a problematic one. John Ellis suggests that the star image is paradoxically incomplete, relying for its completion on the filmic performance.[24] This raises the question of how the star-oriented discourse – for instance, interviews, backstage stories, gossip – should be weighed against the film performance. Of course, the star persona is not constructed on the basis of the performances of the star and the film alone; the extra-filmic discourse that is produced by the cinematic institution is additionally fed into the persona, always making it something more than the film itself. Therefore, a film performance must be perceived as containing extra-filmic elements as well. The star serves as an intermediary between the audience and the world that the extra-filmic elements construct. The presence of the star on the one hand helps give that world a unity and on the other hand regulates the desire of the audience. So far as Turkish audiences were concerned, the American dream to which Dyer refers would always be read specifically in terms of nationality. For American audiences, Lana Turner was a star, but for Turkish audiences she was an *American* star, an image which was not only articulated in the diegesis of whatever film she was making but also coalesced with the wider American dream Hollywood presented to all its spectators. As the surveys discussed above revealed, however, the 'America' that Turkish audiences saw and constructed was very much a product of their own imagination and desire. Rather than being a remote, abstract conception, it reflected Turkish values, in the sense that all this was aimed at an identity seeking to re-build itself in what it is not. To Turks, indeed, it was in the most literal sense 'our America'.

Wherever national culture has to articulate a difference and fantasy has to play on this difference, the distance between the object of desire and the subject must be continuously and carefully maintained and disavowed at the same time. America must neither be too close nor too remote. Hollywood presents a fantasy screen to Turkish audiences but it is important that the screen is kept at the right distance. In this case, the correct distance between the screen and the audience is maintained by the mental machinery of the cinematic institution. This becomes clear from the analysis of letters sent to the editors of Turkish movie magazines and the published responses. Generally, the letters themselves fall into two categories: requests (for a missing issue of the magazine or an autographed picture) and enquiries (for the birth date or the correspondence address of a star). One frequently asked question in the second category was 'How can I go to the States?' The magazines' responses were invariably discouraging:

> It is impossible to go to America right now. And even if it was possible I wouldn't advise you to do so. It would oblige you to speak a language and complete at least [an] intermediate education . . . Do not let yourself be deceived by dreams. The country needs young people . . . In previous issues, I dwelled on this frequently and some of my readers got mad at me for not having encouraged them . . .

> Even if you can go to the States, success is a matter of luck. And to say 'let me give it a try' equals saying 'let me throw myself to the abyss in the dark, maybe I will be saved'.

> You cannot go to Hollywood now . . . The present circumstances are not convenient for your ambitions.[25]

Almost everything else these magazines did negated this practical advice. Outside the correspondence columns, they continued to construct their highly appealing images of America.[26] Having first acknowledged an impossibility, they then posed it as an object of desire. The ambivalence is made even more evident in announcements of this type:

We are looking for a Betty! A Betty, but a Betty of beautiful Istanbul.

'A Hedy or a Clark – what is it that they've got and you do not?' Instead of dreaming of going to Hollywood to become a star and wasting time with this dull dream, shake up and show yourself! We are giving you the golden key to the doors of our studios.[27]

At the same time as these magazines denied the practicability of any Turk being able to go to America, they encouraged the democratic myth that anyone (even from Turkey) could succeed in becoming a Hollywood star.

Sanitised to some degree by distance, the magazines also dealt with issues such as the immorality of some stars' lifestyles. Such immorality would normally be condemned by Turkish social codes, but escaped such condemnation by being presented essentially as fantasy. According to one magazine in 1946:

If Hollywood were left free, it could have been a city where all moral values were abandoned and it might even have surpassed Sodom . . . An enormous income and a life exempt from authority were beginning to seduce the young beautiful girls, handsome young men and the clever businessmen of the land. Crazy meetings, which Americans call 'wild parties', were once very popular. These parties were so crazy that everyone felt free to do whatever he/she wished.[28]

'Enormous income', 'beautiful girls', 'young men', 'a life exempt from authority' and 'wild parties' created a series of fantasy images where everything was allowed.

Many of the male writers on the magazines were plainly fascinated by the issues of how important women were to American cinema and how they were presented in Hollywood films. As one noted, in the first issue of a new magazine:

Aren't vogue and luxury, that the woman loves most, already the two basic elements of the cinema? We see the cinema from her perspective, we see the vogue and luxury in the best possible way. And from the perspective of the film-maker, the woman is an important thing. Otherwise, the most beautiful women of the world would not have gathered in the well-known studios of the world. Is it possible not to envy our colleague Hikmet Feridun Es who is in Hollywood now? To live in the land of beauties, to be in such an atmosphere – even as a viewer; this is what everyone longs for. The woman and the cinema are one inseparable issue. No one can omit the woman from the cinema. If you do not put the woman into the cinema, neither the woman nor the cinema will have a meaning any more . . . In short, it is a must to believe in the force that attracts the woman to the cinema and to believe in the woman that attracts us to the cinema.[29]

Ironically, Hikmet Feridun Es, whom the writer envied for being a Turkish correspondent in Hollywood, later recalled a story that underlines the difference between the image and the reality of Hollywood. Invited to the wedding party of Bette Grable and Jackie Coogan, he was informed that many stars were going to be present. At the reception in a well-known hotel, he vainly looked for the famous people he expected to see. Finally, he spoke to the head waiter, who suggested that he had not recognised the stars themselves because, in person, they were 'less beautiful than their images in your mind'.[30]

Es's story does not undercut the spell of Hollywood. Instead, it stresses what may be seen as the cinema's capacity for producing glamour, transcending the difference between, for instance, Dorothy Lamour the person and the 'Dorothy Lamour' of the movies. What did such glamour itself mean to Turkish audiences? The magazine *Prenses (Princess)* published a letter to Ingrid Bergman from a youthful admirer. He had already asked his mother to get an autographed picture of Bergman in case she met her in America. When his mother returned with the picture (probably given by the studio?), he wrote a letter to Bergman not only to express his appreciation but also to disclose his love:

> I know you receive many letters every day. And I know that this letter will be opened by your secretary. But I also know that you are going to read this letter . . . I feel that with an intuition coming from the depths of my soul.
>
> Listen to me Ingrid . . . listen to me, I LOVE YOU MADLY.
>
> Do not let your wonderful lips allow a scorning smile . . . Ingrid, I have been loving you for years like crazy . . . Any reasonable person can argue that one cannot live with a dream in his mind. But . . . indeed . . . do you think I am an exception? . . . I have not ceased dreaming of you for a single moment, Ingrid![31]

By printing the letter, with its odd mixture of realism and unrequited passion, the magazine presented such behaviour as normal, perhaps even praiseworthy in terms of its emotional commitment to Bergman as a star.

Turkish male journalists who actually visited Hollywood frequently promoted the idea of 'Turkey' as a matter of curiosity and interest to Hollywood stars themselves. Necded F. Uran wrote for the long-established film magazine *Yildiz (Star)*. Uran was shown around the Warner Bros. studio by a Miss Sanchez, secretary to the head of Warners' International Department. During the course of this visit, they met Bette Davis, who was filming *The Corn is Green*. 'When Bette Davis learned that I was a Turkish journalist', Uran recalled, 'she smiled and motioned me to a seat. "Please, [I'll answer] anything you would like to ask . . . But let me add, I would like to know a few things about your country in return." '[32] Another writer, Ridvan Mentes, told how he danced with Maria Montez (though, this time, not in Hollywood but in the Hotel George V in Paris). As Mentes recalled:

> I was paralysed the moment I saw her. My mind was struck with amazement, only my heart began to pound violently. This mature and worldly wise lady, who understood the state I was in, kindly began to speak to me and ask questions. I was gradually feeling more relaxed. At one moment, she asked about my nationality. When I said that I was a Turk, there was an immediate sincerity in her looks and in the way she spoke . . . I shyly asked her to dance with me. She didn't refuse. When my arms got around her waist and

gently held her close to me, I realised that my legs were trembling. I was trying not to make the smallest mistake and the effort made me perspire. Today, when I remember this I cannot help laughing at my situation and smell the scent of that sweet memory.[33]

Although the first story lacks the erotic overtones of the second, both articulate nationality in terms of sexuality: the female star is interested in the male character when she learns that he is a Turk.

## Constructing Hollywood's 'Turkish' Star: The Case of Turhan Bey

The ways in which Turhan Bey, a 'Turkish' star in the Hollywood of the 1940s, was represented to Turkish audiences, shed considerable light on the manner in which film writers constructed a Turkish national identity in relation to Hollywood films. Turhan Gilbert Selahattin Sahultavy, son of a consultant to the Turkish ambassador and a Czechoslovakian mother, was born in Vienna in 1920. The family moved to Istanbul when he was a small child. When his parents split up in the 1930s, Turhan moved to the US with his mother and, after studying acting at Ben Bard's School of Dramatic Art and at the Pasadena Playhouse, he began a Hollywood career. Soon he became a popular leading man with his 'exotically handsome looks and well modulated voice'.[34] He starred in some exotic films, such as *Mummy's Tomb* (1942), *Arabian Nights* (1942), *Sudan* (1945), *A Night in Paradise* (1946*)*, *Out of the Blue* (1947), *The Amazing Mr X* (1948), *Song of India* (1949) and *Prisoners of Casbah* (1953). When his popularity diminished, perhaps due to the decline of the genre, he left Hollywood for Vienna to start a career in photography.[35]

After his films began to be distributed in Turkey in the mid-1940s, film magazines introduced Turhan Bey as the first and only Turkish star of Hollywood. He became a focus of attention. Readers demanded more information and the magazines were eager to print anything about him. American film companies apparently missed no opportunity to feed the Turkish press publicity. A letter sent by David Blum, the director of the News Service Department of M-G-M, to a popular Turkish film magazine reveals that the studio scanned the media carefully and compiled reviews and news about stars and then mailed them to magazines.[36] M-G-M had recently signed a contract with Turhan Bey and apparently launched a campaign to promote him. In the same issue of this magazine, there is another section devoted to Turhan Bey's life story, along with two photographs showing him with his mother in one, and with Maria Montez and two Turkish celebrities in the other.[37]

Turhan Bey was constructed in Turkish film periodicals as 'our man in Hollywood'. The magazines were careful to stress his origins and relate him to a national identity:

Particularly, *Dragon Seed* [M-G-M, 1944] [which] he created together with the great American drama actress Katharine Hepburn suffices to prove that he is going to be a most powerful and brilliant actor in the future. He has spent the first six months of his stay in America learning English. But he has remained faithful to his home country and told us that he would return to Turkey to establish the film industry after the war. Can there be any better news to delight us? Indeed, Turhan Bey has picked a very important issue for our country . . . It is impossible for us not to await his return to his homeland soon . . . It is the right of every Turk to be proud of Turhan Bey.[38]

Turkish journalist Falih Rifki met Turhan Bey in Hollywood. He had the impression that Bey did not look particularly Turkish, describing him as having a face which would best suit 'Chinese stories or 1001 Nights' tales, and also observed that he could not speak Turkish ('But I feel I live within it', Bey ingeniously asserted, and 'two months there would enable me to have good command of the language').[39] The crucial issue here is not whether or not Turhan Bey was Turkish, but the degree to which he was *constructed* as a Turk. The signifier 'Turk' had been attached to him to make him serve as an agent of fantasy as far as Hollywood and its independent-minded women were concerned. Turhan Bey himself played an active role in helping that construction. When asked by Falih Rifki what he thought about 'these Los Angeles marriages', he responded:

> Marrying in Los Angeles? But whose woman will your wife be in the morning and in the evening? If you want to get married, you bring your wife from Turkey and keep her in your home. A woman that you can possess.[40]

Turhan Bey's own affair with Lana Turner was widely known when this interview was conducted – he was referred to in gossip columns as 'Lana Turner's Shadow' and she was described (this time offering US readers their own quasi-orientalist fantasy) as the 'American harem girl'. When Turhan Bey was criticised by one reviewer, Turner herself sprang to his defence, calling the journalist and reproaching him for being unfair. 'I have not met anyone as gentle as Turhan Bey in Hollywood,' she claimed. 'I do not understand why you hate this young Turkish actor who comes from an untainted and noble family'.[41] Fantasy clearly allowed ambivalent situations. Turhan Bey was the fiancé of Lana Turner. He made friends with Maria Montez and other actresses. In other words, he had access to female Hollywood stars. Yet, some Turkish film writers observed, emphasising the gap between fantasy and 'reality', in the end he would probably not marry any of them, preferring a Turkish girl for that purpose. In his interviews, Turhan Bey played on the Turkish moral code when marriage was on the agenda. This made him a perfect object of identification for Turks themselves. A Turkish news report about the possibility of Turhan Bey coming to Turkey noted that:

> According to the recent American magazines Turhan Bey will be coming to Turkey to do his military service. Turhan Bey told the journalists that 'I cannot serve in the US Army, otherwise I will lose my Turkish nationality. And I cannot go to Turkey due to the difficulties of travelling. I am awaiting a permit for my departure.' The journalist continues: 'Everyone was expecting that Turhan Bey would be marrying Lana Turner next August. So what is going to become of them if he goes to Turkey?' Let us add something to this: 'So, what? She will pack and follow Turhan Bey to Turkey. And they will marry here.'[42]

Clearly, as far as Turkish movie writers were concerned, his affair with Lana Turner could only be socially affirmed and legitimated when she was not in Hollywood, but in Turkey. Fantasies were associated with Hollywood; the real was for Turkey and marriage, according to these writers, was no issue of fantasy. Although the magazines repeatedly announced that Turhan Bey would arrive at any moment in his 'homeland', by his own admission Hollywood's archetypal 'Turkish' actor never 'returned' to

Turkey.[43] His story, however, illustrates the ways in which Hollywood was made more 'accessible' by subjecting it to a degree of fictional 'Turkification': Turhan Bey himself helped to promote identification, while his (Turhan Bey, the Turk's) woman (in this case Lana Turner) served to encourage desire. Turhan Bey's absence from Turkey and presence in America created just the right geographical and psychological distance for Turkish viewers of Hollywood to both identify with and fantasise about him. It was this alternation between identification and fantasy on the part of such Turkish spectators generally, indeed, that allowed them to construct the idea of 'our' (Turkish) America.

## Notes

I wish to thank Peter Krämer and Lewis Johnson for their help.

1   Murat Belge, 'Turkiye'de Gunluk Hayat', *Cumhuriyet Donemi Turk Ansiklopedisi* (Istanbul: Iletisim, 1995), p. 863.

2   *Gezerek Gorduklerim* (Istanbul: Devlet Kitaplari, 1970), p. 251.

3   Kim Philby, *My Silent War* (London: Grafton, 1989), p. 198.

4   Ibid., p. 197.

5   David J. Alvarez, *Bureaucracy and Cold War Diplomacy: The United States and Turkey 1943–1946* (Thessaloniki: Institute for Balkan Research, 1980), p. 107.

6   Ibid., p. 110. Ertegun was the father of Ahmet Ertegun, the current head of Atlantic Records.

7   Nezih Erdogan and Dilek Kaya, 'Institutional Intervention in the Distribution and Exhibition of Hollywood Films in Turkey', *Historical Journal of Film, Radio and Television*, vol. 22, no. 1 (2002), p. 47.

8   Burcak Evren corrects a common mistake that it was a 'D. Hanri' (as indicated in an advertisement), who organised the first public screening in Sponeck, and not Sigmund Weinberg, but Weinberg contributed effectively to the promotion of cinema in Turkey by opening a Pathé office. Evren, *Sigmund Weinberg: Turkiye'ye Sinemayi Getiren Adam* (Istanbul: Milliyet, 1995), p. 74.

9   Ibid.

10  Giovanni Scognamillo, *Cadde-i Kebir'de Sinema* (Istanbul: Metis, 1991), p. 98.

11  Ahmet Gurata, 'Imitation of Life: Cross-cultural Reception and Remakes in Turkish Cinema', unpublished doctoral thesis, London Consortium/University of London, 2002.

12  Scognamillo, *Cadde-i Kebir'de Sinema*, pp. 67–77.

13  *Yesilcam'dan Once Yesilcam'dan Sonra* (Istanbul: Antrakt, 1996), p. 27.

14  Scognamillo, *Cadde-i Kebir'de Sinema*, p. 54.

15  Andrew Higson, 'The concept of national cinema', *Screen*, vol. 30, no. 4 (1989), p. 39.

16  Burcak Evren, *Baslangicindan Gunumuze Sinema Dergileri* (Istanbul: Korsan, 1993).

17  *Sinema Alemi*, vol. 1, no. 1 (1944), p. 3.

18  Apparently, some of them were university students who posed as professional journalists.

19  Scognamillo, *Cadde-i Kebir'de Sinema*, pp. 68–77.

20  Richard Dyer, *Stars* (London: BFI, 1986), p. 39.

21  'Acaba yildiz olabilir misiniz?', *Holivut Dunyasi*, no. 66 (February 1945), pp. 13–14.

22  *Holivut Dunyasi*, no. 94 (November 1945), p. 10.

23 Hikmet Feridun Es, *Hollywood'da 300 Gun* (Istanbul: publisher unknown, 1943), pp. 78–9.

24 John Ellis, *Visible Fictions* (London: Routledge and Kegan Paul, 1982), p. 93.

25 From the *Biz Bize* column of *Hollywood Dunyasi, passim*. The editor was anonymous.

26 Nilgun Abisel complains about this attitude in her *Turk Sinemasi Uzerine Yazilar* (Ankara: Imge, 1994), p. 41 n. 71.

27 *Salon-Hollywood Sesi*, no. 1 (November 1946), p. 25.

28 Sezai Solelli, *Yedigun*, no. 673 (27 January 1946), p. 12.

29 Selim Cavit Yazman, 'Kadinin Arkasindan Kostugu Seyler', *Yeni Holivut Magazin*, no. 1 (March 1948), p. 6.

30 *Hollywood'da 300 Gun*, p. 34.

31 Translated into Turkish by Prenses Melike Beyza, *Prenses*, vol. 1, no. 1 (August 1947), p. 7.

32 'Warner Bros.'ta neler gordum?', *Yildiz*, vol. 14, no. 157 (August 1945), p. 14.

33 'Maria Montez'le bir dans', *Prenses*, vol. 1, no. 1 (August 1947), p. 2.

34 Bill Tacacs (kinephile@aol.com), http://us.imdb.com/cache/person-all/a14415, accessed 22 December 1997.

35 Forty years later, he returned to America and made guest appearances in a number of television series, also acting in films such as *Skateboard Kid II* (1995) and *Virtual Combat* (1996).

36 'Our Weekly News Service has come across an interesting article about Turhan Bey, with whom our company has proudly signed a contract to accompany Katharine Hepburn with an admirable role in *Dragon's Seed*.

   I am enclosing this review with the hope that it will arouse your interest as well as those of your readers. Respectfully yours

   David Blum

   The Director of News Service, MGM'

   Turhan Bey 'in yukselisi', *Prenses*, vol. 1, no. 1 (August 1947), pp. 18–19. My translation endeavours to preserve the style of the Turkish version.

37 Perin (translating from the late Cevdet Erdem), 'Turhan Bey'i Takdim ederiz', ibid., p. 4.

38 Azmi Turhan, 'Turhan Bey', *Holivut Dunyasi*, no. 62 (January 1945), pp. 15–16.

39 *Gezerek Gorduklerim*, p. 236.

40 Ibid., pp. 242–3.

41 'Lana Turner Turhan Bey'in Avukati', *Yildiz*, vol. 13, no. 150 (May 1945), pp. 15–16.

42 'Turhan Bey Turkiye'ye Geliyor!', *Yildiz*, vol. 13, no. 155 (July 1945), p. 2.

43 Nezih Erdogan, 'Turhan Bey'i Takdim ederiz', *Geceyarisi Sinemasi*, no. 4 (spring, 1999), p. 42.

# 8
# Popular Films and Colonial Audiences in Central Africa*

Charles Ambler

During the 1940s and 1950s no visitor to the copper-mining cities of colonial Northern Rhodesia (Zambia) in central Africa could escape the visible marks of the impact of American films.[1] In the vast company compounds that housed African miners and their families on the Copperbelt, groups of African boys, 'dressed in home-made paper "chaps" and cowboy hats, and carrying crudely carved wooden pistols', were a ubiquitous presence running through the streets and alleys in endless games of cowboys and Indians. Others appeared 'more sinister . . . with a black mask over the eyes and a wooden dagger in the belt'. As they engaged in their mock battles, they could be heard shouting 'Jeke, Jeke', a local corruption of Jack, the universal term among urban moviegoers in the British central African colonies for the heroes of cowboy films.[2] In the same streets, young men often affected styles of dress that plainly showed the influence of Westerns and gangster films, wearing – amongst other things – ten-gallon hats and kerchiefs.[3]

This phenomenon of 'Copperbelt cowboys' and its manifestation in urban areas across much of British-ruled Africa vividly demonstrates the rapid and pervasive penetration of mythic Hollywood screen imagery into even remote corners of the Empire.[4] In the early 1950s, the industrial development of the Copperbelt and the concomitant creation of urban settlements was scarcely two decades old. Even those who regarded themselves as permanent town residents still had strong ties to the countryside.[5] Yet by the late 1930s, film shows, known locally as 'the bioscope', were a well-established feature of life in the copper-mining towns and company compounds. Thousands of women, men and children crowded into open-air cinemas each week to watch film programmes that mixed entertainment and current events;[6] and many young town-dwellers were avid bioscope fans, valuing films above all other forms of entertainment.[7]

The remarkable persistence of Copperbelt audiences in their affection for cowboy films and the styles drawn from them draws attention not only to the apparently inexorable dispersion of elements of western popular culture but also to the deeper processes of media globalisation.[8] This chapter takes up the history of film entertainment in Northern Rhodesia in order to explore the broad question of the transmission and reception of western mass culture in the context of colonialism. The story of movie-going in Northern

---

\* An earlier version of this chapter appeared in the *American Historical Review*, vol. 106 (February 2001), pp. 81–105. It appears here with the kind permission of the American Historical Association.

Rhodesia places in particularly sharp relief issues defining the movement and appropria-tion of media images as they travel across the boundaries of culture, ethnicity and race – in this case the profound economic and cultural chasm that separated African residents of the Copperbelt from the centres of media production in the United States and Britain.

The people who crowded into outdoor cinemas on the Copperbelt generally had lit-tle if any formal education. Few had travelled outside the territory. Most were little edu-cated in the symbols, customary behaviours and settings that contextualised these films for western audiences or even for relatively better-off and better-educated Africans across southern Africa. Certainly, few moviegoers had sufficient knowledge of collo-quial spoken American or British English to comprehend the dialogue – even if it had been audible in the noisy atmosphere that characterised these film shows.[9] In any case, censors had cut films shown on the Copperbelt to ensure that African audiences were not exposed to images or story lines that they imagined might inspire challenge to the white supremacist colonial order – a tall order given the violent rituals that character-ise the plot of a typical Western.[10] The resulting celluloid butchery apparently left more than a few movies devoid of discernable narrative. One official noted as late as 1956 that substantial cuts meant that 'many films which you may have seen are sadly lacking in continuity'.[11] The result was that most members of the audience could make little sense of film plot lines and consequently experienced these movies in quite different ways from moviegoers in North America. If censorship and noise obscured plots and dia-logue, what was it then that drew African filmgoers to Hollywood Westerns and how did these filmgoers comprehend or consume these films across the sharp cultural and class divide between film-maker and filmgoer?

Movies emerged as popular entertainment in Northern Rhodesia at the same time as social critics in the United States and western Europe began to give serious attention to the impact of films on 'impressionable' audiences – chiefly youths, immigrants and the urban poor. Scholars linked to the Frankfurt School argued that movies constituted a kind of trivial mass deception.[12] In more concrete terms, studies such as those financed by the Payne Fund accumulated data to document charges that movies encouraged anti-social behaviour among young people, sustaining debates about the impact of media that still thrive.[13] The rise of movie attendance in the 1930s inspired many white residents of the Copperbelt and more than a few prominent Africans to express similar concerns about what they saw as the negative and potentially dangerous effects of Hollywood's products on the impressionable African youths who festooned themselves in cowboy gear.[14] Because censors in both South Africa and Northern Rhodesia had already reviewed and often cut the films that were approved for African audiences, such worries were presumably exaggerated.[15] But if attempts to link filmgoing to criminality, sexual violence, a decline in deference and the erosion of traditional values strain cred-ulity, the popular passion for these films that persisted among urban youths for several decades was nevertheless a remarkable sign of the passionate engagement of urban audiences with films. Yet scholars have largely ignored the complicated interplay between African audiences and popular films.[16]

Equally, they have largely ignored the question of how colonised people interpreted the West through the prism of the popular Hollywood movies that drew them to thea-tres week after week.[17] Film scholarship has tended not only to dodge the issue of audi-ence response to popular cinema, but also has typically avoided sustained analysis of the characteristically cinematic elements of such films – the very elements that apparently drew residents of Northern Rhodesian towns into the theatres.[18] Instead, film scholars have most often 'read' films almost as conventional literary narratives – in effect as scripts disengaged from film images and techniques.[19] These readings embody a contradiction that links film scholars in an ironic intellectual alliance with those who demanded movie censorship. Both scholars and censors have confidently extracted the putative narrative meanings of films, largely ignoring the visual images that convey those narratives, while at the same time investing the film medium with transcendent didactic power rooted in those same dazzling visual qualities.[20]

Imperial propagandists likewise became convinced that films invested with appropriate narrative messages could bolster Empire loyalty and help promote colonial 'development' objectives. These films, though rather feeble, have nevertheless attracted considerably more interest from scholars than typical Hollywood fare.[21] Like most film studies, this scholarship generally incorporates a textual determinism that effectively marginalises the audience.[22] Yet in practice, and notwithstanding the best efforts of paternalistic imperial bureaucrats, African moviegoers generally had little patience with films on postal savings banks, 'Better Hides and Skins', and proper tooth-brushing procedures.[23] For them movies meant the bioscope – the high-action products of Hollywood dream factories.[24]

Empirical observations about the experience of watching movies in Northern Rhodesia converge persuasively with a new scholarship that argues for a radical rethinking of the complicated relationship between viewer and subject that would embed the reception of 'film texts' in specific historical circumstances. Locating the history of the bioscope in this way implies shifting the perspective from the films themselves, and the objectives of those controlling their distribution and exhibition, and instead focusing attention on audiences. Such an emphasis on spectatorship requires in turn exploring the 'cultures' of film viewing and extending the meanings of a film in networks of information transmission beyond the theatre. Cinema then becomes 'a particular public sphere . . . a space where viewing communities are constructed in a way that involves both acculturation to social ideals and the affirmation of marginality'.[25] This new literature on spectatorship, rooted in feminist scholarship, is strangely silent, however, on issues of race, culture and class.[26] The work that purports to explore the racial dimensions of spectatorship is in fact mostly concerned with isolating stereotypical imagery in films whose subject matter is identifiably race rather than reading the reception of mass-audience films in race- or culture-conscious terms.[27] Still, the impulse that has led scholars to feminist readings of audience engagement with horror films holds considerable promise for analysis of the often raucous outdoor film showings that were regular features of the urban landscape of Northern Rhodesia during the 1940s and 1950s.[28] Just as women and men may experience the apparently misogynist themes and images of horror movies in ways that confound confident assumptions, so too African audiences seem to have appropriated elements of Westerns and other action movies in ways that subverted the narrative and racially defined principles of censorship.

The recent and dramatic growth of the distribution of imported video cassettes across Africa has attracted a few scholars to the complex phenomenon of audience response to popular films.[29] Whether exploring the popularity of Indian movies among audiences in northern Nigeria or the appeal of romance films to secluded Muslim women on the

Kenya coast, this work focuses attention on the complicated processes through which films are seen across cultural divisions.[30] Likewise, audiences on the Copperbelt in the 1930s, 1940s and 1950s were by no means passive consumers of cinema. They absorbed exotic images and discussed the actions and motivations of characters, but they also appropriated and reinterpreted film images and action in their own terms. To the young women and men who flocked to film shows on the Copperbelt, the often disjointed and exotic images of the 'Wild West' that Hollywood films conveyed comprised a crucial repertoire of images through which to engage notions of modernity – a vital concern for residents of this industrial frontier.[31] In the networks of film distribution, the Northern Rhodesian mining district lay on the extreme margins, a distant outpost for a South African distributor.[32] The introduction and spread of film entertainment in Northern Rhodesia followed rapidly on the development of the copper mining industry in the late 1920s, as colonial officials and mine management sought to provide 'appropriate' leisure activities for an African work force that was for the most part unaccustomed to the temporal and spatial constraints of industrial employment. After the first public film showing in 1928, the bioscope spread steadily across the Copperbelt.[33] By the mid-1930s tens of thousands of Africans lived in municipal African townships and mining company residential compounds in the mining district, and cinema shows had become a commonplace feature of town life.[34] Throughout the early 1930s British and American silent films dominated screens, but by 1935 the paucity of silents in distribution had forced the mine companies to introduce sound.[35] World War II brought a rapid expansion of film showings across the British Empire under the aegis of the Colonial Film Unit, as imperial officials strove to mobilise support for the war effort.[36] In 1942, the Northern Rhodesia Information Service began a mobile cinema service in the countryside.[37] In 1944, when the African population of the entire territory numbered about 1.3 million, approximately 17,000 Africans saw films each week in the established municipal and mine-company cinemas; in addition, the mobile cinema van reached about 80,000 people during the year.[38] By 1947, the film library had expanded to 650 titles and six mobile units and fifteen outdoor theatres provided films to Africans in Northern Rhodesia. Seventeen private exhibitors also showed movies from time to time.[39] Thus, by the 1950s, a large segment of the African population in Northern Rhodesia had some knowledge and experience of films, and an established audience of filmgoers had emerged in towns.[40]

The government recognised the development of a local movie audience by launching a 'Northern Spotlight' 35-millimeter current events magazine series and by permitting the establishment of film societies and film showings in clubs.[41] These efforts to reach an influential segment of the African population coincided with the emergence of bitter opposition among Africans in Northern Rhodesia to the amalgamation of Northern and Southern Rhodesia and Nyasaland in a Central African Federation dominated by white settlers, and with a broader campaign by the mining companies and the state to nurture a privileged class of relatively well-paid and well-educated African workers.[42] Private movie-theatres in Northern Rhodesia, however, remained reserved for whites, and regulations thwarted even private showings of films for groups that included whites and Africans until all public facilities were desegregated in 1960 in anticipation of majority rule.[43]

The mythology of the birth of film celebrates stories of spectators screaming and running from auditoriums in terror at the destruction of the distinction between the real and imaginary that motion pictures putatively represented. Film historian Tom Gunning has argued that vivid and exaggerated early accounts, and the persistent theoretical assumptions drawn from these stories, have typically portrayed early film showings as the dramatic confrontations of naifs with a frightening unknown force, replicating 'a state usually attributed to savages in their primal encounter with the advanced technology of Western colonialists, howling and fleeing in impotent terror before the power of the machine'.[44] Gunning effectively situates these early film shows as a 'cinema of attractions' in a history of spectacle. He persuasively re-reads the myths of reactions to moving images of on-rushing trains 'allegorically rather than mythically', arguing that 'screams of terror and delight were well prepared for by both showmen and audience'.[45] Audiences in the mining compounds and at rural film shows experienced films in much the same way as European audiences at the turn of the century. The movies shown in Paris and New York at that time aimed to amaze – like the magic shows that preceded them – not to tell stories. By 1905, narrative films had entirely supplanted this early genre, but exported to Northern Rhodesia and shown in censored form, mainstream movies were often perceived viscerally as disconnected series of exotic, exciting and frighteningly pleasurable images and special effects. At film shows on the Copperbelt, the audience members continually engaged with the action: 'men, women, and children rose to their feet in excitement, bending forward and flexing their muscles with each blow the cowboys gave. The shouting could be heard several miles away'.[46] Accounts of film showings invariably emphasise the enthusiastic engagement of audiences, but they provide little evidence of the existence of 'primitive' machine terror.[47] African audiences may have had no specific experience of magic attractions, but they could nevertheless locate films in an indigenous tradition of plays and other kinds of performances and enjoy them in the context of a story-telling tradition that was by no means rooted in linear narrative.[48]

If audiences seem in fact to have rapidly accommodated film technology, colonial cinema policy remained rooted in deeply held assumptions about the powerful, emotional effect of films on Africans. Even as late as 1960, as the colonial government attempted against considerable settler resistance to engineer a transition to majority rule, many white colonial officials remained absolutely convinced of the continued need to censor films on a racial basis. When Harry Franklin, long-time Director of Information in Northern Rhodesia, had the temerity to argue that 'the idea that the white female leg or the safe blowing crackman shown on the screen encourages Africans more than any other people to immorality or crime is outmoded', the official reviewing the memorandum pencilled in defiantly, 'But it's still true'.[49]

Ironically, it was educated people, both European and African, rather than the mass African audience, who were most dazzled by the medium and convinced of its powerful potential for harm and good. As late as 1960, an African government official could still aggressively defend racial censorship in public testimony, citing the deleterious impact of 'scenes of crime or violence being shown to the unsophisticated, uneducated mass of the African people'. He went on to assert that:

> such films have an adverse effect emotionally . . . The primitive African is always being told of the advantages of assimilating Western Civilisation, but when he sees Europeans in a film indulging in sexual and criminal misbehavior doubts are raised in his mind.[50]

Even if in retrospect it seems laughable that the state would have found it necessary to protect African audiences from 'Fitness Wins the Game', or 'The Lavender Hill Mob',[51] the assumptions that sustained such actions and the criticisms of them inscribe critical debates about the relationship between the nature of film media on the one hand and on the other the evolution of class and race difference. Moreover, the practice of censorship had a direct, material effect on the actual experience of film attendance, while the ideas that shaped the practice provide an essential context for reading the accounts of African filmgoing – texts that were largely the product of white officials and observers and which often took the form of ritualised encounters of 'the primitive' and technology.[52] Thus, a white businessman proposing the establishment of commercial cinemas for Africans in the 1950s noted casually that 'from a health point of view' it was essential that such film shows be in the open air.[53] Similarly, a description of mobile cinema shows in Northern Rhodesia in 1950 contained the warning that 'on no account should an attempt be made to give a demonstration in a confined space unless the attendance can be effectively controlled. The larger the space the better.'[54] These concerns about space reveal plainly the danger that Europeans saw in film shows for Africans, where it was imagined emotional surges provoked by moving images might inspire irrational, immoral or criminal acts.[55]

From the very beginning of film showing in the early 1930s, government officials insisted on some form of race-defined censorship, and in the late 1930s, as the number of film showings increased quickly, they created a special board to censor films for African audiences.[56] The principles that governed the board's actions flowed from a number of sometimes contradictory understandings of the interplay between African audiences and film. Employers and many government officials held that only 'action' could hold the interest of African spectators and that settings and meaningful plot lines were often irrelevant.[57] Such officials regarded action movies as 'healthy amusement' for urban workers and could be contemptuous of those who saw the entire genre as lacking in value or even as dangerous.[58] In contrast, the activities of the Carnegie-funded Bantu Educational Cinema Experiment (BECE) and subsequent experiments with educational film were rooted in an opposing perspective.[59] As early as 1932, the report of an investigation of conditions on the Copperbelt sponsored by the International Missionary Council waxed rapturous on the possibilities that Soviet media campaigns had demonstrated for Christian education and development through film. Mesmerised by the power of film, and in particular the power of film over 'primitive' audiences, those involved in the BECE and its successors such as the Colonial Film Unit believed deeply in the educational and developmental potential of film and were profoundly disturbed by what they believed to be the economic and social consequences of the popularity of commercial movies.[60] During its brief existence between 1935 and 1937, the BECE concentrated on the production of didactic 'entertainment' films with local actors and settings that would be shown especially in rural areas in British east and central Africa.[61]

The development of programmes of educational film distribution in Northern Rhodesia and other British African colonies incorporated a distinctive imperial folk theory of African visual cognition that surfaced repeatedly in the pages of the official periodical, *Colonial Cinema*. An article published in 1943 emphasised that, to gain and maintain the attention of the African audience, a film-maker had to employ a 'technique which is skilfully related to the psychology of the African'. That meant that images had to be 'needle sharp' and subjects correspondingly straightforward. Above all it was critical that 'tricks' used in film-making to convey elapsed time or to shift scene be avoided:

> visual continuity from scene to scene should be sustained. Every new shot without a visual link with its predecessor starts another train of thought which may exclude everything that has gone before . . . To the illiterate such a technique leads to utter confusion; their minds are not sufficiently versatile to comprehend these swift and sudden changes.[62]

Similarly, films that framed a distance shot of a moving boat with a swaying tree branch closer up would supposedly confuse African filmgoers, who would focus on the moving branch rather than the boat.[63] Certainly, the BECE placed particular emphasis on the importance of using recognisable film settings and avoiding exotic locales, a perspective maintained by the officials of the Colonial Film Unit: 'Fun and games in the snow do not look so funny to an audience which thinks snow is sand and wonders how it sticks together'.[64] The enormous popularity of American Westerns – in which such techniques were commonplace – would seem effectively to dispose of these outlandish theories.[65] But perhaps not. The evaluation of the effects of film techniques invariably made narrative comprehension the measure of a movie's quality; but, in a cinema of attractions, individual sequences and powerful imagery supercede questions of narrative and continuity.

If whites in Northern Rhodesia debated the dangers and entertainment value of ordinary Hollywood fare, virtually all agreed that certain categories of films and film images were inappropriate for African viewing. While no statutory guidelines governed censorship decisions, the definition of what was suitable for African audiences remained quite consistent over time, although political concerns seem to have become more prominent after 1945.[66] Scenes 'invariably cut from films' in 1946 included women in swimsuits and other scanty attire, 'women of easy virtue, manhandling of women, prolonged embraces, fights between women, crimes readily understood by Africans [and] scenes of drunkenness'.[67] A list dating from 1951 included those same categories but stressed the censorship of scenes involving violence, laying special emphasis on those ritual scenes in which American Indians captured and tied up white pioneers. Objections were also raised to films including scenes of war atrocities, violent battles, arson, masked men, or rioting and demonstrations.[68] A 1956 summary of the Censorship Board's criteria for cutting or banning films also included 'deliberate murder, wanton killing and knife scenes', as well as any films 'with religious references which might be misunderstood and thereby reflect poorly on any church'.[69] By the mid-1950s, the Board reviewed as many as 200 films a year and cut scenes from perhaps half. A number of films were banned outright for African audiences.[70]

The public discourse on censorship imputed a powerful relationship between moving images of violence and sexuality and impulsive, aggressive and violent forms of behaviour on the part of male, working-class Africans. This preoccupation expressed itself especially in terms of the repression of black male sexuality and a defence of white womanhood. Any kind of display of white women's bodies or female sexuality, it was argued, undermined Africans' respect for white morality. One defender of tight censorship maintained that 'the safety of the [white] women and girls in Northern Rhodesia hangs upon their being respected by the Africans'.[71] Perhaps more to the point, the security of white male authority required that respect. Censorship was in fact defined essentially as a male domain. White women were included on the Censorship Board, beginning in the 1930s, but only reluctantly because it was difficult to find men with the spare time to devote to a task that – despite the rhetoric – was regarded as essentially frivolous. Moreover, officials privately argued that the presence of a woman member would 'disarm criticism' if any 'unpleasant crime by natives in this area should be attributed to anything seen on the films'.[72] The message was clear: this (male) official did not really believe that any such connection was likely to exist. The token female members of the Board were, meanwhile, tolerated as ineffectual observers of base imagery, as it was argued that they did not recognise scenes of 'rank indecency' readily identified by their male counterparts.[73] The all-white Board was very anxious, however, to include male African members, arguing that such men would bring a special insight into what was for many whites an unfathomable world of African taste.[74] By 1945, two of the ten unofficial Board members were Africans, whose perspectives differed little from 'moderate' white members in their concentration on the impact of film on urban youth.[75] Interestingly, none of the series of commissions appointed to investigate urban discontent and labour activism on the Copperbelt made mention of movies as a source of urban criminality or aspirations.[76]

Actions taken on which films to pass or ban often struck perplexed observers as arbitrary or even ludicrous. In the late 1950s, a letter to the governor on the subject questioned permitting distribution of *West of Zanzibar*, a film on the Indian Ocean slave trade which included a scene of African slaves throwing overboard 'slick Indian lawyers and a villainous Arab dhow captain', while at the same time the Board banned *Frontier Trail*, a Western that followed a 'half caste American Indian sneaking through the snows and conifers of Canada to ambush a posse of "Mounties".'[77] If the proposition that African audiences would be more likely to identify with a slave mutiny than American Indians defending their land seems obvious, the banning of *Frontier Trail* possessed a certain tortured logic in the provincial and racially charged context of Northern Rhodesian censorship: the Mounties were, after all, British Empire policeman, and they were white; the slavers were Arabs, and they were represented as criminals.[78]

White residents of the colony often emphasised the dangers they saw in exposing Africans to typical cowboy movies with their scenes of lawlessness and violence, including violence that pitted 'one bunch of Europeans against another'.[79] Some censors were even uneasy about films depicting combat during World War II or resistance to the Nazis.[80] A film such as *Town Meeting of the World* might be banned for the dangerous democratic and internationalist sentiments it was likely to convey, but much more threatening was the American Western that included a train hijacking and seizure of weapons – 'poisonous stuff' in Northern Rhodesia when increasingly bitter conflict over political power challenged the race hierarchy and threatened public order.[81] Many whites saw all popular films as intrinsically dangerous in that they eroded the fundamental culture of deference by encouraging 'the idea that to stand and speak to anyone with hands in pockets, lounging, and possibly giving the hat – firmly on the head – an insolent backward tilt is to show a high degree of sophistication'.[82]

In an interview conducted in 1990, South African actor John Kani described his childhood encounter with Hollywood films: 'Just to sit in this dark place, and magic takes place on the wall. For a moment, we forgot apartheid, we forgot there was another world that wasn't good, we sat there and were carried away by the dream of these American movies.'[83] As actor Djimon Hounsou from Benin has recently recalled, going to the movies in African cities differed strikingly from the experience in the United States or Europe. The film was usually a dated Western, but 'it was amazing . . . We'd climb the walls to get in, and you'd see people packed in . . . Here, people refuse to sit in the first row of the theatre. In Cotenou [Benin's capital] there were kids pressed up against the screen.'[84] Children in Ghanaian cities would pool their change to raise enough money to buy a single movie ticket for the one boy or girl who could be counted upon to absorb the film and describe in detail the hero's dress and gait and repeat his memorable phrases.[85] Elderly Zambian city-dwellers hold similar memories of escapist pleasure in their recollections of the bioscope. One African woman became particularly animated as she recounted hours spent watching Westerns. She did not care for the other important diversions that town life had offered her: she did not drink or attend dances, 'I only liked the bioscope. Horses, cowboys, big hats, America.'[86]

Film attendance in Northern Rhodesia grew rapidly during the 1940s – the same time that the movies reached their peak as an attraction in America and Britain. Many thousands of Africans were paying a small admission price to see films each week and with 'African cinemas well equipped and supervised, especially in the Copperbelt, a generation of regular "film fans" [was] in the making'.[87] The campaign of the various information arms of the British imperial state to develop a base of support for the war effort brought film to a much wider area of the country at the same time that the intensifying movement between rural home areas and urban industrial employment spread knowledge about the character of urban life and its amenities, such as cinema.[88] This was by no means, however, the same cinema that attracted many millions of patrons in Europe and the United States. Simple outdoor amphitheatres or mobile cinema vans or barges stood in for luxuriously appointed movie palaces. And whereas marquees and posters attracted spectators in America and Britain from shopping streets in urban business districts into an enclosed world, in Northern Rhodesia it was the setting up of apparatus and the gradual transition from dusk to dark that drew people into the film world. In both urban and rural areas until well into the 1950s, Africans saw movies almost exclusively out of doors. At the Roan Antelope Mine in the mid-1950s, 2,000 or more would gather for weekly film shows that were social events as much as entertainment.[89]

'At seven o'clock on a clear evening,' wrote anthropologist Hortense Powdermaker,

> adults and children lined up for their tickets – 'thruppence' (three pennies) for adults and a penny for children – at the large, unroofed white stone amphitheater connected with the mine Welfare Hall . . . As the theater began to fill up, friends greeted each other, some young men attempted to make assignations with young women, children jostled and pushed each other and were told to be quiet and to make way for their elders. There was a continuous hubbub. The large audience spilled over into the center aisle, sitting on the steps of the inclined floor. Late-comers stood by the walls. Talk, laughter, and a sense of expectation pervaded the theater.[90]

Cinema shows attracted mainly children and young adults, although older people were certainly found among the audiences. A survey of film attendance conducted on the Copperbelt in the 1950s suggests that a majority of town-dwellers attended movies at least occasionally, and that a sizeable minority went to film shows on a weekly basis. Males clearly predominated, but substantial numbers of young women were also dedicated moviegoers. Copperbelt residents with more education and better jobs were more likely to go to movies than their less-educated counterparts and probably more likely to be dedicated fans, but it was still working-class male youths with relatively little education who made up the core of film audiences.[91]

The programme typically began with 'The African Mirror', a magazine series that showed elements of African life such as first-aid teams at a mine, traditional dancing and commercial agriculture. This was followed by 'The Northern Spotlight', a Northern Rhodesian newsreel, and then British news. Animal cartoons, known as *kadoli* and favoured by small children, preceded the main feature, usually a dated or 'B' cowboy film or occasionally a *Superman* film. Although each week brought a new feature, the cheap Westerns that dominated film shows for three decades were generally instantly recognisable to audiences. In film after film, cowboy heroes faced brutish outlaws and badmen in a series of confrontations. Sometimes the hero himself was disguised as an outlaw, or the villain was a supposedly respectable citizen, or stereotypically bloodthirsty Indians were called upon to take to the warpath in opposition to the heroes. Although major Hollywood Westerns became increasingly complex and sophisticated during the 1940s, the B-movies that dominated the Copperbelt outdoor cinemas remained remarkably consistent, offering uninterrupted series of vignettes of fights, chases and horseback stunts.[92] By the time the chase was over and the hero victorious, it was 9.30pm, the show was over and the audience drifted home on foot and bicycles.[93]

Even as African audiences became more accustomed to film entertainment and some became regular moviegoers, the film experience in Northern Rhodesia still involved aspects of the wonder and amazement that were characteristic of first encounters with motion picture technology. The absurd imperial mythologies of natives struck dumb by moving images and disembodied voices emanating from black boxes may have been largely products of Europeans in the thrall of the medium, but film shows did provide novel and sometimes thrilling experiences as darkness fell and the images and sounds brought familiar scenes to the screens or exposed audiences to exotic, incomprehensible settings. Europeans argued that the lack of understanding of the technologies that produced these films meant that Africans regarded movies in the 'same category with the miracle of an airplane'.[94] But evidence of African audience behaviour reveals little sense of such mystery and alienation.

In the Roan Antelope mine compound in the early 1950s, 'going to the movies was a social experience . . . There was an excitement in being part of a movie audience of more than a thousand people, constantly commenting to each other, shouting their pleasure and booing their displeasure.'[95] In place of the regimented and reverential silence imposed on filmgoers in North America and Europe, African films shows were characterised by the noise, commentary and engagement typical of spectacles.[96] Scenes of mineworkers produced loud commentaries on the quality and energy of the workers; portrayals of 'traditional' dances led to debates on changing mores; a newsreel on Kenya produced discussion of mountains in the tropics and memories of war service; but the greatest and most enthusiastic involvement was reserved for the featured Western.[97] The dynamic of these film shows underscores Lawrence Levine's argument that, in nascent industrial communities, 'people enjoyed popular culture not as atomized beings vulnerable to an overpowering external force but as part of social groups in which they experienced the performance or with which they shared it after the fact'.[98] Although the characters and plots varied, Northern Rhodesian audiences always called the hero 'Jack'.[99] This convention, so at odds with American and British preoccupations with particular characters and the actors who portrayed them, reflects a deeper divide in film spectatorship.

African audiences in Northern Rhodesian for the most part seem to have ignored or dismissed plots, made murky in any case by the unfamiliar language or accents, the crowd noise and the censor's shears.[100] Moviegoers watched the films for the stock scenes that amused and delighted, in one form or another, in film after film: the characteristic stride, the fighting style, the memorable phrase. These elements were observed and appreciated according to well-defined standards of action taste, at least according to young male viewers. As one satisfied patron noted as a film came to an end, 'this is the kind of Jack we want'.[101] Although whites were often dismayed by films that portrayed hold-ups and murders, descriptions of film shows suggest that audiences viewed and appropriated elements of these in isolation from the narrative or plot. In a protest to the Northern Rhodesian Department of Information in the mid-1950s, one employer charged that showing cowboy action films was 'nothing less than criminal folly'. The concern was well placed in the sense that audiences focused on the scenes of stagecoach hold-ups and various murders in isolation, paying little attention to the fact that the heroes eventually brought the villains to justice: 'With two thirds of the cast galloping all over the place at breakneck speed . . . I can promise you', this critic wrote, 'that the plot was not understood by the audience. I have taken the trouble to make quite sure of this fact by questioning the one more intelligent individual, a bricklayer, who did attend. What *was understood*, was the fact that film portrayed utter lawless and indiscriminate use of revolvers and rifles.'[102] But it is equally clear from audience response that these scenes conveyed general styles of masculine bravado, rather than literal models of behaviour.[103]

Fight scenes drew especially favourable response, with one man describing how he liked 'to see cowboys run after one another on horses, and the fighting. Jack beats his friends skilfully, and it pleases me to see him plant blows on other men's faces'. Another liked 'best the cowboy films, because they teach us how to fight others and how to win lovers'. A young, educated man explained that he felt 'as if I am fighting. I always want to see how strong Jack is and whether he can be knocked out early. But I expect the hero, Jack to beat everyone and to win every time.'[104] Such reactions often perplexed whites. To a researcher in the 1950s, the connection that a group of teenagers made between the appearance of Superman with his cape and a Roman official in a toga in a movie about the crucifixion demonstrated an inability on the part of African viewers to understand the representational nature of film.[105] But to audiences who watched films as disconnected series of scenes, with close attention paid to styles of clothing and action, such comparisons made perfect sense. Similarly, such an appreciation of movies as intrinsically disconnected from the linear and the real partly explains the apparent overwhelming preference of African audiences for black and white films when colour films were initially introduced.[106] The first colour movies shown tended to be locally made and didactic, but the preference apparently went beyond that to an assertion that colour films were not 'natural-looking'. The conjunction of the use of colour and the introduction of local settings also took films in the direction of the mundane, where plainly they did not belong. Hortense Powdermaker reported a deep reluctance among school children and some adults to accept that films were staged and claimed that audiences reacted with irritation when an actor, shot dead in a previous film, turned up alive in another.[107] But the very conventions of naming the hero Jack and analysing and comparing the stock sequences argue in fact for a fine appreciation of films as fantasy.

Audiences invariably responded insistently and angrily to the occasional attempts of paternalistic officials to vary programmes and broaden local film taste.[108] In 1953, the white managers at the Luanshya municipal residential compound experimented with a showing of *Cry the Beloved Country*. Shown on a programme that included a *Superman* movie, the film drew a very large audience. The screening was preceded by a synopsis in a local language, Chibemba, and three educated African men were asked to mingle with patrons and collect reactions. The audience engaged the film in typical fashion, with general comments and open discussion, rather than the reverential silence that Europeans expected for serious movies. People in the audience continually complained about the film and demanded 'cowboys'. Uproarious laughter greeted the scene in which Mr Jarvis is informed of the murder of his son, and audience members were 'visibly delighted when Mrs Jarvis was grief-stricken at the news of the death of her son'. Rev. Kumalo's appearance elicited loud and derisive comments like 'church', 'Christianity' and 'we want cowboys'.[109] Such seemingly callous responses might be represented in part as 'oppositional' statements. Certainly, the reaction to Kumalo conveyed some of the resentment that working-class African men felt towards the church leaders and other 'respectable' men in their community; but it is unlikely that antipathy to white domination, however bitter, would translate into derision of the emotional grief of a white mother and father over the loss of their son. Unable or unwilling to comprehend the dialogue, audience members largely ignored character development and plot, and probably in this case reacted to extreme facial expressions. They experienced or 'read' the film as they would have the cowboy movie they had anticipated seeing – as a series of action scenes. In a slow-moving and rather pretentious film like *Cry the Beloved Country* there was little 'action' and audiences reacted viscerally to the few scenes that stood out. As the report of the showing makes clear, a very substantial proportion of the audience demonstrated their boredom simply by walking out.[110]

The world of films, and especially cowboy films, spilled out into the popular culture of Northern Rhodesian urban communities and followed filmgoers into the streets and their homes and eventually back to their rural home villages. When members of the audience got back to their rooms or houses or met friends at work or at other social occasions, films were often the subject of discussion.[111] As in Ghana, youths talked over the films in the days that followed, paying particular attention to the styles of dress and fighting techniques that were central to the appeal of Westerns. Oral recollections reveal the same flow of Hollywood imagery into Cape Town's District Six community. There, people waiting in line for tickets could be overheard sprinkling their conversation with terms like 'pardner' and 'howdee', and motifs drawn from films often surfaced in the costumes of the annual New Year carnivals.[112] Certainly, in rural areas of Northern Rhodesia, the mobile cinemas left a great many images in their wake for audiences to savour and rehearse before the van returned, even if many of the residents had in fact spent considerable time in towns and would have been fairly familiar with film shows.[113]

A film show in a remote rural area was, of course, much more of a special event, since mobile cinemas did not reach a given village or town much more often than once or twice a year in the 1940s or once a month in the 1950s. The entertainment began with the arrival of the van. Crowds began to assemble in the afternoon to watch and assist in setting up the projector and screen, eventually numbering from one hundred to 3,000. Before the film show itself, members of the mobile cinema staff gave educational talks illustrated with film strips on topics such as malaria eradication. They tuned in to the national radio station and piped it out to the crowd on loudspeakers; and they sold various books and newspapers.[114] Consistent with the non-commercial, educational mission of the mobile cinema, the main programme did not include 'unsuitable' Westerns or other adventure movies. But the staff was careful to alternate 'entertainment' films with more didactic ones. The programme usually began with 'one or two amusing films, followed by an instructional film. The next film is usually something else of particular interest, not necessarily comedy. It might be a short film on game or a "musical" with catchy tunes'. If ten reels were shown, half would be solely for entertainment, three 'really educational' and the remaining two general interest films and regionally oriented newsreels.[115] By the 1950s, rural audiences had become substantially more sophisticated in their film tastes, as the mobile cinema programme expanded and as more people spent time in the urban areas. Local 'respectable' men and women shared the distaste of the mobile cinema staff for cowboy films, regarding them as a dangerous influence; but younger people were increasingly caught up in cowboy craze that had taken root in the Copperbelt, even though Westerns themselves were still not usually shown by the mobile cinema.[116]

African audiences often disturbed European officials by the ways that they used material from films to make judgments about the outside world, the nature of imperialism and the character of European culture. Seemingly innocuous footage of healthy cattle in Southern Rhodesia, for example, inspired commentary from Northern Rhodesian moviegoers in the 1950s on racial segregation and the inferiority of the diet of Africans in comparison to whites. A Northern Rhodesian newsreel showing the dedication of a home for the aged elicited comments in the crowd that these had to be for whites: 'do you think they can build houses for Africans like that?'[117] Depictions of whites engaged in manual labour invariably inspired sarcastic, critical commentary.[118] Although the active white settler proponents of censorship often advanced the shibboleth of black sexuality to defend the need to subject films to close scrutiny, colonial officials were much more concerned that scenes of half-dressed and philandering white women would become the evidence for critical judgments on white morality.[119] Scenes of kissing or scantily clad women were more offensive than sexually provocative. A discussion of a scene of courtship in a European café led one man to ask: 'are these proper ladies or are they clowns?' Another responded: 'It is the behaviour of white ladies. They are not ashamed.' Men and women swimming together was denounced: 'I do not like it. It encourages immorality.' But, at the same time, movie patrons paid careful and detailed attention to a distinctively modern style of dancing that might be reproduced later at a local party.[120]

As the cowboy phenomenon makes plain, film made its most distinctive impact on local youth culture. During the 1930s and 1940s, when primary schooling was not yet entrenched in urban areas, young boys often were at loose ends. They roamed around in gangs, whose leaders gave themselves names like Jack, after the cowboy hero, and Popeye. Among the main occupations of these gangs were 'cowboy games' where rivals pretended to shoot each other. By the early 1950s, all children were expected to attend school and many more organised activities had become available.[121] But filmgoing was still very popular, and that popularity was reflected in the styles of dress of school-age boys as well as young men.[122] 'Respectable' Africans as well as whites generally found these styles reprehensible, associating them in their minds with insolent attitudes if not outright criminality.[123] In the industrial areas of South Africa, local hoodlums often appropriated the names of film stars or notorious characters in Westerns or gangster movies.[124] In 1947, a prominent member of the Northern Rhodesian African Representative Council demanded to know in a debate whether the government was aware that 'the films shown to African children in bioscopes at present are harmful to their characters?'[125] In Dar es Salaam, it was claimed that 'the cult of cowboy clothes is the safety-valve of the dangerous mob element'.[126] Fear of the spread of such behaviour certainly motivated many of the paternalistic believers in educational cinema. Indeed, it was almost an article of faith that if good films could be effective tools of education and development, bad ones would produce the juvenile delinquents that many saw as a growing Copperbelt problem.[127] What the authorities feared, of course, was that African town-dwellers would appropriate immoral and criminal behaviour from cowboy and gangster movies. Official files on film censorship contain a report from the late 1940s that appeared to justify such fears. A group of six young African men, convicted of robbing and beating a man in the mining town of Mufulira, claimed in their defence that they had seen similar acts in films and wanted to copy them. Whether or not exposure to cowboy movies inspired criminal activities, these young hoodlums were resourceful enough to play on stereotypes by rationalising their actions in terms of film allusions. It is also possible that they understood that paternalistic officials might go more easily on unsophisticated youths who were believed to be highly susceptible to the power of film imagery.[128]

For young crooks, as for the mass of Copperbelt youth, film offered a repertoire of images, characters and behaviours that could be drawn on to define and navigate modern, urban life. Descriptions of audience behaviour draw attention not only to the enthusiasm that filmgoers showed for fights and other action sequences, but to the close attention spectators paid to the material contents of films. Notwithstanding the efforts of the Colonial Film Unit, audiences showed little patience for films that depicted rural life and the potential for the development of agriculture. Movies represented an escape from the harsh realities of urban life, especially in an increasingly repressive South Africa, but notwithstanding the exotic locales of gunfighter epics, film also provided a kind of guide to urban modernity and sophistication. Published memoirs of urban black South Africans reveal the powerful and romantic appeal of Hollywood products, but it is clear as well that audiences drew the characters into urban southern Africa, weaving witchcraft and kinship politics into discussions of the meanings of particular sequences. As one filmgoer from the Copperbelt noted, 'the cowboy has medicines to make him invisible . . . Cowboys show respect. And Jack is also the son of a big man.'[129]

Older men and women who regarded themselves as more mature often dismissed the bioscope as a trivial pastime appropriate only to children. One Copperbelt woman in her thirties defined films as a distinctly urban phenomenon, only appealing to those who had been raised in the city:

> Cinema shows and radio are there to entertain youth. We people of old age cannot attend such things where small boys go. Our form of entertainment is beer . . . How can

I develop the habit of going to cinema now? The people who enjoy it are those who have been born here.[130]

In the urban areas of central and southern Africa, the divide between those who self-consciously remained oriented towards their rural homes and those who committed to a distinctively modern world view surfaced very visibly in leisure activities: people who conceived themselves as 'modern' participated in church activities and organised sports and were bioscope enthusiasts, while those who rejected modernity dismissed such pastimes and generally preferred to spend their leisure time in informal socialising and drinking.[131]

In the last, bitter years of colonial rule in Northern Rhodesia, some Africans and their liberal white allies directly challenged the censorship of films on racial lines, as part of a broader assault on the colour bar.[132] Some of the younger and better-educated town residents, in particular, found the bioscope unappealing and were anxious to see more sophisticated and varied movies in more sedate surroundings.[133] In 1957, the chairman of the inter-racial Capricorn Africa Society drew attention

> to the fact that large numbers of educated Africans are profoundly dissatisfied with the programmes being shown on the African locations. They wish to see the films that Europeans, Indians and Coloureds are seeing but the decisions of the Board are preventing them from doing so.[134]

When the Board chose to ban newsreels for African viewing that depicted the resistance of Hungarians to the Soviet invasion and the demonstrations that followed in various European cities, the controversy reached the floor of the British House of Commons. There, a government spokesman vigorously defended censorship with the assertion that 'Africans were more likely to be impressed by moving pictures.'[135] The opening of a multiracial cinema in 1957 in Lusaka provided an opportunity for Africans to see a wider range of films in the more genteel atmosphere of an indoor theatre, but the continued application of censorship rules meant that African patrons still risked being turned away at the door if a particular film had not been passed for African audiences.[136] For this small, but highly influential group, the humiliation of being forbidden to see films that had been approved for viewing by whites, including children, was a stark reminder of the continued ascendancy of racial hierarchy and made a mockery of promises of 'racial partnership' and non-racialism.[137] Yet as late as 1960, on the eve of the legislated desegregation of public facilities in Northern Rhodesia, Roman Catholic bishops still vigorously defended racial censorship:

> Material reasons like uniformity of treatment, economy, convenience and such ought not be allowed to weigh against the need to safeguard from evils of the moral order of the African people, the vast majority of whom have . . . primitive ideas of morality affecting public order and decency.[138]

This tenacious devotion among whites in Northern Rhodesia to the spectre of film's power over Africans reveals not only a deeply entrenched racial order but an unquestioning confidence in the powerful force of the medium of film as an instrument of cultural subversion. The claims advanced in colonial Northern Rhodesia and across colonial Africa that movies, and popular culture generally, undermined traditional authority and custom belong to a powerful intellectual tradition of modern imperialism enshrined in administrative terms by the British in the form of the doctrine of indirect rule and more broadly in the ideal of trusteeship.[139] The strong attraction of African audiences to a vision of Europe and North America inscribed in Hollywood Westerns and other action movies subverted cherished colonial notions of Africa as Britain's 'Wild West'.[140] This colonial antipathy to the global consumerism of urban Africans, decried as evidence of dangerous 'detribalisation' or 'westernisation', has survived in post-colonial discourse in the context of debates over cultural imperialism. Ranging across the ideological and disciplinary spectra, scholars and critics lament the disruption of societies, characterised variously as traditional or backward, and in particular stress the role of mass media in projecting the ideological messages of international capitalism and demand for global consumer commodities at the expense of traditional values and practices.[141]

Ariel Dorfman and Armand Mattelart's influential early 1970s study of Disney comics in the Third World, *How to Read Donald Duck*, drew on dependency theory to argue that such hugely popular but seemingly innocent media products in fact have extended American global hegemony by conveying to unsophisticated readers principles that bolster capitalist values and thus restrict the emergence of genuine consciousness.[142] In their confident analysis of the meanings of mass media products and assumptions of the power of those products to persuade, Dorfman and Mattelart and other critics of global information flows not only share common ground with liberal critics of global cultural homogenisation but betray a perverse intellectual debt to alarmist imperial rantings against the nefarious influence of Hollywood films. In each case, 'Third World' peoples or audiences are assumed to lack the sophistication to resist popular media images or to engage them critically.

The moviegoing experiences of Africans in Northern Rhodesia challenge such assumptions, suggesting not only that the meanings of films and other pieces of mass media are elusive and contested, but that audiences continually appropriate and re-appropriate such media and subject them to various and fluid readings. The cowboys who populated Westerns emerged from screens on the Copperbelt as characters who were as much rooted in urban Northern Rhodesian communities as in the American West, and the ways that audiences drew on and referred to film images varied as widely as confident official or scholarly pronouncements on their meaning. Seemingly bizarre audience responses to a film such as *Cry the Beloved Country* made perfect sense in terms of local expectations for film shows and constructions of film character behaviour. Certainly, highly politicised informal audience commentaries on film depictions of life in African colonies demonstrated a keen appreciation on the part of African moviegoers of the manipulative power of film. Although very little research has directly addressed the global appeal of popular media, the work that has been done, especially that exploring the seemingly inexplicable universal popularity of the American television programme *Dallas* and its supposed glorification of wealth, has suggested how 'naïve and improbable is the simple notion of an immediate ideological effect arising from exposure to the imperialist text'.[143] Like movie patrons in colonial Northern Rhodesia, *Dallas* viewers sometimes drew on the programme to criticise American excess, or saw in the programme a guide to style, or simply responded to the basic morality plays that drove the narratives. But reliance on immediate reactions in con-trolled circumstances very much limits the validity of this kind of audience research, no matter how stimulating the findings.[144] The Copperbelt audiences who crammed into noisy outdoor cinemas analysed and debated the elements of films as they watched them, drew film images into their lives as they adopted and modified modes of dress, speech and behaviour, and then took those sensibilities back into the theatre in a pro-cess that was difficult to capture at the time and now, in the age of video, resembles in popular memory a kind of quaint nostalgic relic. But as the fragmentary evidence of audience response suggests, moviegoers sought in films not only entertainment and sources of style, but an opportunity to engage and critique the colonial order they inhabited and to appropriate and synthesise notions of modernity that they believed would facilitate urban life. As Hortense Powdermaker observed of the Copperbelt film shows, 'whatever was seen was commented on, interpreted, criticized. Questions were asked'.[145]

## Notes

1 The British colony of Northern Rhodesia became Zambia at independence in 1964. During the 1950s Northern Rhodesia was linked with Southern Rhodesia (Zimbabwe) and Nyasaland (Malawi) in a Central African Federation dominated by white settler interests.

2 H. Franklin, 'The Central African Screen', *Colonial Cinema*, vol. 8, no. 4 (December 1950), p. 85. Jack was supposedly a tribute to the actor, Jack Holt. See also H. Franklin, 'The Cinema in Northern Rhodesia', *Colonial Cinema*, vol. 2, no. 6 (June 1944), p. 22.

3 R. J. Allanson to Director, Deptartment of Information, Lusaka, 27 January 1956, NAZ: Sec 5/16, I no. 88.

4 According to a 1956 survey, in Dar es Salaam 'there has grown up, as elsewhere in East Africa, the cult of the cowboy . . . The young man . . . soon acquires the idioms of tough speech, the slouch, the walk of the "dangerous" man of the films; the ever-popular Western films teach him . . . ' J. A. K. Leslie, *A Survey of Dar es Salaam* (London: Oxford University Press, 1963), p. 112; and Rob Nixon, *Homelands, Harlem, and Hollywood: South African Culture and the World Beyond* (New York: Routledge, 1994), pp. 31–5.

5 For an introduction to the large literature on the history of the Copperbelt, see Jane L. Parpart, *Labor and Capital on the African Copperbelt* (Philadelphia: Temple University Press, 1983).

6 Already, by the early 1930s, twice-weekly film shows at the Roan Antelope Compound in Luanshya drew average attendance of more than 1,000. Charles W. Coulter, 'The Sociological Problem', in J. Merle Davis (ed.), *Modern Industry and the African* (London: Macmillan,1933), p. 72.

7 Hortense Powdermaker, *Copper Town: Changing Africa: The Human Situation on the Rhodesian Copperbelt* (New York: Harper and Row, 1962), p. 227. In the District Six neighbourhood of Cape Town, movies were 'unquestionably the most popular form of paid entertainment in the inter-war years'. Bill Nasson, ' "She preferred living in a cave with Harry the snake-catcher": Towards an Oral History of Popular Leisure and Class Expression in District Six, Cape Town, c. 1920s–1950s', in Philip Bonner, Isabel

Hofmeyr, Deborah James and Tom Lodge (eds), *Holding their Ground: Class, Locality and Culture in Nineteenth- and Twentieth-Century South Africa*, (Johannesburg: Witwatersrand University Press, 1989), p. 286.

8  The globalised power of media and its role in transmitting American culture is probably more assumed than it is studied. For an exception, see Peter Manuel, *Cassette Culture: Popular Music and Technology in North India* (Chicago: University of Chicago Press, 1993), esp. pp. 2–18. In practice, the study of media 'development' in Africa has been shaped by assumptions associated with modernisation theory. See, for example, Graham Mytton, *Mass Communication in Africa* (London: Edward Arnold, 1983), pp. 4–18; Robert L. Stevenson, *Communication, Development, and the Third World: The Global Politics of Information* (New York: Longman, 1988).

9  Powdermaker, *Copper Town*, p. 259.

10  NAZ: Sec 2/1121, 'Censorship of Films for Natives, 1932–48' and subsequent files.

11  Response to Mr R. J. Allanson, 28 February 1956, NAZ Sec 5/16, no. 88.

12  Alan O'Shea, 'What a Day for a Daydream: Modernity, Cinema and the Popular Imagination in the Late Twentieth Century', in Mica Nava and Alan O'Shea (eds), *Modern Times: Reflections on a Century of English Modernity* (London: Routledge, 1996), pp. 243–5.

13  See, for example, Herbert Blumer, *Movies and Conduct* (New York: Macmillan, 1933). The tendency to look for sources of violence and anti-social behaviour in media is noted in a recent analysis in the *New York Times*, 'Rampage Killers: A Statistical Portrait', 8 April 2000.

14  Franklin, 'The Central African Screen', p. 87.

15  NAZ: Sec 2/1121, 'Censorship of Films for Natives, 1932–48' and subsequent files.

16  Although not centrally concerned with film, Debra Spitulnik's 'Anthropology and Mass Media', *Annual Review of Anthropology*, vol. 22 (1993), pp. 293–315, provides an effective introduction to some of the theoretical assumptions shaping media studies on Africa.

17  Cynthia Erb raises some of the critical theoretical issues in *Tracking King Kong: A Hollywood Icon in World Culture* (Detroit: Wayne State University Press, 1998) but does not move beyond close interpretative readings of various versions of the story.

18  Richard Maltby, 'Introduction', in Melvyn Stokes and Richard Maltby (eds), *Identifying Hollywood's Audience: Cultural Identity and the Movies* (London: BFI, 1999), p. 3. Also, Robert Stam and Louise Spence, 'Colonialism, Racism and Representation: An Introduction', *Screen*, vol. 24 (1983), pp. 4–20.

19  Janet Staiger, *Perverse Spectators: The Practices of Film Reception* (New York: New York University Press, 2000), esp. pp. 43–57. Also see Shaun Moores, *Interpreting Audiences: The Ethnology of Media Consumption* (London: Sage, 1993), p. 6; Miriam Hansen, *Babel and Babylon: Spectatorship in American Silent Film* (Cambridge, MA: Harvard University Press, 1991), pp. 3–7; and David Bordwell, *Narration in Fiction Film* (Madison: University of Wisconsin Press, 1985), esp. p. 29.

20  This critique might be extended to the scholarship on the representation of history in film. See Robert Rosenstone (ed.), *Revisioning History: Film and the Construction of a New Past* (Princeton: Princeton University Press, 1995); and Tony Barta (ed.), *Screening the Past: Film and the Representation of History* (Westport, CT: Praeger, 1998).

21 Rosaleen Smyth, 'The British Colonial Film Unit and Sub-Saharan Africa, 1939–1945', *Historical Journal of Film, Radio and Television*, vol. 8 (1988), pp. 285–98; Rosaleen Smyth, 'Movies and Mandarins: the Official Film and British Colonial Africa', in James Curran and Vincent Porter (eds), *British Cinema History* (London: Weidenfeld and Nicolson, 1983), pp. 129–43; Rosaleen Smyth, 'The Development of British Colonial Film Policy, 1927–1939, with Special Reference to East and Central Africa', *Journal of African History*, vol. 20, no. 3 (1979), pp. 437–50; Rosaleen Smyth, 'The Central African Film Unit's Images of Empire, 1948–1963', *Historical Journal of Film, Radio and Television*, vol. 3 (1983), pp. 131–47; Rosaleen Smyth, 'The Feature Film in Tanzania', *African Affairs*, vol. 88, no. 352 (July 1989), pp. 389–96.

22 A partial exception is Megan Vaughan, ' "Seeing is Believing": Colonial Health Education Films and the Question of Identity', in her *Curing Their Ills: Colonial Power and African Illness* (Oxford: Polity, 1991), pp. 180–99.

23 'Films for the Colonies', *Corona*, vol. 1, no. 5 (June 1949), p. 20. Even the officials charged with organising film shows for circulation in rural areas acknowledged the need to include some 'suitable' commercial entertainment films to make the propaganda palatable. W. Sellers, 'Mobile Cinema Shows in Africa', *Colonial Cinema*, vol. 9, no. 4 (September 1950), pp. 77–8.

24 Surprisingly, the growing literature on the social and cultural history of southern African urban communities, including studies of sports, drinking and popular theatre and music, largely ignores the bioscope, which novels and memoirs make clear formed a vibrant element of town life. See, for example, Ezekiel (Es'kia) Mphahlele, *Down Second Avenue* (London: Faber and Faber, 1959) and Ezekiel (Es'kia) Mphahlele, *Africa My Music: An Autobiography, 1957–1983* (Johannesburg: Ravan Press, 1984); Modikwe Dikobe, *The Marabi Dance* (London, 1973); and Godfrey Moloi, *My Life: Volume One* (Johannesburg: Ravan Press, 1987). Social historian Bill Nasson suggests some of the possibilities in 'Towards an Oral History of Popular Leisure and Class Expression in District Six', pp. 285–309, esp. pp. 287–95.

25 Judith Mayne, *Cinema and Spectatorship* (London: Routledge, 1993), pp. 8–9, 17, 65. See also Hansen, *Babel and Babylon*, pp. 3–5.

26 Linda Williams (ed.), *Viewing Positions: Ways of Seeing Film* (New Brunswick, NJ.: Rutgers University Press, 1994). But see the essays in the section on 'Black Spectatorship' in Manthia Diawara (ed.), *Black American Cinema* (New York: Routledge, 1993), pp. 211–302. Some of the work on early film audiences in North America and Europe has focused attention on perspectives of working-class and immigrant audiences. See Judith Thissen, 'Jewish Immigrant Audiences in New York City (1907–1914)', in Melvyn Stokes and Richard Maltby (eds), *American Movie Audiences: From the Turn of the Century to the Early Sound Era* (London: BFI, 1999), pp. 15–28; Roy Rosenzweig, *Eight Hours for What We Will: Workers and Leisure in an Industrial City, 1870–1920* (Cambridge: Cambridge University Press, 1983), pp. 191–221; and Elizabeth Hahn, 'The Tongan Tradition of Going to the Movies', in Kelly Askew and Richard R. Wilk (eds), *The Anthropology of Media: A Reader* (Oxford: Blackwell, 2002 [1994]), pp. 256–69.

27 See, for example, E. Ann Kaplan, 'Film and History: Spectatorship, Transference, and Race', in Ralph Cohen and Michael S. Roth (eds), *History and Histories within the Human Sciences* (Charlottesville: University of Virginia Press, 1995), pp. 179–208. Also

see Stuart Hall, 'Cultural Identity and Cinematic Representation', *Framework*, vol. 36 (1989), pp. 68–81.

28 See, for example, Carol J. Clover, *Men, Women, and Chain Saws: Gender in the Modern Horror Film* (Princeton: Princeton University Press, 1992); and Barbara Creed, *The Monstrous Feminine: Film, Feminism, Psychoanalysis* (London: Routledge, 1993). The issues raised by these scholars have not yet made their way into studies of filmgoing in Africa. The special issue of *Matatu*, no. 19 (1997), devoted to 'Women and African Cinema' included no article that explored the female film audience or interpreted spectatorship in gendered terms.

29 For the role of imported videos in local cultures see Minou Fuglesang, *Veils and Videos: Female Youth Culture on the Kenyan Coast* (Stockholm: University of Stockholm, 1994); and Brian Larkin, 'Indian Films and Nigerian Lovers: Media and the Creation of Parallel Modernities', *Africa*, vol. 67 (1997), pp. 406–40. Most of the work on video concentrates on local production and distribution and on the analysis of video film content. The most important studies are Onookome Okome and Jonathan Haynes, *Cinema and Social Change in West Africa* (Jos: Nigerian Film Corporation, 1995); and Jonathan Haynes (ed.), *Nigerian Video Films* (Jos: Nigerian Film Corporation, 1997).

30 Martin Allor, in 'Relocating the Site of the Audience', *Critical Studies in Mass Communication*, vol. 5 (1988), pp. 217–33, traces the development of theoretical approaches to the relationship between medium and audience.

31 According to Leo Charney and Vanessa R. Schwartz, 'Cinema, as it developed in the late nineteenth century, became the fullest expression and combination of modernity's attributes'. Charney and Schwartz (eds), 'Introduction', *Cinema and the Invention of Modern Life* (Berkeley: University of California Press, 1995), p. 1; also pp. 1–3. For a stimulating analysis of ideas of 'the modern' see Nestor Garcia Canclini, *Hybrid Cultures: Strategies for Entering and Leaving Modernity* (Minneapolis: University of Minnesota Press, 1995). The reception of film images was linked as well to the development of a mass-consumption economy. See Timothy Burke, *Lifebuoy Men, Lux Women: Commodification, Consumption, and Cleanliness in Modern Zimbabwe* (Durham, NC: Duke University Press, 1996).

32 F. Spearpoint, Compound Manager, Roan Antelope Mine, Luanshya to General Manager, 2 October 1935, 'Films for Compound Bioscope', RACM WMA/94 204.2, Zambia Consolidated Copper Mines, Archives, Ndola (ZCCM); and 'Film in Northern Rhodesia', *Colonial Cinema*, vol. 11, no. 4 (December 1953), p. 81.

33 Powdermaker, *Copper Town*, p. 255.

34 Commissioner, N. R. Civil Police to Chief Sec., 22 August 1932, NAZ Sec 2/1121 no. 1; and 'The Cinema in Northern Rhodesia', *Colonial Cinema*, vol. 2, no. 6 (June 1944), p. 22.

35 Spearpoint, 'Films for Compound Bioscope', 1935, ZCCM, RACM WMA/94, 204.2.

36 'The Colonial Film Unit', *Colonial Cinema*, vol. 5, no. 2 (June 1947), pp. 27–31; and African Film Library Purchasing Committee, List of Films Purchased, 1942, NAZ, Sec 2/1122, 84/1.

37 Note for Finance Committee, 29 May 1945, NAZ, Sec 2/1121 (5) no. 245; and 'The Cinema in Northern Rhodesia', p. 22.

38 Ibid., p. 22.

39 *Colonial Cinema*, vol. 6, no. 3 (September 1948), pp. 56–7.

40 Extract, 6 January 1956, ZCCM, RACM WMA/94, 204.2 (2).

41 'Film in Northern Rhodesia', *Colonial Cinema*, vol. 11, no. 4 (December 1953), p. 82. For discussion of the development of clubs generally, see Charles Ambler, 'Alcohol and the Control of Labor on the Copperbelt', in Jonathan Crush and Charles Ambler (eds), *Liquor and Labor in Southern Africa* (Athens: Ohio University Press, 1992), p. 352.

42 D. C. Mufulira to P. C., Ndola, 23 December 1954, NAZ, Sec 5/16 (3) no. 53/1. Frederick Cooper connects these local policies to broad questions of labour and decolonisation in *Decolonization and African Society: The Labor Question in French and British Africa* (Cambridge: Cambridge University Press, 1996), pp. 336–48.

43 Extract from *Central African Post*, 5 November 1956, NAZ, Sec. 5/16, no. 107a; Rev. George Shaw (Member Film Censorship Board), 23 February 1960; and J. V. Savanhu (Parliamentary Secretary to the Minister for Race Affairs), 18 March 1960 in Enclosed File, 'Film Censorship: Evidence Submitted to Federal Working Party, 1960', NAZ, Sec 5/15, 16.

44 See Tom Gunning, 'An Aesthetic of Astonishment: Early Film and the (In)Credulous Spectator', reprinted in Williams, *Viewing Positions*, p. 115.

45 Gunning, 'An Aesthetic of Astonishment', p. 129.

46 Powdermaker, *Copper Town*, p. 258.

47 'The Cinema in Northern Rhodesia', p. 22.

48 Harry Franklin (former director, N.R. Information Service), 12 February 1960, evidence submitted to Federal Working Party, NAZ, Sec 5/15, 16. Vanessa Schwartz argues in a study of early film audiences in Paris that 'cinema's spectators brought to the cinematic experience modes of viewing which were cultivated in a variety of cultural activities and practices'. 'Cinematic Spectatorship before the Apparatus: the Public Taste for Reality in "Fin-de-Siècle" Paris', in Charney and Schwartz, *Cinema and the Invention of Modern Life*, p. 298.

49 Harry Franklin (former director, N.R. Information Service), 12 February 1960, evidence submitted to Federal Working Party, NAZ, Sec 5/15, 16.

50 J. V. Savanhu, 18 March 1960, evidence submitted to Federal Working Party, NAZ, Sec 5/15, 16.

51 African Film Library Purchasing Committee, List of Films Purchased, 1942, NAZ, Sec 2/1122, no. 84/1; and extract from *Northern News*, 9 May 1957, NAZ, Sec 5/16, no. 170.

52 'The Mobile Cinema in Northern Rhodesia', *Colonial Cinema*, vol. 6, no. 2 (June 1948), p. 44.

53 H. Stelling to Committee for Local Government, 16 March 1955, NAZ, Sec 5/16(3), no. 69/1.

54 W. Sellers, 'Mobile Cinema Shows in Africa', *Colonial Cinema*, vol. 9, no. 4 (September 1950), p. 80.

55 These concerns of course resemble fears inspired by immigrant, working-class and youth audiences in the United States and Europe. See Rosenzweig, *Eight Hours for What We Will*, pp. 191–215. Recent public debates about theatre location and selection of films in contemporary American cities reveal the persistence of assumptions about the effects of movies on racially and age-defined audiences. *New York Times*, 28 December 1998 and 31 January 1999.

56 D. C. Kitwe to P. C., 25 November 1937, NAZ, Sec 2/1121 (2), no. 54/1.

57  Letter from Interested Citizens, 8 February 1960, evidence submitted to Federal Working Party, NAZ, Sec 5/15, 16; and Memorandum on Native Film Censorship, 12 December 1947, Sec 2/1121 (7), no. 348.

58  J. D. Cave, Native Welfare Officer (and Film Censorship Board member) to D. C. Kitwe, 7 August 1940, NAZ, Sec 1/1121 (3), no. 130/4.

59  Smyth, 'The British Colonial Film Unit'; Smyth, 'Movies and Mandarins'; and Smyth, 'The Development of British Colonial Film Policy'. Also see Thomas G. August, *The Selling of Empire: British and French Imperialist Propaganda, 1890–1940* (Westport, CT: Greenwood Press, 1985), pp. 101–2.

60  J. Merle Davis, 'The Problem for Missions', in Davis, *Modern Industry and the African* (New York: A. M. Kelley, 1968), p. 323.

61  Smyth, 'The British Colonial Film Unit'; Smyth, 'Movies and Mandarins'; and L. A. Notcutt and G. C. Latham (eds), *The African and the Cinema: An Account of the Work of the Bantu Educational Cinema Experiment during the Period March 1935 to May 1937* (Edinburgh: n.p., 1937).

62  'Films for African Audiences', *Colonial Cinema*, vol. 4, no. 1 (June 1944), pp. 1–2. See also James Burns's recent book on the culture and practice of the production of didactic films for colonial African audiences, *Flickering Shadows: Cinema and Identity in Colonial Zimbabwe* (Athens: Ohio University Press, 2002).

63  *Colonial Cinema*, vol. 1, no. 3 (May 1943), p. 1.

64  *Colonial Cinema*, vol. 1, no. 2 (December 1942), p. 3.

65  'Films for African Audiences', *Colonial Cinema*, vol. 1, no. 4 (June 1944), pp. 1–2.

66  See Corrigan, 'Film Entertainment as Ideology', p. 29.

67  Acting Chief Secretary to Government Secretary, Mafeking, 8 March 1946, NAZ, Sec 2/1121 (6), no. 297.

68  Minutes of a Meeting of the Native Film Censorship Board, 31 August 1951, NAZ, Sec 5/16, no. 12A.

69  Memorandum on Film Censorship, n.d. (1956), NAZ, Sec 5/16, no. 121.

70  Ibid.

71  Mr Shaw, Lusaka, 28 July 1959, evidence submitted to Federal Working Party, NAZ, Sec 5/15.

72  D. C. Kitwe to J. D. Cave, Native Welfare Officer, 6 August 1940, ZNA, Sec 2/1121 (3), no. 130/3.

73  J. D. Cave, African Welfare Officer, to D. C. Kitwe, Nkana, 7 August 1940, NAZ Sec 2, 1121, no. 130/2.

74  Censorship Board, Lusaka, minute, 20 June 1945, ZNA, Sec 2/1121, no. 246.

75  General Notice 596 of 1945, 16 September 1945, NAZ, Sec 2/1121, no. 269.

76  Notably, Great Britain, Report of the Commission Appointed to Enquire into the Distrubances in the Copperbelt [Russell Commission] (Lusaka, 1935).

77  H. A. Fosbrooke, Rhodes Livingstone Institute to Governor Arthur Benson, 5 March 1957, NAZ, Sec 5/16, no. 147.

78  Similarly, the Director of Information argued in clear racial terms for banning the movie, *Huckleberry Finn*. Director of Information to Chief Secretary, 8 December 1940, NAZ, Sec 2/1125, no. 19.

79  R. J. Allanson to Director, Department of Information, Lusaka, 27 January 1956, NAZ, Sec 5/16, no. 88.

80 'Guiding Principles for the Use of Native Film Censorship Board', n.d., NAZ, Sec 5/16, no. 121.

81 Rev. George Shaw (Member, Censorship Board), 23 February 1960, evidence submitted to Federal Working Party, NAZ, Sec 5/15, 16.

82 R. J. Allanson to Director, Department of Information, Lusaka, 27 January 1956, NAZ, Sec 5/16, no. 88.

83 Quoted in Peter Davis, *In Darkest Hollywood: Exploring the Jungle of Cinema's South Africa* (Athens: Ohio University Press, 1996), p. 23.

84 In the *New York Times*, 7 December 1997.

85 Emmanuel Akyeampong, personal communication, January 1998.

86 Interview, Mrs W., Kamwala, Lusaka, 5 July 1988.

87 'The Cinema in Northern Rhodesia', p. 22.

88 Capt. A. G. Dickson, 'Effective Propaganda', *Colonial Cinema*, vol. 3, no. 4 (December 1945), pp. 82–5.

89 Roan Antelope Mine Welfare Office, Annual Report, 1952–1953, 26 September 1953, ZCCM, RACM 1.3.1C.

90 Powdermaker, *Copper Town*, pp. 255–6.

91 Ibid., pp. 337–8.

92 George Fenin and William K. Everson, *The Western: From Silents to the Seventies* (New York: Penguin Books, rev. edn, 1977), pp. 31–42, 199.

93 Powdermaker, *Copper Town*, p. 258.

94 Ibid., pp. 228–9.

95 Ibid., p. 256; also see Michael O'Shea, *Missionaries and Miners: A History of the Beginnings of the Catholic Church in Zambia with Particular Reference to the Copperbelt* (Ndola, Zambia: Mission Press, 1986), p. 246.

96 J. H. G., 'My First Visit to the Cinema', *Colonial Cinema*, vol. 8, no. 3 (September 1950), pp. 60–1.

97 Powdermaker, *Copper Town*, pp. 256–8.

98 Lawrence Levine, 'The Folklore of Industrial Society: Popular Culture and its Audiences', *American Historical Review*, vol. 97 (1992), p. 1396.

99 Powdermaker, *Copper Town*, p. 261; 'The Cinema in Northern Rhodesia', p. 22; and Franklin, 'The Central African Screen', p. 85.

100 O'Shea, *Missionaries and Miners*, pp. 245–6; and Powdermaker, *Copper Town*, p. 259.

101 Ibid., p. 258.

102 R. J. Allanson to Director, Department of Information, Lusaka, 27 January 1956, NAZ Sec 5/16, I, no. 88.

103 See Yvonne Tasker, 'Dumb Movies for Dumb People: Masculinity, the Body, and the Voice in Contemporary Action Cinema', in Steven Cohan and Ina Rae Hark (eds), *Screening the Male: Exploring Masculinities in Hollywood Cinema* (London: Routledge, 1993), pp. 230–44.

104 Powdermaker, *Copper Town*, pp. 260–1.

105 Ibid., p. 264.

106 Ibid., p. 260. In contrast, George Pearson, Director of the Colonial Film Unit, claimed that it was evident that 'coloured films help tremendously in getting a story across to Colonial peoples . . . We know from the reactions of the audiences there that these films are greatly appreciated'. Quoted in David R. Giltrow, 'Young Tanzanians and the

Cinema: A Study of the Effects of Selected Basic Motion Picture Elements and Population Characteristics on Filmic Comprehension of Tanzanian Adolescent Primary School Children', PhD dissertation, Syracuse University, 1973, p. 17. Giltrow's own study showed audience preference for colour but no real difference in didactic terms (p. 15).

107 Powdermaker, *Copper Town*, pp. 263–4. In the 1960s, Tanzanian school children who had rarely attended films had little trouble identifying objects and actions represented on screen. Giltrow, 'Young Tanzanians and the Cinema', p. 132.

108 Roan Antelope Mine Welfare Office, Annual Report, 1952–53, 26 September 1953, ZCCM, RACM 1.2.1C.

109 Welfare Officer, Luanshya Municipal Board to Chairman, African Film Censorship Board, 6 November 1953, NAZ Sec 5/16 no 44/1.

110 South African black intellectuals had criticised the book on which the movie was based for its negative view of urban life and the 'religiosity, deference, and the urban incompetence' of the central character, Rev. Kumalo. Nixon, *Homelands, Harlem, and Hollywood*, p. 27.

111 J. H. G. 'My First Visit to the Cinema', p. 61.

112 Nasson, 'An Oral History of Popular Leisure and Class Expression in District Six', p. 289.

113 Lawman, 'Information Research', pp. 59–61.

114 *Colonial Cinema*, vol. 4, no. 3 (September 1946), pp. 64–5; and Louis Nell, 'The Mobile Cinema in Northern Rhodesia', *Colonial Cinema*, vol. 6, no. 2 (June 1948), pp. 43–6.

115 Nell, 'Mobile Cinema', p. 45.

116 Tony Lawman, 'Information Research: An Experiment in Northern Rhodesia', *Colonial Cinema*, vol. 10, no. 3 (September 1952), pp. 56–61.

117 Powdermaker, *Copper Town*, p. 257.

118 Ibid., p. 269.

119 Ibid., pp. 168, 267; Rev. George Shaw (Censorship Board Member), 23 February 1960, Evidence submitted to Federal Working Party, ZNA, Sec 5/15; and Lawman, 'Information Research', p. 59.

120 Powdermaker, *Copper Town*, p. 267.

121 Ibid., pp. 196–7.

122 Franklin, 'Central African Screen', p. 85; 'Cinema in Northern Rhodesia', p. 22; and R. J. Allanson to Director, Department of Information, Lusaka, 27 January 1956, NAZ: Sec 5/16, I, no. 88.

123 Lawman, 'Information Research', pp. 56–61.

124 Nixon, *Homelands, Harlem, and Hollywood*, pp. 12, 31–35; and Don Mattera, *Sophiatown: Coming of Age in South Africa* (Boston: Beacon Press, 1989), p. 75.

125 Nelson Namulango, African Representative Council Debates, 1 July 1948, excerpted in NAZ Sec 2/1121 no. 346.

126 Leslie, A. *Survey of Dar es Salaam*, pp. 112–13.

127 Powdermaker, *Copper Town*, p. 198.

128 Extract from Mufulira Monthly Police Report, 1947, Rex vs. John Kandu and Five Other Africans, NAZ, Sec 2/1121 no. 346/1. In the end, however, each received a punishment of twelve strokes.

129 Film spectators quoted in Powdermaker, *Copper Town*, pp. 263, 256–9. Among a number of memoirs, see, for example, Bloke Modisane's *Blame Me on History* (London: Thames and Hudson, 1963) refers repeatedly to the allure of cinema and its importance in constructing elements of cosmopolitanism.

130 Powdermaker, *Copper Town*, p. 298.

131 Philip Mayer, *Townsmen or Tribesmen: Conservatism and the Process of Urbanization in a South African City* (Cape Town: Oxford University Press, 1961), esp. pp. 111–17.

132 Film censorship had a parallel in the regulations that restricted African consumption of European-type alcohol. Africans were forbidden to consume spirits until late in the colonial period. See Michael O. West, ' "Equal Rights for all Civilized Men": Elite Africans and the Quest for "European" Liquor in Colonial Zimbabwe, 1924–1961', *International Review of Social History*, vol. 37 (1992), pp. 376–97.

133 A few private clubs sponsored by mining companies provided relatively privileged Africans the opportunities to see films not approved for African audiences. Memorandum on Film Censorship, Cinema Officer, n.d. (c. 1956), ZNA: Sec 5/16, no. 121.

134 Mr Kemple, Chairman, Capricorn Africa Society to Native Film Censorship Board, Lusaka, 10 March 1957, NAZ: Sec 5/16.

135 Extract, *Central African Post*, 10 May 1957, NAZ: Sec 5/16, no. 171a.

136 H. A. Fosbrooke to Governor, 5 March 1957, NAZ Sec 5/16.

137 Mr Kemple, Chairman, Lusaka Branch, Capricorn Africa Society to Chairman, Native Film Censorship Board, Lusaka, 10 March 1957, NAZ Sec 5/16.

138 Northern Rhodesia Bishops Conference, Secretary General, 9 March 1960, evidence submitted to the Federal Working Party, NAZ: Sec 5/15.

139 Mahmood Mamdani, *Citizen and Subject: Contemporary Africa and the Legacy of Late Colonialism* (Princeton: Princeton University Press, 1996), pp. 62–90.

140 Barbara Bush, *Imperialism, Race and Resistance: Africa and Britain, 1919–1945* (London: Routledge, 1999), pp. 28–38.

141 Tomlinson, *Cultural Imperialism*, pp. 1–33.

142 Ibid., pp. 35–45.

143 Ibid., p. 47. Note especially Ien Ang, *Watching 'Dallas': Soap Opera and the Melodramatic Imagination* (London: Methuen, 1985).

144 Tomlinson, *Cultural Imperialism*, pp. 50–57.

145 Powdermaker, *Copper Town*, p. 270.

# 9
# 'It's the Language of Film!': Young Film Audiences on Hollywood and Europe

Philippe Meers

This chapter, which is part of a larger research project on young film audiences in Belgium, examines the attitudes of young Flemish viewers towards Hollywood, European cinema and national cinema.[1] Inevitably, it engages with the issue that Thomas Elsaesser has described as 'the founding myth' of the discipline of film studies, the opposition between Hollywood and European cinema, which it views through the everyday life experiences and views of actual audiences in their social and cultural context.[2] In doing so, it considers the whole spectrum of film consumption, including television and video, something which is particularly important in considering Hollywood, since Hollywood films and their by-products in popular culture predominate in other media.[3] Broadening the field in this way helps to draw a richer picture of the kaleidoscopic experiences of film audiences, providing new insights on how audiences recreate and use discursive constructions of Hollywood, European and national cinema.

Some commentators have explained the hegemony of the US film industry over the European market as a form of cultural imperialism, while other scholars attribute Hollywood's success to its narrative and formal qualities.[4] Media reception scholars nuance both positions, but almost all these reception studies focus on television rather than film audiences.[5] The survey on which this chapter is based examines what Andrew Higson calls a 'national reception culture', using an approach that studies 'the activity of national audiences and the context within which they give meaning to the movies they watch'.[6] The audience examined is situated in Flanders, the Dutch-speaking part of Belgium, a fact that in itself problematises common definitions of 'national' cinema. Belgium is a small federal country in the heart of Europe. Its two main communities are Dutch-speaking Flanders and French-speaking Wallonia, with Brussels, the European capital, being bilingual. This ethnic and linguistic division has created significant differences in film culture between the two communities. On the level of production and policy, each has its own legislation and subsidy system. On the level of reception, there are related differences, mainly concerned with language issues, and the top ten box-office movies in the two parts of the country are very different. In Wallonia, most films are dubbed, whereas the only films not subtitled in Flanders are children's animation films; this holds true for films on television as well as in the cinema. Flanders has some of the biggest multiplexes, owned by the European-wide Kinepolis Group; as in other parts of Europe, small town cinemas are well on the way to extinction. There are clear-cut distinctions between commercial multiplexes, arthouse cinemas (mainly in the big cities such as Antwerp, Ghent and Brussels), film museums (Antwerp and Brussels) and cultural centres screening films as part of their overall programming.

The range of films on offer to audiences includes an enormous number of Hollywood films in the multiplexes, a far smaller number of Flemish and Belgian films, some French films (especially in Brussels and the French-speaking community) and a few other European films. Hollywood films also feature prominently on prime-time television. Although the almost fully cabled Belgian television service offers more than thirty channels (Dutch, British, French, German, Spanish, Italian), the Flemish commercial and public channels are by far the most popular. Amongst these, the commercial channels VT4 and Kanaal 2 are aimed at a young audience and show primarily US films. Although Flanders is heavily dependent on US films, its geographical location makes it possible for the survey to study how young people interact with a cultural web in which not just American but French, German, Dutch, British and other films are available and accessible through various media channels.[7] The objective of the survey was

> to get a grasp of our contemporary media culture, particularly as it can be seen in the role of the media in everyday life, both as a topic and as an activity structured by and structuring the discourses within which it is discussed.[8]

Young people were selected as the focus for the survey because they are the core target group of contemporary mainstream (Hollywood) cinema. The survey's concern was with mainstream youth culture, rather than underground or marginal subcultures.[9] By taking a broader view of the role of film as a cultural product in young people's everyday lives, the survey offers insights into their cinematic preferences, patterns, opinions and attitudes.[10] It also encourages a detailed analysis of cross-cultural relationships in film reception, and a comparison of marketing and press discourses with those of the audience.[11] The survey illuminates the ways in which Hollywood is a formative part of popular film culture in Flanders, interacting with young people's national and regional identities.

In spring 2001, in-depth interviews were conducted both with twenty-eight adolescents (seventeen girls and eleven boys with an average age of seventeen and a half) in their last year or second last year of secondary school, and also with their family members.[12] The educational level of those interviewed included students preparing for tertiary study (ASO), technical education (TSO), and those taking vocational courses (BSO). The level of film consumption varied widely within the sample, ranging from the rare filmbuff who watches films on a regular basis and collects film on video, to people who hardly ever go to the cinema or rent a video and for whom the experience of film is limited to watching films on television. Although the sample cannot be considered to be wholly representative of young people in Flanders, it does reflect an existing variety in class, gender, level of education and location.

Because interview data is never transparent, it inevitably poses problems when it comes to interpretation and evaluation. 'Interview talk is the rhetoric of socially situated speakers', remarks Thomas Lindlof, 'not an objective report of thoughts, feelings, or things out in the world'.[13] Every attempt has been made in this chapter to seek a balance, as Thomas Austin writes, between 'avoiding both the naive positivism of treating audience research as a source of unmediated access to film viewing experiences, and a defeatism that too readily abandons empirical inquiry.[14] In summarising research findings, direct quotations are used to illustrate the points made while staying as close to the respondents' discourse as possible.[15]

## Hollywood, Europe and National Cinema: Discursive Dichotomies

The survey's clearest finding was the overwhelming preference for Hollywood films displayed by a young mainstream audience, and the relative lack of interest in European and local Flemish films. For these audience members, as for the teenage boys studied by Martin Barker and Kate Brooks, Hollywood is 'a widely-shared mental construct which summarises a place of tinsel and tin, glamour, money and power' but also a site of power towards which interviewees feel ambivalence.[16] An analysis of young people's discourses brought to light a range of associations between particular notions of form, style and narrative and a particular style of American, European or Flemish film-making. While respondents paid little detailed attention to 'European' cinema as too abstract a category, a pattern of dichotomies between Hollywood and Flemish movies emerged on the levels of production, distribution, film characteristics and reception (see Figure 1).

On the level of production, respondents knew that only Hollywood has the know-how and the financing to make worldwide blockbusters. Big budgets have their own implications in terms of the use of special effects, settings and actions. On the level of distribution, Hollywood films are considered to be highly visible in the media, in the cinemas, in the videotheques and on television. This high visibility is associated with box-office success and a diverse audience range. Most respondents, however, focused on the differences in characteristics among the films. The most frequently articulated opposition was one of quality: Flemish films were considered 'low' quality while Hollywood meant 'high' quality. A comparable stylistic dichotomy emerged between 'primitive' national film and 'sophisticated' high-tech Hollywood. Some respondents contrasted the old-fashioned Flemish 'reality' with modern American 'fantasies'. A similar opposition also appeared in generic associations, where Flemish drama and historical film were perceived as very different from Hollywood's action, thriller and horror genres. National origin was, indeed, itself linked with the idea of genre. 'Hollywood cinema' was perceived by many as itself a broad genre, namely mainstream commercial cinema, as opposed to national cinemas, which were often dismissed as narrow or irrelevant. One respondent observed that 'Flemish film is not at all my film genre' and another confessed that 'I have never seen a real Belgian action movie, simply because they don't have the means to do that.' A film's setting was also understood as a generic element. Banal Flemish reality was often contrasted with Hollywood's attractive foreign, exotic settings, while the acting in Flemish films was considered amateurish and artificial in comparison to Hollywood's professional and spontaneous performances. Only Hollywood, some respondents believed, featured real movie stars. A similar contrast was constructed on more technical levels, such as sound and image, although the young people in the survey did not usually possess an adequate vocabulary to describe this difference and talked rather of 'ugly' and 'beautiful' images with special effects. Many connected the use of Dutch language to the notion of poor acting, regarding it as clumsy and artificial when compared to American English, the film lan-

Figure 1: Discourses on Flemish cinema vs Hollywood cinema: a schematic overview

| Level | Subject | Local Flemish film | Hollywood film |
|---|---|---|---|
| **Production** | Budget | Cheap | Expensive |
| **Distribution** | Visibility | Low | High |
| | Success (box office) | Low | Blockbusters |
| **Film characteristics** | Quality | – Low | + High |
| | | + Good within a small budget | – low considering the enormous budget |
| | Style | – Primitive, simple | + Sophisticated, high |
| | | + Simple but OK | Tech, – Exaggerated |
| | Genre | – Drama, historical | Action, comedy, |
| | | + Teenpics | thriller, horror |
| | Subject | (Banal) reality | (Unreal) fantasy |
| | | Old fashioned | Modern |
| | Setting | (Banal) Flemish scenery | Attractive foreign setting |
| | Acting | Amateurish, artificial | Professional, spontaneous |
| | Actors | TV-celebrities | Movie stars |
| | Image and sound | Poor quality | High quality |
| | Language | Artificial | The film language |
| | Form | Ugly, grim | Beautiful, special effects |
| | Link with everyday life | High | Low |
| | Filmic/narrative realism | Low | High |
| **Reception** | Identification | Low | High |
| | Suspension of disbelief | Low | High |
| | Horizon of expectation | Low | High |
| | Context of exhibition | Multiplex | Multiplex |
| | Point of reference | Old films on television | Recent films in cinema |
| | Context of consumption | TV and rarely video | Cinema, video and TV |

guage par excellence. Flemish movies were closely linked to daily reality, while Hollywood signified a fantasy world, but one considered more 'real' in that it was regarded as convincing within cinematic conventions. The young people surveyed constructed a clear-cut dichotomy between Hollywood as a sensational dream factory and Flemish film as small and not particularly attractive window on mundane reality. The existence of these attitudes has repercussions on the reception processes of both categories of film. Popular identification with Hollywood movies is much higher, entailing a higher suspension of disbelief. The horizon of expectation is much lower for Flemish film. Hollywood movies are consumed across all media, from cinema to the internet, while Flemish films are viewed mainly on television. The points of reference for Flemish movies are 'not so recent' films shown on television while, for Hollywood, reference is usually to the latest blockbuster.

## The Hollywood Blockbuster as Classic

When audiences talk about 'American' film, they clearly mean mainstream Hollywood movies. Frequently, respondents did not distinguish between American cinema as a whole and Hollywood. This should come as no surprise, since only Hollywood fare reaches Flemish multiplex screens, and the rare US arthouse or independent production ends up in the kind of arthouse cinemas that few teenagers attend. Most young people explain the dominance of American cinema primarily in terms of Hollywood's enormous budgets, while more critical viewers point to its hegemonic presence in the Flemish media. Hollywood's supremacy also means that peer pressure forces viewers into watching such movies, in order to be able to talk about them.[17] This peer pressure is clearly linked to the hype created around blockbuster movies:

> *Marie* [eighteen-year-old school girl]: . . . thrillers such as *Scream* . . . I don't really like those films, but sometimes you have to because otherwise you're not up to date, what can you talk about if you haven't seen *Scream*? . . . *Hannibal* was the sequel of *Silence of the Lambs* and I hadn't seen it and then people said 'Oh no! you haven't seen it?'

For ordinary moviegoers, Hollywood occupies a category of its own – 'mainstream cinema' – somewhere between a genre and a style and with specific characteristics. The dichotomy between Hollywood and European film also involves a distinction revolving around genre:

> *Kristien* [eighteen-year-old school girl]: It's a different genre. Those American films, they mostly deal with issues, that's always action and violence. European films are less violent.

A more surprising element in the responses concerned the discussion of 'classic movies':

> *Marie* [eighteen-year-old school girl]: I'm not a film freak, but some films you just have to have seen them, otherwise it's a gap in your culture . . . Like *Jurassic Park* and *Star Wars*, those films, you know, classics . . .

People regularly use the word 'classic' to describe their favourite movies, referring more often than not to Hollywood movies of the 1980s and 1990s. For these young people, the most important criteria for a classic appear to be the repeated experience, the quality and the story. These films 'never lose their attraction', and the intensity of the experience remains high. To have watched these movies ten times is not exceptional, although many viewers have only seen the 'classics' on television or video. As with the cinephile video-collectors in the research of Uma Dinsmore-Tuli, people take pleasure in acquiring a detailed knowledge of the text, reciting the dialogue and song lyrics during the viewing process, and from the repeated discovery of new things in the same movie.[18] The distinction between regular films and classics also affects video collecting. While some cassettes are used for constant recording, others are reserved for collecting Hollywood 'classics':

> Gert [eighteen-year-old school boy]: I have a box or two full of cassettes with films I recorded the last years. I find it hard to erase those films, I want to keep them, those are good movies, the classics. For instance last week I recorded *The Godfather* series. I'm certainly going to keep them, those are classics, as a film fan I have to have them in the house.

Although there were no clear gender differences in the viewers' genre preferences, differences emerged in their discussion of 'classic' movies, with girls commonly citing *Grease* (1978), *Dirty Dancing* (1987) and *Pretty Woman* (1990). The identification of the classic was in some cases passed on from mother to daughter: one mother mentioned *Grease* and *Dirty Dancing* as her own favourites as well as her daughter's: '*Grease*, I went to see it four times a week, until they stopped playing it.' Boys, on the other hand, were more inclined to cite *The Matrix* (1999), *The Silence of the Lambs* (1991), *Hannibal* (2001) and *Star Wars: Episode One* (1999). *Braveheart* (1995) was a favourite for both sexes. The few highbrow or more alternative moviegoers preferred films such as *Festen* (1998), *Pulp Fiction* (1994) or *Gummo* (1997). In hardly ever mentioning directors when they talked about films, respondents resembled the US audiences researched by Tom Stempel.[19] For all the critical discussion and promotion of directors over the years, interviewees focused either on the movies themselves or on the actors. For Flemish young people, stars such as Julia Roberts, Bruce Willis and Steven Seagal epitomised Hollywood.

Although the positive discourse on Hollywood cinema was clearly dominant, there were also certain undertones of criticism. Mostly higher-educated people considered Hollywood film to be 'predictable, slick, superficial, exaggerated, over the top, form over content'. This minority vision injects a number of nuances into the straightforward Hollywood/European dichotomy:

> *Interviewer*: What is your typical Hollywood movie?
> *Christel* [nineteen-year-old school girl]: Big names, special effects, you notice there's a lot of money in it, probably also big-name directors. But since I prefer movies with content, I would rather watch the European films.

> *Interviewer*: And if you compare in general European films to American films?
> *Inge* [seventeen-year-old school girl]: Yeah that's a big difference. I find American films to be much more commercial, mostly with big budgets, and you notice it in the special effects and they use much more, so they are more successful. But if you peel off all that and just keep the story, it's just a simple story. I find European scenarios more original because with American movies, I often get the feeling I already know how it's going to end.

Other respondents expressed strong irritation at 'too promising' Hollywood trailers that turn the experience of watching the film itself into a disappointment:

*Cor* [nineteen-year-old school boy]: They take five minutes of the movie, where all the action is, they push it in a trailer and show it. And that's what people go to see, and then most of the times the movie is disappointing, because the action is spread all over the movie and they squeeze it in five minutes and show it time and again. And the Americans have the money to show it over and over again.

The fact that films are frequently made to showcase particular actors disturbed some. The acting itself was often considered superficial:

*Cor*: Most [American] films are built around actors, they put a big action giant there and then they build a film. Instead of making a film and then finding the best actor, they pick the actor first and then the movie.

It is important to keep in mind, however, that although some interviewees were critical of Hollywood cinema, they continued to consume a diet of primarily American movies.

## European Cinema: the (In)signifcant Other

European cinema was at first a vague abstraction during the interviews. It was only after it was juxtaposed with Hollywood and specified as French, German or British that the concept became clearer. On the whole, however, young people displayed a combination of ignorance, indifference, dislike and even aversion towards European cinema:

*Interviewer*: What do you think of if you hear European film?
*An* [eighteen-year-old school girl]: Yeah, European film . . . if I think French film, I think boring. But it's probably the language, and German the same. But I really wouldn't know, like Spanish films or Italian films, I wouldn't know . . . if they exist [laughs].

The established view of European cinema as fundamentally art/auteur /intellectual cinema persists, creating an impression that it is difficult and less accessible: 'it forces you to pay attention and think'. There is also a clear association with particular arthouse cinemas:

*Kristien* [eighteen-year-old school girl]: European films are shown in smaller cinemas . . . there's much less advertising and they deal with subjects that don't interest everybody. American films are made for large audiences and European films are less easy for everybody and make you think.

Notwithstanding the negative attitudes towards European cinema, there also existed a minority opinion which viewed European cinema as a valid alternative to Hollywood. For some respondents, the technical and formal advantages of Hollywood cinema counted for little by comparison with the content of European cinema. Oppositions between form and content or predictability and originality were frequently mentioned, on the basis of a general cultural tendency to value auteur cinema rather than a range of exposure to European films. As in the marginal critical discourse on Hollywood, a respondent's level of education appeared to be an important factor in determining his or her attitude, although most interviewees showed an appreciation of the realities that led to the success of Hollywood films and the failure of European ones:

*Gert* [eighteen-year-old school boy]: European films are at a higher level, foreign films compared to Hollywood films. Hollywood films will have a weak story but great special effects. And because of the budget they can make a weak story popular, while European films have more content, and a deeper meaning, and they fail at the box office.

It is striking that this interviewee uses the term 'foreign' films in opposition to Hollywood, as if the US-centred discourse is already interiorised to such a degree that foreign simply means 'not American'.

Clichés about nationality – for example comments about 'the endless talking of the French' – were common in discussions of French cinema, which was considered to be the typical 'European' cinema:

*Nora* [seventen-year-old school girl]: Most French films are not interesting I think, always the same topic, very monotonous.
*Interviewer*: And what topic is that?
*Nora*: Well, mostly about relations and everyday life and the description of each day. There is a lot of talking and very little story in it.

Peer group attitude was an important influence. The few people who did like French films were met with incomprehension or rejection:

*Inge* [seventeen-year-old school girl]: I don't know why but I like French films . . .
*Interviewer*: And do you find it strange that you like them?
*Inge*: I don't know, if I say to my friends, yeah, I rented two French movies, they say: 'What!? You rent French movies?'

School programmes dedicating time to film education typically discuss French film, but such analyses are, as one person comments, 'not applicable to the Hollywood movies I watch in the cinema'.[20] The association of European cinema, and French cinema in particular, with school not only fails to stimulate interest in a cinema that departs from the Hollywood mainstream, but also helps produce an active dislike of European cinema.

The importance of the language factor is highlighted by the fact that most French-speaking Belgian films such as *Rosetta* (1999) and *Le Huitième Jour* (1996) are often considered as French films. Furthermore, the 'raw realism' of the French-Belgian cinema is seldom appreciated, even by people who declare themselves to be open-minded towards European cinema generally. This is a different film language with which they are not familiar and do not appreciate, because it does not correspond to their definition of a pleasurable film experience:

*Christel* [nineteen-year-old school girl]: We have often been forced to go to the cinema with the school. *Rosetta*, that was a bad film! . . . Maybe as cult film it was good, I mean, they filmed it this way and that way and it's different from the usual, but I came out and I felt so depressed. It was a beautiful day and I was depressed as hell. Maybe, probably even, this was the intention of the makers.

*Kristien* [eighteen-year-old school girl]: French-spoken Belgian films, I have seen a few,
I usually find them a bit too negative . . . Like *Rosetta* or *La Promesse*, they're always
in the same atmosphere, mostly poor people, I don't have anything against it, but
they're often too negative.

The fate of other European national films was even worse. Except for a few mentions
of *Lola Rennt* (1998), German cinema was completely unknown. Italian film shared the
same fate. The *La Vita é Bella* (1997) effect had completely disappeared.[21] British film
was a partial exception to the rule, but this had much to do with the language.
Interviewees were also aware of the very limited offerings of European films that were
available in the multiplexes. The most evident factor affecting cinematic tastes was the
respondent's level of education, with more educated interviewees showing a slight incli-
nation towards European films, although it would be fairer to describe this weak preference as displaying a less negative view of European film than that of other
interviewees, rather than demonstrating a really positive attitude.[22]

## Local Flemish Film and Mundane Realism

One might have expected a more positive view towards the local culturally specific
Flemish films by comparison to non-domestic European cinema, but this was not the
case. There is a very low level of consumption of Flemish film, almost exclusively on
television. Most respondents had not seen more then one or two Flemish films in their
lives, and usually referred to television showings of films such as *Daens* (1992), or to
historical film adaptations of classical Flemish literature made in the 1970s and 1980s
and depicting 'the peasant life', such as *Het gezin van Paemel* (1986). This image of
Flemish cinema corresponds with the 'peasants in clogs' representation of Flanders in
older television fiction.[23] Flemish cinema is perceived on the one hand as being too
common in its depiction of everyday life, but at the same time too artificial in its acting
and language. The budget was one of the main issues mentioned when it came to discussing differences in style between Hollywood or Flemish movies, In thinking about
genre, style, setting and atmosphere, young people evaluate Flemish films in accordance
with what they perceive as characteristic of Hollywood films: action, suspense and an
intense cinematic experience. Key concepts were 'simple' and 'uncomplicated':

*An* [eighteen-year-old school girl]: Maybe it [*Team Spirit*] was a bit silly and a bit
simple, but I liked it, because Flemish films are more simple than American films but
for me it's as good as an American film . . . for instance, when it's about football, in
other movies, it's with a lot of fuss, and a huge stadium and a lot of blabla, and in a
Flemish movie, it's just a small football field. This doesn't mean it's worse, it's just
represented in a more unsophisticated way.

In commenting on the relatively small number of Flemish films they had seen, interviewees at times dismissed the acting as unprofessional and artificial. They also noticed
a difference in image and sound quality, although they were unable easily to define
them. They believed that a Flemish movie could be recognised through its particular
atmosphere and its image. All these perceived characteristics resulted in an extremely

low horizon of expectation. One of the most frequent comments was: 'It's not bad for a Flemish movie':

> *Kristien* [eighteen-year-old school girl]: Maybe because its Flemish, you think, it won't be much of a film . . . you know they don't have the means to make mass production, but that's not necessary, but they have less means and money to make films and mostly you know the actors from television. You don't go with mega-expectations to the cinema, because you know how they act and you know the stories from the newspaper, so it's no big surprise. If it's good, it can be a nice surprise, because you don't have high expectations.

Finally, Flemish film has a limited generic range. Respondents did notice the complete lack of some genres – there are, for example, no Flemish action films. Discourses of comment and criticism, therefore, are consequently based on the interaction between genre preferences and genre availability. Many interviewees discriminated between different genres of Flemish films. The most striking example was *Team Spirit* (2000), a 'teenpic' by Flemish director Jan Verheyen and the only Flemish film that gained regular mention. This movie was constructed as a media event especially marketed for adolescents, with an *avant-première* for the contestants in the *Big Brother* (2000) house on commercial television channel Kanaal 2. *Team Spirit* was regarded by many as an atypical Flemish movie; one respondent described it as 'a Flemish movie with an American script'. Flemish cinema, like Hollywood cinema, was seen as a genre in itself with formal and content conventions. But, as one interviewee declared, 'Flemish cinema is not my genre'. Another thought that a Flemish film such as *Team Spirit* and a Dutch film such as *Costa* were successful because they appeared partly American. But she predicted that 'a real Flemish film, not like the Hollywood stuff, will have less success'.

As with European cinema in general, more positive reactions existed among a minority of respondents. Some young people recognised a number of specific characteristics of Flemish film and appreciated the quality, especially in the light of the many limitations that Flemish film-makers had to face. As one interviewee put it, 'In fact [they are] pretty good, if you look at the material and the capital that is invested in it, compared to American films, they can do a whole lot with a very small amount of money.'

## Language on Screen

Language is a crucial factor influencing film appreciation. The survey found a clear equation between, on the one hand, the knowledge of a language and habit of listening to it and, on the other, the choice and enjoyment of film. American English was considered by interviewees to be the film language par excellence:[24]

> *Interviewer*: And if you compare in general: European or American film?
> *Dirk* [nineteen-year-old school boy]: Then American is better. The language, you start understanding it automatically, American . . . if you get English lessons, then you start talking English immediately. If you're used to it from the movies and stuff . . . it's the language of film.

> *Francine* [eighteen-year-old school girl]: The way they act and talk, I think, in
> American [English], they have more effect than if you would say it in French or
> Dutch . . . because I really think that you can express yourself better in American
> than in Dutch. On the one side it's not so direct, because when you say for example
> 'Ik zie u graag' or 'Ik hou van u' while in American you just say 'I love you' or
> something . . . I find that easier . . . in French, it's a beautiful language, but I really
> don't have that feeling with it. And German, absolutely not.

Our respondents were used to American English, which sounded 'good, spontaneous, cool', whereas French was 'too fast, ugly' and Dutch sounded 'artificial'. One family preferred to watch German film *Das Boot* (1981) on DVD with English language dubbing. When people do not possess an adequate level of knowledge of a European language, they are not able to enjoy films produced in that language. Failure to comprehend the dialogue does not merely reduce enjoyment in a particular film, it also promotes a negative attitude in general towards films in that language. The preference for a particular language is linked to respondents' familiarity with it and this frequently has to do with the social environment. People who have French-speaking friends (for example, those going to school in Brussels) are open to the language and also tend themselves to reach a certain level of expertise.

Arguments relating to levels of linguistic competence can, however, hardly be used for films in Dutch, the mother tongue in Flanders. The negative attitude found here derived more from the difference between the artificial standard Dutch and spoken (Flemish) dialects, the habituation to American English as the archetypal film language and the unusual nature of Dutch in film. Dutch was considered an ugly language, not appropriate for movies. The use of standard Dutch – in contrast to the informal dialects young people use – adds to the aversion.

> *Gert* [eighteen-year-old school boy]: Flemish in a film sounds rather strange,
> amateurish because it's Flemish, it sounds so un-Hollywood-like, because of the
> language, so yes, I prefer American films to Flemish films.

The use of the interviewees' own language in this context, therefore, somewhat surprisingly is a disadvantage.

Respondents identified a clear link between acting and language. Both are usually perceived as either 'spontaneous and realistic' or 'artificial and affected':

> *Francine* [eighteen-year-old school girl]: In Dutch, it often does not give such a real
> impression, it seems more real when I watch an American film.

Dubbing and subtitling are equally linked with the language issue. Respondents attach great importance to subtitles. When English-language films are subtitled, they do not normally have to read them all, but subtitled French or German films often present them with difficulties in following the story. Even when Hollywood (animated) movies are dubbed into Dutch, the interviewees seem to have preferred the original English-language version. This was also true of television. The fact that foreign channels show dubbed (Hollywood) movies was regarded as reason enough for ignoring or changing away from the channel concerned:

> *Jakobien* [eighteen-year-old school girl]: James Bond or something, dubbed in French, that really is stupid, with those French voices, it destroys everything. And English or American is easier to understand, and the voices are better compared to French, or German, that's like an American film dubbed in German, not subtitled, its not at all the same, the voices. I prefer the original American.

From the survey, therefore, it seems that American English has become young people's *lingua franca* when it comes to film consumption. As one respondent put it bluntly: 'It doesn't matter where the film comes from, as long as it's English or American spoken, I don't care.' So far as respondents are concerned, other languages do not work on the screen. It is perhaps surprising that the mere sound of the language can have such an impact on the image of a country's cinema, even from people who may have studied up to four languages in school (Dutch, French, English, German or Spanish). A small number of these people say they are more open to different kinds of European film and that the precise language is not important. They claim that what matters is the story of the film itself. In practice, however, most of them also end up watching primarily Hollywood films too (and to much lesser extent French films) because so few films in other languages are actually available.

## Screen Language: Reel Realism vs Realistic Fantasy

As well as highlighting a clear-cut opposition in young people's approach to language in film, the survey also foregrounded contrasting discourses on realism between Hollywood and European cinema. These discourses can be broadly divided in two main clusters. On the one hand, young people talk about the close link between films and the reality of everyday life, which we might call 'thematic realism'. On the other hand, another discourse focuses on the realistic and convincing character of the filmic narration, which we might call 'filmic realism'. The young people perceived Hollywood as creating a sensational but realistic fantasy world. By contrast, Flemish film offered a small and hardly attractive window on mundane reality:

> *Dirk* [nineteen-year-old school boy]: [Flemish film] is more weeping and moaning, Flemish films are more family dramas, a real family; someone runs away or is kidnapped. In America . . . there [is] something added, that normally never is [here]. Flemish films, television, is just what really happens. In America, there is a whole lot fantasised that you think normally is not possible, they like that, you know. Loads of unreality added, fantasies.

Hollywood is on the one hand more exotic, fantastic, far away and remote from everyday reality. On the other hand, the narrative and the whole film language is so convincing that the level of spectatorial identification with the fantasy is higher. Thus it becomes a realistic – that is, a believable – fantasy. The narrative realism is articulated through 'cool', 'spontaneous', 'convincing' acting, lavish and exotic settings, fast pace and uncomplicated stories. The attractive exotic aura has much to do with the characteristics of the setting and the background that situates the narration far away, but at the same time makes it more convincing. This is related to the technical possibilities – for instance, when making a thriller or horror movie with 'realistic' special effects. The thematic realism of the Flemish film is regarded as 'mundane' and 'common' while the 'suspension of disbelief' is much higher in Hollywood cinema. The ambiguous relationship of these two concepts of realism, and how young people negotiate them, is illustrated in the following quote:

> *Patricia* [eighteen-year-old school girl]: American movies are more spectacular, terrorists and bomb attacks and plane crashes, and *Team Spirit*, that's just a simple football team they interview, the content is different, the stories, it's less spectacular and more kept to everyday life.
>
> *Interviewer*: And does that make it more interesting or less interesting?
>
> *Patricia*: It's something different, it's more interesting, because you know it's a movie, yeah, it's different from daily life, but if you watch a Flemish movie, then you say this is better because you can better identify with the movie, but you also say it's maybe worse because it's just what you experience everyday.

Ien Ang's concepts of 'emotional' and 'empiricist realism' are useful in this context.[25] Flemish film, representing local Flemish reality, provides an empiricist conception of realism, in which the emphasis is on the extent to which the representation corresponds to external reality. In emotional realism, the setting of the story is disregarded, and the focus is on whether the characters, models of action and conflict situations are believable within the context of one's own life-experiences. Hollywood film appears to offer mainly realism of this kind. As Geoffrey Nowell-Smith suggests, the realism of European cinemas that reflect their national-cultural distinctiveness is a mirror of everyday reality.[26] But this is not the kind of realism young audiences require of the cinema. Hollywood fantasy turns out to be much more entertaining and relaxing than European realism. This view is confirmed by the striking contrast between Flemish cinema and television. It is perhaps surprising that some of the most convinced fans of Hollywood blockbusters are equally fond of Flemish soap opera. On the small screen, however, they see this as a totally different genre, with other conventions, where the ties with everyday Flemish reality can be appreciated:

> *Interviewer*: On television you watch foremost Flemish series, and if you choose a film, it's mainly American?
>
> *Geertrui* [eighteen-year-old school girl]: Yes, but a film is different from a series, sometimes also unrealistic things happen in a series like in film, but it's different.
>
> *Interviewer*: And different in what sense?
>
> Geertrui: I don't know, like *Thuis* [a popular Flemish soap opera] is Flemish and those are things that could happen here too. And in America, it's different, those things usually can't happen here.

## International Audiences, Transparent Narration and Cultural Dominance

Since Belgium has traditionally been seen as occupying a central position in Europe in geographical terms, and since a wide range of media windows for cinema are available there, it might be thought that young people would have a truly multinational experience of film. The findings of the survey on which this chapter is based do not, however, confirm this speculation. The analysis of young people's discourses on Hollywood, European cinema and Flemish cinema exposed a series of uniform discursive constructions centred on a number of oppositions between the clearly dominant Hollywood and its European and national counterparts. Hollywood is the one and only norm for cinematic experiences in Flanders, and is also paid considerable attention on television channels directed at teenagers. Hollywood blockbusters serve as markers for a new definition of the 'classic film'. European cinema is an insignificant Other: there is a general lack of knowledge and interest in it, and the few discourses on European cinema refer to its association with school and intellectual practice. The local Flemish film is seen as the discursive opposite of Hollywood, a rather unsophisticated form of film that only marginally touches upon the popular mainstream film culture.

As Thomas Elsaesser has noted, the Hollywood blockbuster plays an important role in the everyday film culture of European young people:

> The blockbuster as an event film becomes the engine of the contemporary media culture. We read about it, hear about it, get to see exiting trailers long before the exhibition, our experience is intensified and we have something to talk about and be a part of.[27]

Blockbuster movies are viewed in the cinemas, on video and television, and they intersect with other popular cultural phenomena and merchandising products. European and local films, on the other hand, are viewed almost exclusively on television and video. Moreover, because the quality or intensity of the viewing process differs, the fact that Hollywood blockbusters are seen in cinemas while, by and large, Flemish and other European movies are not, makes American cinema seem doubly dominant: young people watch more Hollywood films in general and especially more in the cinema, where the intensity is higher.

Since (American) English is regarded as the core film language, language performs an ambiguous role as a barrier for cultural product flows. In the distribution of European television fiction, linguistic and cultural affinity continue to play a decisive role in the success and appreciation of the programmes concerned.[28] But Hollywood is able to transcend such national boundaries. Indeed, young people's discourses are strikingly similar to those of the dominant Hollywood media industries and mainstream press institutions. As Janet Wasko and Eileen Meehan conclude in their cross-cultural reception study on Disney, film experiences and discourses remain largely demarcated by the industry.[29]

In the discursive dichotomy between Hollywood and Europe, many of the responses echo established distinctions in film criticism between mainstream Hollywood cinema and the European art film as its main stylistic and narrative opponent.[30] The contemporary vision of Hollywood on the part of Flemish young people strongly parallels David Bordwell, Kristin Thompson and Janet Staiger's definition of the classical Hollywood cinema as 'an excessively obvious cinema' marked by a set of strict codes, an 'imperceptible and unobtrusive' narration, and a categorisation into well-defined genres that helps the audience to position the story and facilitates its comprehension. For

Bordwell, Thompson and Staiger, these characteristics make Hollywood cinema accessible for audiences from different cultures, which in large part explains why it developed
into the international standard.[31] In a more recent study, Kristin Thompson argues that
contemporary Hollywood cinema still displays the classical narrative features of narrative clarity and coherence that assure high attractiveness.[32] For Thompson, the fact that
Hollywood's international market has expanded in the 1990s demonstrates that the
contemporary Hollywood film is not the fragmented post-classical object described by
some post-modern film theorists:

> Could 'fragmented' Hollywood films appeal to audiences even in countries such as Iran,
> which nominally have cultures totally opposed to US values? The fact that such films
> are so easily comprehensible makes them more accessible . . . The films of countries like
> France, or Iran are, for better or for worse, the niche-audience product.[33]

The survey also suggests that Janet Staiger was right when she said that, considered
from the perspective of reception studies, notions such as national cinemas become significant interpretative strategies.[34] Defining a film by its national production circumstances offers viewers as much a strategy for comprehending the movie as, for example,
genre. In the case of Flemish movies, this results in a low horizon of expectation combined with little interest in the domestic films on offer, although on television European
audiences prefer domestic soap opera, indicating a difference in the modes of experience and narrative between the two media. Cultural discount provides a disadvantage
for European film, but a benefit for the small, everyday narratives of soap opera and
television series. As in most media research, social context, cultural capital and education also play a significant role.

As Geoffrey Nowell-Smith argues, it seems as if 'much mouthed banalities about
Hollywood as dream factory are not only true but important'.[35] Hollywood is the
biggest 'fabricator of fantasy' and that remains its enormous and unchallenged strength.
The perception of Hollywood as the norm for international cinema is reflected in the
ways in which Flemish young people receive cinema. The survey also underlines a one-
sided pattern of film consumption, and demonstrates Hollywood's hegemony in framing young people's cinematic fantasies. Narrative transparency thus does not exclude
notions of cultural imperialism. Ultimately, the language factor – language in film and
film language – is an issue of power. While the text may be transparent, issues of power
relations and unbalanced media flows remain. The extremely efficient and sustained
marketing efforts of the Hollywood majors in Europe are very well reflected in the discourses of young Flemish people on what cinema means for them.

## Notes

The author wishes to thank Daniël Biltereyst for his comments on a previous version of
this chapter.

1 Philippe Meers, 'De Europese film op zoek naar een publiek' ['European Cinema in
  Search of an Audience'], PhD thesis, Ghent University, 2003. Few studies have been
  published on contemporary audiences for Hollywood cinema, mostly focusing on one
  film, one genre or one particular audience group. See, for example, Jaqueline Bobo,

'*The Color Purple*: Black Women as Cultural Readers', in E. Deidre Pribam (ed.), *Female Spectators: Looking at Film and Television* (London: Verso, 1988), pp. 90–109; Valerie Walkerdine, 'Video Replay: Families, Films and Fantasy', in J. Burgin and C. Kaplan (eds), *Formations of Fantasy* (London: Methuen, 1986), pp. 167–99; Martin Barker and Kate Brooks, *Knowing Audiences: Judge Dredd, its Friends, Fans and Foes* (Luton: John Libbey, 1998); Martin Barker, Jane Arthurs and Ramaswami Harindranath, *The Crash Controversy: Censorship Campaigns and Film Reception* (London: Wallflower Press, 2001); Annette Hill, *Shocking Entertainment: Viewer Response to Violent Movies* (Luton: John Libbey, 1997); Thomas Austin, *Hollywood, Hype and Audiences* (Manchester: Manchester University Press, 2002); Göran Bolin, 'Film Swapping in the Public Sphere: Youth Audiences and Alternative Cultural Publicities', *Javnost-The Public*, vol. 7, no. 2 (2000), pp. 57–73; Rajinder Kumar Dudrah, 'Vilayati Bollywood: Popular Hindi Cinema-going and Diasporic South Asian Identity in Birmingham', *Javnost-The Public*, vol. 9 (2002), pp. 19–36.

2   Thomas Elsaesser, 'Putting on a Show. The European Art Movie', *Sight and Sound*, vol. 4, no. 4 (1994), pp. 22–7.

3   Mark Jancovich, Lucy Faire with Sarah Stubbings, in their study of a century of film consumption in Nottingham, deliberately choose the term 'film consumption' because it is larger than just cinemagoing, and includes other forms of distribution and exhibition: television (broadcast, satellite, cable), video rental and purchase, internet etc. It also is broader than the mere act of film watching: 'film consumption is about far more than simply the viewing of films'. *The Place of the Audience: Cultural Geographies of Film Consumption* (London: BFI, 2003), pp. 4–5. In *Hollywood, Hype and Audiences* (p. 8 n. 3), Austin also explicitly integrates films on video and television as part of popular film culture.

4   For a recent overview of the debate on Hollywood, see Toby Miller, Nitin Govil, John McMurria and Richard Maxwell, *Global Hollywood* (London: BFI, 2001); Scott Robert Olson, *Hollywood Planet: Global Media and the Competitive Advantage of Narrative Transparency* (Mahwah, NJ: Lawrence Erlbaum, 1999).

5   Ien Ang, *Watching 'Dallas': Soap Opera and the Melodramatic Imagination* (London: Methuen, 1985); Tamar Liebes and Elihu Katz, *The Export of Meaning: Cross-Cultural Readings of Dallas* (Cambridge: Polity, 1995); Daniël Biltereyst, 'Qualitative Audience Research and Transnational Media Effects. A New Paradigm?', *European Journal of Communication*, vol. 10, no. 2 (1995), pp. 245–70. One of the rare examples of cross-cultural research into film reception is Janet Wasko, Mark Phillips and Eileen R. Meehan (eds), *Dazzled by Disney: The Global Disney Audiences Project* (London and New York: Leicester University Press, 2001) on the reception of Disney in several countries.

6   Andrew Higson, 'The Concept of National Cinema', *Screen*, vol. 30, no. 4 (1989), pp. 36–46.

7   Els De Bens and Hedwig De Smaele, 'The Inflow of American Television on European Broadcasting Channels Revisited', *European Journal of Communication*, vol. 16, no. 1 (2001), pp. 51–76.

8   Pertti Alasuutari, 'Introduction: Three Phases of Reception Studies', in Alasuutari (ed.), *Rethinking the Media Audience: The New Agenda* (London: Sage, 1999), p. 6.

9   David Buckingham, 'Introduction', in Buckingham (ed.), *Reading Audiences: Young People and the Media* (Manchester: Manchester University Press), p. 12.

10 A similar approach is adopted to that of Charles Acland in considering everyday life outside the home context, focusing on the 'everyday' consumption of film in all its contexts. Charles Acland, 'Cinemagoing and the Rise of the Megaplex', *Television and New Media*, vol. 1, no. 4 (2000), pp. 375–402.

11 We use the concept of 'audience', fully aware that, as Ien Ang has shown in *Desperately Seeking the Audience* (London: Routledge, 1991), the audience is as much a discursive as a social phenomenon, since individuals are constructed as audience members through industry attempts at marketing research, advertising, promotion, the décor of movie theatres, etc.

12 The respondents were selected out of a larger representative survey sample of young people. In a first quantitative survey (spring 2000), 1,088 secondary school students (aged sixteen to eighteen) in thirty-nine schools across Flanders and Brussels filled in a sixteen-page questionnaire on their media use, their leisure activities, their opinions on and experiences of film in different consumption contexts. The names of the twenty-eight respondents have been changed, due to the guarantee of anonymity offered respondents. The seventeen girls and eleven boys come from all five provinces of Flanders. They come from working-class (sixteen) and higher and lower middle-class (eleven) backgrounds. They live in villages or small towns (fifteen), middle-range towns (eleven) or large cities (two). They are all white. Questions of sexual orientation were not addressed. Their mother tongue is Dutch (with a Flemish accent). Only two are bilingual and speak French at home. All but one live at home with their parent(s).

13 Thomas Lindlof, *Qualitative Communication Research Methods* (Thousand Oaks and London: Sage), p. 165.

14 Austin, *Hollywood, Hype and Audiences*, p. 68.

15 Interviews were transcribed and analysed with Nud*ist, a software program for qualitative analysis, allowing systematic and precise selection and coding of statements.

16 Barker and Brooks, *Knowing Audiences*, p. 77.

17 Cf. Hill, *Shocking Entertainment*, p. 20.

18 Uma Dinsmore-Tuli, 'The Pleasures of "Home Cinema", or Watching Movies on Telly: An Audience Study of Cinephiliac VCR-use', *Screen*, vol. 41, no. 3 (2000), pp. 315–27.

19 Tom Stempel, *American Audiences on Movies and Moviegoing* (Lexington: University Press of Kentucky, 2001), p. 141.

20 This finding corresponds with the distinction made by students between films 'that can be analysed' and films 'for mere entertainment' based on the intentions of the producer in Naomi Rockler, 'Messages between the Lions: The Dominance of the Transmission Paradigm in Student Interpretations of *The Lion King*', *Journal of Communication Inquiry*, vol. 25, no.1 (2001), pp. 6–21.

21 In the survey conducted during the previous year, *La vita é bella* was an important factor in boosting the knowledge and appreciation of Italian film.

22 In interviews with parents, nostalgia for old popular European movies and stars tends to emerge: French action and thriller heroes such as Alain Delon and Jean-Paul Belmondo, comedy stars such as Fernandel and Louis de Funès.

23 Alexander Dhoest, 'Peasants in Clogs: Imagining Flanders in Television Fiction', *Studies in Popular Culture*, vol. 23, no. 3 (2001), pp. 11–24.

24 Young audiences in Flanders, of course, are accustomed to seeing and hearing television fiction and films with subtitles.

25  Ang, *Watching 'Dallas'*.

26  Geoffrey Nowell-Smith, 'Introduction', in Nowell-Smith and Steve Ricci (eds), *Hollywood and Europe: Economics, Culture and National Identity 1945–95* (London: BFI, 1998), pp. 1–18.

27  Thomas Elsaesser, 'De blockbuster als motor van de hedendaagse mediacultuur', in Elsaesser with Pepita Hesselberth (eds.), *Hollywood op straat: Film en Televisie in de hedendaagse mediacultuur* (Amsterdam: Vossiuspers AUP) pp. 27–44.

28  Daniël Biltereyst, 'Language and Culture as Ultimate Barriers? An Analysis of the Circulation, Consumption and Popularity of Fiction in Small European Countries', *European Journal of Communication*, vol. 7 (1992), pp. 517–40; De Bens and De Smaele 'The Inflow of American Television'.

29  Janet Wasko and Eileen. R. Meehan, 'Dazzled by Disney? Ambiguity in Ubiquity', in *Dazzled by Disney*, pp. 329–43.

30  Cf. Bordwell, *Narration* and Wendy Everett, 'Introduction: European Film and the Quest for Identity', in Everett (ed.), *European Identity in Cinema* (Exeter: Intellect, 1996), pp. 7–12.

31  David Bordwell, Kristin Thompson and Janet Staiger, *The Classical Hollywood Cinema: Film Style and Mode of Production to 1960* (London: Routledge, 1985), p. 370; Bordwell, *Narration*, p. 157.

32  Kristin Thompson, *Storytelling in the New Hollywood: Understanding Classical Hollywood Narrative* (Cambridge, MA: Harvard University Press, 1999), p. 10 *et. seq.*

33  Thompson, *Storytelling in the New Hollywood*, p. 347.

34  Janet Staiger, *Interpreting Films: Studies in the Historical Reception of American Cinema* (Princeton: Princeton University Press, 1992), p. 95.

35  Nowell-Smith, 'Introduction', pp. 12–13.

# Index